The Wonga* Coup

* Wonga *n*. Early twenty-first century British slang for money, usually a lot of it. A large splodge of wonga: great quantities of cash. Probably from the Romany word 'wanger', meaning coal. Coal served as a slang term for money in eighteenth- and nineteenth-century England.

Praise for *The Wonga Coup*

"In a remarkable piece of reporting told in lucid prose, Roberts unravels this folly, which winds up implicating Mark Thatcher (son of Margaret) as well as best-seller Jeffrey Archer (who denies the involvement). As in so many African stories, no side emerges unsullied." —*Entertainment Weekly*

"The book—far more instructive than a thousand foundation-commissioned 'good governance' reports—is an account of a tragic farce that took place a couple of years ago. . . The Wonga Coup can be read as a case study of the African failure." —*The Wall Street Journal*

"In his well-researched new book, *The Wonga Coup: Guns, Thugs, and a Ruthless Determination to Create Mayhem in an Oil- Rich Corner of Africa*, Economist correspondent Adam Roberts describes how the purported plotters of 'assisted regime change' in Equatorial Guinea stood to win control of one of the richest patches of oil and gas in Africa." —*Slate.com*

"The book is filled with meticulous reporting on the planning the coup and gets inside the world of African mercenaries, arms suppliers, and intelligence traders." —*Seattle Times*

"As one might infer from the misadventures in Iraq, potential oil riches can inspire some pretty bodacious behavior. In the case of Simon Mann, the disgraced, Eton-bred former officer at the center of Adam Roberts' gripping expose *The Wonga Coup*, it becomes reason enough to plot a regime change in the tiny West African nation Equatorial Guinea." —*Time Out New York*

"An irresistibly lurid tale, [it] is peopled with bellicose profiteers, particularly of the neocolonialist sort from Europe and South Africa, with long histories of investment in oil, diamonds and war-for-profit." —*Publishers Weekly, starred review*

"For the real [coup] story one must turn to Adam Roberts' gripping, well-researched and—given the ludicrous ease with which African tyrants have been able to milk the English libel laws—legally very bold book." —*London Review of Books*

"Roberts' lively narrative is well served by characters from central casting, and his story reveals much about contemporary Africa and its international relations." —*Foreign Affairs*

"The characters in Adam Roberts' book *The Wonga Coup* are as preoccupied with oil as if they'd sprung from the black stuff themselves. . . Roberts' portrait of Thatcher as a bumbling, petulant boy-prince. . .is a major joy of *The Wonga Coup*. . . Roberts presents Mann's hubris and fall in workaday language, leaving the conclusions largely up to his readers. Still, the implications of his scrupulously researched narrative are clear. . .Reading Roberts' book, we are reminded over and over that oil addiction affects all levels of global society, and carries bloody consequences wherever it strikes." —*Plenty magazine*

"Roberts' discoveries allude to the crazy mirror game that goes on between real soldiers of fortune and the popular entertainments (books and movies) that glorify them. . . . *The Wonga Coup* offers a window into the demimonde of African soldiers for hire." —*Salon.com*

"One of the many pleasures of this mesmerizing tale is its glimpse inside modern Africa."–San Diego Union-Tribune

"Meticulously researched, vividly told, unsparing in its assignment of blame, *The Wonga Coup* will leave you shaking your head at the audacity and avarice its players display. At times their schemes read like political satire—*The Year of Living Dangerously* meets *Dr. Strangelove*." —*Cleveland Plain Dealer*

The Wonga Coup

Guns, Thugs, and a Ruthless
Determination to Create Mayhem
in an Oil-rich Corner of Africa

ADAM ROBERTS

PublicAffairs
New York

To E and M

First published in Great Britain in 2006 by PROFILE BOOKS LTD
www.profilebooks.com

Published in the United States by PublicAffairs™, a member of the Perseus Books Group.

Printed in the United States of America.

Typeset in Palatino by MacGuru Ltd
info@macguru.org.uk

Library of Congress Cataloging-in-Publication Data
Roberts, Adam.
    The Wonga coup : guns, thugs, and a ruthless determination to create mayhem in an
oil-rich corner of Africa / Adam Roberts.—1st ed.
    p. cm.
    Includes bibliographical references and index.
    HC: ISBN-13: 978-1-58648-371-5; ISBN-10: 1-58648-371-4
    PBK: ISBN-13: 978-1-58648-500-9; ISBN-10: 1-58648-500-8
    1. Equatorial Guinea—Politics and government—1979- 2. Political corruption—
Equatorial Guinea—History—21st century. 3. Coups d'état—Equatorial Guinea—
History—21st century. 4. Mercenary troops—Equatorial Guinea—History—21st century.
5. Mercenary troops—Great Britain—History—21st century. 6. Mercenary troops—South
Africa—History—21st century. 7. Mercenary troops—Zimbabwe—History—21st century.
8. Petroleum industry and trade—Political aspects—Equatorial Guinea—History—21st
century. I. Title.

    DT620.8.R63 2006;
    967.1803'2—dc22

                                                                          2006047254

10 9 8 7 6 5 4 3 2 1

Contents

Locations of the Wonga Coup, Africa and Europe, 2004

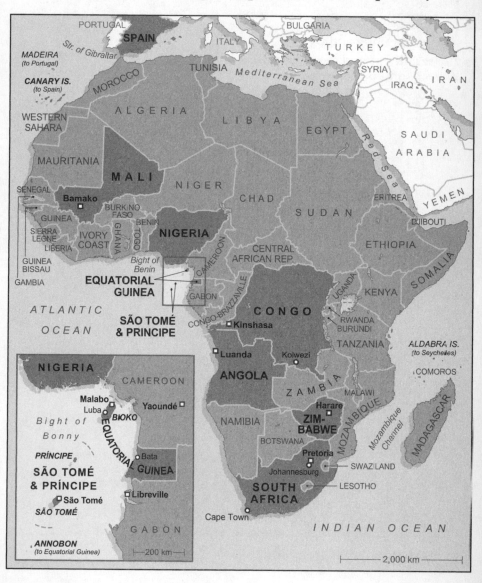

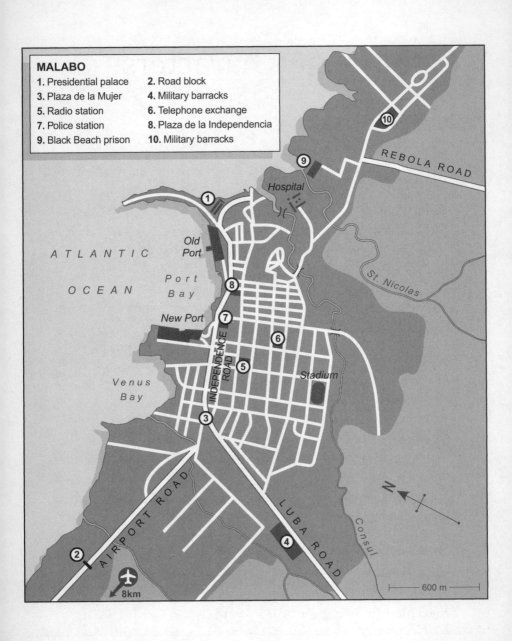

MALABO
1. Presidential palace
2. Road block
3. Plaza de la Mujer
4. Military barracks
5. Radio station
6. Telephone exchange
7. Police station
8. Plaza de la Independencia
9. Black Beach prison
10. Military barracks

REBOLA ROAD

Hospital

ATLANTIC

Old Port

OCEAN

Port Bay

St. Nicolas

New Port

INDEPENDENCE ROAD

Stadium

Venus Bay

AIRPORT ROAD

LUBA ROAD

Consul

8km

600 m

List of Characters

Selected characters, by location, as of Sunday 7 March 2004.

Zimbabwe

Harry Carlse Ex-special forces soldier and former Executive Outcomes employee. Fought beside Simon Mann (below) in Angola; also in Iraq. Ex-nightclub bouncer, assistant to Mann. South African. a.k.a. The Enforcer.

Victor Dracula Decorated soldier of 32 Battalion, long fought in Angola. Naturalised South African.

Simon Mann Ex-Executive Outcomes and SAS. Active notably in Angolan war in early 1990s. Mastermind of the Wonga Coup. Old Etonian and friend of many others involved. British/South African. a.k.a. Captain F.

J. Samukange Lawyer and aspiring politician. Zimbabwean.

Niel Stey Ex-Executive Outcomes in Angola. Grey-haired pilot of Boeing 727 for Indian tycoon. Brother of Crause Steyl (see below, Canary Islands). South African.

Simon Witherspoon Ex-special forces soldier and professional hunter. South African.

South Africa

James Kershaw Mann's young administrative assistant. Friend of Morgan and friend of Smith (below). South African.

Nigel Morgan Intelligence trader and *bon vivant*. Close to South African government, ex-military intelligence. Close friend of Mann and Thatcher (below). British. a.k.a. Nosher, Captain Pig.

Johann Smith   Intelligence trader close to governments of
Equatorial Guinea and South Africa. Ex-military intelligence. South
African. a.k.a. Peg Leg.

Sir Mark Thatcher   Businessman and friend of Mann and Morgan.
Financier of helicopter intended by others for use in coup plot. Son
of Baroness Thatcher. British. a.k.a. Scratcher.

Equatorial Guinea

'Bones' Boonazier   Ex-sergeant major in South African army.
Worked for du Toit (below) in Equatorial Guinea. South African.
First name Marthinus. a.k.a. Bones.

Sergio Cardoso   Ex-South African special forces and mercenary.
Thought to be second in command to du Toit. Sao Tomean.

Nick du Toit   Ex-South African special forces. Arms dealer and
friend of Mann. Front man in Equatorial Guinea. South African.
a.k.a. Niek, Nicky, Nik.

Gerhard Merz   Aviation broker, business partner of du Toit and
chemical weapons trader. German.

Obiang Nguema   Long-standing president of Equatorial Guinea,
nephew of Macias (see below). Equatorial Guinean.

Macias Nguema   Ex-president and genocidal dictator of
Equatorial Guinea (1968–79). Equatorial Guinean.

Teodorin Nguema   Elder son of, and likely successor to, Obiang.
Playboy. Equatorial Guinean.

Armengol Nguema   Younger brother of Obiang and business
partner of du Toit. Equatorial Guinean.

Spain and Canary Islands

Severo Moto Trained priest. Aspiring president of Equatorial Guinea, exiled in Madrid. Friend of Ely Calil (see United Kingdom, below).

Crause Steyl Pilot. Ex-Executive Outcomes. Brother of Niel Steyl and friend of Mann. Self-confessed plotter of the Wonga Coup. South African.

David Tremain Businessman. Friend of Mann and alleged financier and coup plotter. Wanted in South Africa. British.

Greg Wales Accountant. Ex-Executive Outcomes. Friend of Mann and fellow plotter. Wanted in South Africa. British. a.k.a. Oil Slick, Charles Burrows.

United Kingdom

Jeffrey Archer Novelist, politician, member of the House of Lords and convicted perjurer. Accused of putting funds into Mann's bank account a few days before the launch of the coup. British.

Ely Calil Tycoon and friend of Moto, Archer, Mandelson, Mann and Thatcher. Well-connected in west Africa. Accused by Equatorial Guinea of being the chief financier of the plot. Lebanese–Nigerian. a.k.a. Khalil, Smelly.

Frederick Forsyth Bestselling novelist; author of *The Dogs of War*, about a coup plot in west Africa. Suspected plotter of 1973 coup attempt against Equatorial Guinea. British.

France

Henry Page Lawyer for the government of Equatorial Guinea, based in Paris. British.

USA

Simon Kareri African accounts manager, Riggs Bank. Very close to Equatorial Guinea rulers. American.

Prologue

Manyame military base
Harare, Zimbabwe
Sunday, 7 March 2004
6.35 p.m.

There were no stars that night on the Harare airstrip, nor any moon; just the southern African darkness wrapping around him like warm, wet velvet …

A slender, middle-aged man with a military bearing stares at the horizon as a dot of light appears in the south. Right on schedule, the lights of a Boeing 727 flicker in the gloom. He feels a twinge of excitement, the familiar adrenalin. The aircraft lumbers closer and his breathing quickens. This night will see the climax to months of hard preparation.

'Captain F' slips a cell phone into his jacket pocket, spins on his heel and turns his back to the approaching plane. Head up, breathing in the fresh night air, he closes his eyes and – as he has already done so many times before – runs the plan through his mind …

Soon after midnight the forward team will move into position. The sweaty little capital of the target country will be silent as Nick's landcruisers conduct a final reconnaissance. Their beams illuminate Spanish colonnades, palms, the squat concrete houses, the rubbish-strewn streets, the odd drunken soldier. A last drive past the president's palace, then on to the coast road and towards the orange night sky, towards Punta Europa, the gas-flaring complex beside the airport, and then to the airfield itself. Nick and his welcoming committee will enter the tower, take charge, set the radio to the agreed frequency and wait.

Two hours after midnight, west African time, Captain F's team will be approaching the target. Contact will be made with Nick. Touch down and a rapid exit from the customised ex-American government Boeing. The seventy men of the landing team, veterans of mercenary wars in Africa, of some of the bloodiest battles on the continent, have done all this before. They can be trusted with loaded weapons in a pressurised plane. First task on arrival: secure the airport. Second, load the mortars, grenades, ammunition, rocket-propelled grenades (RPGs) and other supplies in the landcruisers.

From the west, skimming the waves of the north Atlantic, another plane will head for the target. In the darkest hours the King Air propeller plane will hop flame-topped oil rigs in the Gulf of Guinea. Its precious cargo, the priest, the man who would be president, will arrive.

From the airport it is a short drive along a toll road to the capital. A small roadblock manned by two drunken soldiers will be swept aside. In the city one unit – perhaps a dozen men at most – will take the first barracks on the road to the south. Sweep into town, past the embassies – expect a light shining in the Spanish one – and into the old quarter. Three smaller units will take the radio station, the telephone exchange and the police station near the central square.

Then the main assault. They may need something big – a fire engine from the airport, perhaps – to flatten the huge iron gate at the entrance to the president's palace. There may be a guard or two waiting, but nothing to stop Nick's seventy men. Inside it will be a different game: the Moroccan presidential guard and a local force. But with mortars, RPGs, his newly trained men well used to urban fighting and house penetration, the attack will take an hour at most. The president's palace is isolated at the east end of town. Another barracks, beyond the Black Beach prison, will be sealed off by a unit of Buffalo Soldiers.

Inside they will need a local guide to take them to the president's chamber. The man may not need to be killed if he offers no resistance. But a bullet in his head is more likely.

Then, by dawn, the priest's speech will be playing on Radio Asonga. Monday morning and the new government – his new government – will be open for business. Those juicy oil revenues will need to be re-allocated. In a few hours history will be made ...

Captain F turns back. The Boeing, safely landed, taxies from the international runway into the military half of the airport, Manyame base. He can make out a familiar face in the cockpit window. He turns and walks towards a parachute hangar and a truckload of weapons. The game is about to begin.

PART ONE

The Ocean of Oil

1

The Rise of Mann

'Everything we've touched turned to gold. Simon is full of ideas.
He finds profitable solutions.'

Crause Steyl on Simon Mann

Beer is the mother of many extravagant ideas and much improbable bravado. The roots of the Wonga Coup draw down into one of the East End of London's largest breweries. Nearly a century ago, the Mann, Crossman and Paulin brewery in Whitechapel was a family affair run by Francis Thomas Mann. He passed it on to his son, Francis George. Young George enjoyed his beer and the brewery served up ale, porter or bitters as fashion changed. Both father and son combined brewing and soldiering – the one fighting in the First World War, the other for the Scots Guards in the Second. Beer, then as now, was capable of giving drinkers the taste for a bit of a scrap.

When peace broke out in 1945, Major George Mann should have returned to the business of brewing, but instead the family's other passion, hardly less combative, intervened. George Mann, though stocky verging on squat, was a cricketer of distinction. And so popular was he with his fellow players that he became captain of the Marylebone Cricket Club (MCC), a quaint English way of saying he led the national team. It was a remarkable feat, since again he was following his father's example. The Mann family claimed a place in the high echelons of British society. Though its wealth came from trade (and beer at that) and there was little sign of royal blood in their veins, the Manns passed as aristocrats. Their sons boarded at Eton, the country's most prestigious public school, where future ministers and royals were caned, slippered and otherwise battered into shape to run the country. When they came of age, the men joined White's, London's most exclusive, if dry as dust, gentleman's club that still counts the Prince of Wales and other members of the English upper classes on its books.

After the war, George led the English cricket team to tour South Africa. They arrived by ocean-going liner and travelled for months by sea and train. He did well enough on the field during the series of high-profile games, though the gentlemen amateurs who had long dominated the game were fast being replaced by professionals. But he performed best on the long cruise home, using the weeks sailing from South Africa to court a young woman. As the ship plodded north, beyond the coast of Portuguese west Africa (now Angola), heading to the swells of the Atlantic and beyond the Gulf of Guinea, turning past the bulge of west Africa at the Canary Islands, setting a course north for the Bay of Biscay and Southampton, George secured himself a wife. By the time the liner docked, he had snared a South African, Margaret Marshall Clark, the product of another high-society family. Her father was chairman of South Africa's railways and a director of De Beers, the world's largest diamond company. It was a happy match. Marriage followed and their son, Simon Francis, was born on 26 June 1952. At around the same time a brewing giant offered to buy the family business. George cashed in and took a seat on the board of the larger company. His son would need another career.

At first, young Simon followed the family tradition. 'Mann is used to wealth and an upper class way of life,' sums up a friend. He passed his childhood at Eton, then took up officer training at the Royal Military Academy Sandhurst. He did not try for university as he lacked academic talent and hungered for an active life, if not a sporting one. By the 1970s, when others grew their hair long, donned flares and protested against war and global injustice, Simon followed his father and took a commission in the Scots Guards. Some later suggested that his family had faintly disapproved. Soldiering for your country at a time of grave threat is an honourable duty; but a career in the army when no war is imminent could smack of desperation.

Mann, though, did well as an officer, and applied to the Special Air Service (SAS), Britain's well-respected special forces regiment. He was promptly accepted and became a troop commander in G Squadron of 22 SAS, where he specialised in intelligence and counter-terrorism. Most officers in Britain's special forces are expected to complete a three-year rotation, which Simon duly did before moving back to his regular army job. His counter-terrorism training would have been useful during a three-year tour of Northern Ireland in the 1970s, when British soldiers struggled to keep apart warring Protestant and Catholic factions. He travelled, facing Soviet opponents at the front line of the Cold War, both in West Germany and in Norway (where British squaddies (privates) were notorious for their capacity for pub brawls). He was also posted to Cyprus, Canada and central America. But by the beginning of the 1980s, after a decade in the army, promotions dried up and Simon tired of life in uniform. 'I think he wanted a new challenge, and after a while some people find army life a little bit mundane,' says an ex-colleague.

Simon Mann turned his hand, maladroitly, to computer software and, more dexterously, to a private military company run by the notorious founder of the SAS, David Stirling, who by the mid 1970s had convinced himself that Britain was in terminal decline and in need of a dose of strong leadership. Mann maintained his privileged life. He mixed with royalty and lingered at White's, though the smoke-filled rooms where geriatrics hurled anecdotes and bread rolls did little to satisfy the restless ex-soldier. When Stirling's private empire became embroiled in scandal at the end of the 1980s over the misuse of charity money, it was time to move on. Saddam Hussein briefly did him a favour, invading Kuwait and kicking off the first Gulf War. Mann re-enlisted, joining the army staff at the headquarters of the British commander in Saudi Arabia, where he liaised with active members of the SAS. Once that war was over Mann was footloose again.

Corporate warrior

Now Mann found his stride as an entrepreneur, largely thanks to an acquaintance with Tony Buckingham, an ex-North Sea oil-rig diver and businessman who liked to spend time with SAS veterans. Buckingham was involved in various oil firms, including one called Heritage and another called Ranger. By 1992 he was trying to break into Angola's emerging oil industry. He and Mann made contacts with Angola's national oil firm just as a rebel group, Unita (Uniao Nacional para la Independencia Total de Angola), overran several oil installations near a town called Soyo, in the north of Angola, seizing assets of the foreign oil firms. Angola's large but ineffective army failed to dislodge the rebels, so Mann and Buckingham stepped in: they volunteered to recruit a small private army

– a crack mercenary force – to fight the rebels and retake the oil assets. Angola's desperate rulers agreed.

Mann and Buckingham joined a long tradition of grizzled white men fighting in Africa. They followed men like Mike Hoare and Bob Denard, the veteran dogs of war. Hoare was a white-haired, stiff-lipped veteran of the Second World War who took ragbag armies of adventurers and crooks to fight in Congo's wars in the 1960s. Denard, a more flamboyant Frenchman, became famous for another mercenary craft: the foreign coup plot. Notably, in the 1970s, he slipped by night to murder presidents and take control of small African states, usually installing a new leader on behalf of France.

Both were moderately successful: Hoare won the hearts of those settlers, missionaries and civilians he rescued in remote corners of Congo. Foreign journalists lionised him. His daring tactics – 'In Congo we would rush around in a flying column, all guns blazing and it worked,' recalls one of his men interviewed in South Africa today – inspired novelists and film-makers. The Wild Geese, a novel and Hollywood film, is a lightly disguised portrayal of his exploits. Denard's craftier deeds were less well celebrated. One Sunday morning in 1977 he took ninety Sten-gun-waving mercenaries in a DC7 to snatch power in Benin, a tiny west African state. They fought for two hours in the capital, seizing the international airport and attacking the president's palace. Eventually Denard cut and ran. A year later he led a small hired army in a similar assault in the Comoros, a tiny collection of islands off Africa's east coast. He took with him fifty men armed with sawn-off shotguns and twenty-four bottles of Dom Perignon champagne. In darkness they landed from a fishing trawler, stormed the beachside palace, killed the president, toasted their success and installed a rival. Eleven years later Denard did the same thing again.

Hoare tried to ape Denard with a similar attack in the Seychelles, in the Indian Ocean, in 1981. He used a commercial plane and a team of South African mercenaries disguised as beer-swilling tourists – the Ancient Order of Froth Blowers. Hoare hoped to reinstall an old president, but he barely left the airport. His hired guns, after too much beer on the plane, started a battle at the arrivals hall. They managed to kill one of their own, endured several hours of fighting around the airport, then hijacked an Air India plane back to South Africa. There were worse examples of bad mercenary behaviour, especially in Angola where trigger-happy – and perhaps deranged – soldiers of fortune ran amok. An odd assortment fought for both sides of Nigeria's civil war. The hired guns generally got a reputation for daring and adventure, if not for effectiveness.

Such was the tradition of the dogs of war in Africa when Mann and Buckingham volunteered to arrange for men to fight in Angola. Mann, however, was a little different. He was as likely to wear a crumpled business suit and rimless spectacles as camouflage or chest webbing. He was an early example of a new sort of mercenary, the type as familiar with company law, bank transfers and investor agreements as with the workings of a Browning pistol. Mann and Buckingham came to represent a new era of corporate fighters, the professional soldier-of-fortune that is prevalent today.

It started with the smallish battle at the oil installations in Soyo, Angola, in February 1993 against Unita. At this time Unita – formerly an ally of the American and South African governments – was isolated while Angola's government had close ties with the west, largely because of its oil. The government agreed to let white South African and British mercenaries, under Mann and Buckingham, lead the fight to retake

Soyo. Officers and footsoldiers were recruited from the ready supply of South African apartheid operatives, both white and black. A small private security firm with the bland name Executive Outcomes, founded in 1989 and with close links to semi-official 'counter terrorism' hit squads in South Africa, provided the corporate structure.

Many who worked for Executive Outcomes were veterans of a South African army unit, 32 Battalion, that had previously fought in Angola (ironically, alongside those same Unita rebels they would now attack). These included Portuguese-speaking Angolans with a reputation for brutally effective warfare techniques. 32 Battalion had been known – as were many mercenary armies in Africa – as 'the terrible ones'. The South African army unit had fought using guerrilla and conventional tactics for more than a decade. Others in Executive Outcomes were drawn from domestic apartheid units: clandestine bodies of police and soldiers who were used to repress black democracy movements. Some were trained in the Koevoet, a terrifying counter-insurgency unit in South African-run Namibia. Others were parachutists, military intelligence, special forces officers and policemen.

From the start Executive Outcomes proved more serious than gentleman amateurs like Hoare and Denard. Most of the recruits at the attack on Soyo were skilled and experienced, though a few did turn tail at the first sign of gunfire. A smaller core of hardened soldiers, barely twenty-five men, led an assault that was backed by the Angolan air force and army. Many of the mercenaries had fought together before, in South African uniform, and some knew the enemy extremely well: they had once helped train and equip the Unita rebels.

The mercenaries favoured a limited selection of weapons – AK-47 assault rifles, PKM machine guns, a 60mm mortar

– that are light and easy to carry, and so are handy for attack. They were flown to their target by Angolan military helicopters, along the Atlantic coast, landing in thick elephant grass a few miles from Soyo shortly after heavy rains had fallen. From there on the mercenaries charged forward, overwhelming startled Unita soldiers, killing two men in a jeep, securing a beachhead a short distance from the Unita-run town, then withstanding a counterattack. With support from the Angolan air force and army, the mercenaries attacked from a direction the rebels little expected and retook the oil town in a couple of days. One South African, a veteran of 32 Battalion, was killed by a grenade when he leapt on to a tank in mid-battle; two more were killed in a fierce exchange of gunfire with the rebels. But Unita withdrew and the mercenaries – and Executive Outcomes – won a reputation for hard fighting.

Now there was no looking back. Angola offered a long term deal: more than $80 million plus diamond mining concessions if the hired guns would continue the war against Unita and help train the national army. Buckingham, Mann and their South African partners agreed. A second battle of Soyo followed and a much larger fighting force was put together by the mercenaries in Angola. 'Executive Outcomes in Angola was a big affair. We had perhaps 1,000 EO people and some 3,000 locals under command for short periods. And we helped run the air force,' explains one man who helped organise it. Mann reportedly co-ordinated much activity from alternate headquarters in Luanda – Angola's capital – and from a hotel in Sandton, Johannesburg, in South Africa. In 1994 he claimed his corporate army's second attack on the rebels at the Soyo oil installation, which again dislodged them, was one of the largest combined ground and air operations in Africa since the Second World War. The soldiers recruited to the private army included pilots, intelligence officers and men with intense and prolonged experience of war in Africa. This was a sophisticated army for hire to the highest bidder, though its leaders took care to choose clients favoured by western governments.

Pilots ferried large numbers of soldiers back and forth between Angola and South Africa. One of those who first took on the job of transporting them, a tousled-haired young Afrikaner called Crause Steyl, used a small Cessna aircraft. It was known as 'Ghost Rider' and had once been used by American drug-runners. Mann also found him contracts servicing Angolan military aircraft and fitting spy cameras. Eventually a larger airline, Ibis Air, was formed to support Executive Outcomes using much larger planes. Helicopter pilots could earn $7,000 a month, hugely more than the South African military would pay. And the soldiers found a tight-knit unit of hired guns provided camaraderie. One described enjoying 'closer bonding than I've had with my mother, my father, with anyone else ... It's like a marriage that doesn't go wrong.'

From 1993 to 1996, the corporate soldiers – led ultimately by Mann and Buckingham – went repeatedly into battle in Angola. Eventually twenty-one foreign mercenaries were killed alongside many more unnamed Angolans. Most notable were assaults against diamond-rich regions in rebel hands, especially in the north of the country. When Unita lost its income from the precious stones, due to a United Nations ban, rebel strength waned. The hired guns did not end the war, which continued until the death of Unita's leader, Jonas Savimbi, in 2002. But Executive Outcomes' reputation continued to grow.

The corporate army fought next in Sierra Leone, another west

African country blighted by internal conflict. Again the rebels of Sierra Leone were funded by the illicit trade in diamonds; again they were a nasty bunch. Soldiers of the Revolutionary United Front were famous for chopping off victims' limbs with machetes – a brutal operation known as 'long sleeves' for those whose hands were amputated, and 'short sleeves' for those who lost a whole arm. Sierra Leone's government hired Executive Outcomes in 1995–96 to fight the rebels and train its own forces. The mercenaries did so, growing popular among ordinary people sick of war. But international pressure grew too strong: African and other rulers officially opposed the use of hired guns. Eventually the mercenaries left and the government promptly collapsed, letting rebels swarm the capital.

But others flocked to hire the mercenary group. Executive Outcomes became a conglomerate of companies, with interests in security, diamonds, oil and other forms of mining. Its various corporate incarnations such as Sandline International, or Branch Energy, had offices in Europe, North America and Asia, as well as in twenty-six African states. Towards the end of the 1990s governments beyond Africa were keen to hire Executive Outcomes. Papua New Guinea paid for it to organise an attack on rebels in 1997, though a storm of public anger (and complaints from the poorly paid local army) eventually forced a withdrawal by the mercenaries. Tim Spicer, a front man for the organisation and friend of Mann, and two others were briefly arrested.

But Executive Outcomes expanded and other corporations were created. Later the corporate army was reborn for operations in other countries. A confusing web was spun of connected companies and holding firms, some related to oil or diamonds, others to military affairs or aviation. Many shared a single operational address in London but were registered in

Guernsey – an island tax haven in the English Channel – where Mann also kept some bank accounts. Mann and Buckingham grew wealthy. Mann proved a good project manager, spending two years developing a mining firm, Diamond Works, in Angola. Such assets were eventually turned into cash when the connected companies were floated on the Toronto stock exchange, earning Buckingham and Mann several million dollars each.

This arrangement kept away prying journalists, rivals and tax men. Some close to Mann say he did less well than the more financially astute Buckingham. But he clearly made a good income. Buckingham was probably worth $150 million by 2005, largely from his diamond and oil incomes, plus property. Mann was not quite in that league, but he reputedly earned as much as $1 million a month on the Angola contract. He came out of it with several million dollars and a growing property portfolio, including an expensive home on Portobello Road, a fashionable corner of west London, and a stately home, Inchmery, set in twenty acres of pasture in Hampshire on the south coast of Britain. The latter, which had long been owned by the Rothschild family, is currently worth more than £5 million. Mann's holding companies bought a private plane and made other investments on his behalf.

Retirement

Executive Outcomes' spokesmen said the army helped bring order to Africa, and only fought for governments. But the mercenaries also broke rules and undermined broader efforts to end wars. In 1998 Sandline International breached a UN embargo on weapons sales to Sierra Leone. Many governments grew uneasy at the clout of these freelance fighters. South Africa's new democratic rulers particularly opposed them. President Nelson Mandela did not want apartheid-era soldiers operating – fighting and killing for profit – out of South Africa. The country longed to shake off its reputation, earned during the apartheid years, as a source of instability in Africa. So, in May 1998, Mandela's government passed an anti-mercenary law, the Foreign Military Assistance Act, which makes it illegal for anyone to offer military aid overseas.

The impact was clear: the corporate army closed doors in South Africa, though it continued to operate elsewhere under different names. Buckingham continued to work in the oil industry, including in Africa. But others considered retiring. One of the South African founders of Executive Outcomes became a horsewhisperer, running a ranch in South Africa where he now offers tourists luxurious riding holidays. A few turned to writing up their adventures or preparing film scripts. Others fished for low-key intelligence work advising African governments.

The black footsoldiers, the former Angolans of 32 Battalion, sought jobs where they could. Many took menial employment as security guards at supermarkets or in office buildings in South Africa. Others returned to a wretched military base, Pomfret, in the desert of north-west South Africa. It is a miserable spot: an abandoned asbestos-mining town at the end of a dry and rutted road, between a distant village called Terra Firma and an even more remote one called Eureka. Birds of prey sit on broken telephone poles, mongoose and duiker scurry over the roads. Many houses have smashed windows; their sandy gardens are strewn with rubbish.

Mann all but retired. He looked for smaller diversions. He and Buckingham – plus a third British businessman and friend, David Tremain – competed in a marathon car race from China to Europe, the Peking-to-Paris Rally. But after weeks of hard driving, Mann and Buckingham grew sick of each other and went their separate ways. Mann had a young wife, Amanda, who enjoyed luxury. Mann already had three children from previous marriages and Amanda produced three more. There were many opportunities for safe, sensible and unglamorous investments: he considered putting money into light indus- trial units being built beside the harbour at Southampton, near his stately pile. He could have made a decent return, but 'I've never seen anyone look so bored', recalls a friend. He was sick of his quiet life in southern England. So, in search of something new, Mann and his wife moved to a large rented house in a fashionable corner of Cape Town, South Africa.

Mann's father died in 2001 and the son was ageing, too, nearing fifty. He had a hip replaced. He dabbled with various investments, including gold mines in South America. A friend recalls that 'Simon was always involved in several projects at once. There was a big one, Placer Gold, a mine in Guyana. Simon was very involved in that one.' He took whatever chances arose. In 2001 he agreed to play a role in a British film drama, a gritty reconstruction of Bloody Sunday, the day (30 January 1972) when British troops shot unarmed Catholic protesters in northern Ireland. Mann thought the shootings a 'cock-up', and played the part in the film of Colonel Derek Wilford, the British commander. He said he hoped to help the Northern Ireland peace process and spoke to the press under a slightly altered name, as Frank Mann. The film's director, Paul Greengrass, called him thoughtful, courageous and 'a humane man, but an adventurer. He is very English, a romantic, tremendously good company,' he suggested. It was a typical assessment.

Mann felt as drawn to the daredevil lives of Hoare and Denard as to the new breed of corporate warrior. He could not settle to light industrial units or a sleepy retirement. The romantic side of his character wanted excitement, the thrill of adventure, the old fashioned hunt for treasure and fame. By 2003 he was hungry, looking for an opportunity where he could find action, and money, once more. He was looking for the Big Chance. That would come in a small country in west Africa with a longstanding reputation for violence and a more recent reputation for wealth.

2
Mad Uncle Macias

'Those were the Days, My Friend'
Mary Hopkin song, played at executions in Equatorial Guinea

At about the time Simon Mann signed up for the Scots Guards, a brutal murder took place. Far away in a tiny patch of American territory in the sweaty capital of a west African microstate, two diplomats were closing their consulate for the day. It was late afternoon in August 1971. A balding bespectacled diplomat told his colleague, another grey-suited employee of the State Department, to tidy up his papers and prepare to leave. Their office was composed of just a few rooms with a vault – a secure space with a radio set and valuable documents – and a reception. The two diplomats had spent the previous hours sending telegrams to their superiors warning of a dangerous conspiracy against America.

Now the elder diplomat, Alfred Erdos, suddenly snapped into a rage. He pushed his startled companion into a chair in the vault and unleashed a terrifying attack. Erdos grabbed some electrical cord and tightened it around Donald Leahy's neck. The younger man struggled free, leapt from his chair and stumbled to the reception room. But before he could scrabble for the front door, Erdos snatched a pair of office scissors and plunged them into his colleague. He stabbed gingerly at first, later recalling the skin was tough as leather. But as the men struggled, Erdos thrust the scissors more fiercely – ten times in all – eventually killing Leahy with a bloody blow to the neck.

Brought to Washington DC and put on trial the following year, Erdos offered a defence of insanity. He had been driven mad, he said, by brutal conditions in one of the most awful countries in Africa. The country where the two men served was a wretched spot where violent death was all too common. He suffered 'acute paranoid psychosis' as his home over-looked the main police station of the capital city. He came to fear that he and his family would be murdered. He 'could hear the comings and goings, the sounds of torture inside and see the bodies carried away', explained his lawyer. It did little good. The jury showed no interest in his *Heart of Darkness* defence, nor in the slaughter in the African country. Instead, Erdos was convicted of involuntary manslaughter following a homosexual affair with the victim.

Whatever the cause of the attack, the trial briefly cast a light on a tiny country that might reasonably claim to be the most wretched on earth. If you look at a map, Equatorial Guinea sits in the armpit of Africa, a small patch of land divided between a square of mainland territory and a scattering of islands in the Gulf of Guinea. The jungle-covered part on the continent borders Gabon and Cameroon; on one of the islands, Bioko, is the capital city, Malabo. Almost nobody has a good word for the place. If you see a man limping on both legs, quipped one American ambassador, you know he has been to Equatorial Guinea. 'Devil Island', as it is sometimes known, is unlike much of modern Africa. Senior churchmen and politicians talk of the 'magical powers' of the rulers; there are said to be regular witch-burnings. It is both sleepy and sinister, where the vicious rivalries of village politics are elevated to the national level.

For two centuries Spain owned the territory, but showed almost no interest in its only tropical African possession. Twice the colonial power tried to sell the island part of the colony, Fernando Po (now Bioko). In 1824 Thomas Fowell Buxton, who led a British anti-slavery party, said Britain should buy it and 'hold it for no other purpose than the benefit of the African'. Fernando Po should be 'a counterpart to Singapore' and a centre for 'enterprise plus native industry', he argued. But when Spain finally offered to sell for £60,000, in 1839, Britain sniffed at the price. In 1901, a proposed sale to Germany also folded. Only France grabbed some of Spanish equatorial Africa, stealing some mainland territory for its own colonies.

The Victorian explorer Henry Morton Stanley called Fernando Po a 'pearl of the Gulf of Guinea', but added he would not give a penny for a 'jewel which Spain did not polish'. In 1936 the British novelist Graham Greene, who was generally fond of west Africa, dismissed 'the little dreadful Spanish island' where there existed a 'mild form of slavery that enabled a man to pawn his children'. Towards the end of its two centuries of rule, Spain did a little to improve the lives of those it ruled. The colonial power set up an economy based on cocoa plantations and a reasonable school system; health campaigns reduced the impact of tropical diseases, at least on Fernando Po. By the second half of the twentieth century, Equatorial Guineans were less poor than most Africans thanks to exports of cocoa. But few Spaniards settled and native Africans were denied political rights and economic chances. When independence loomed, the Spanish organised hasty polls to find a new government. Spain, under its own dictator General Franco, was hardly qualified to promote democracy and Equatorial Guinea was ill-prepared when, late in 1968, it became the 126th member of the United Nations.

After independence things really went wrong. Its citizens were soon desperate to escape. A sleepy-eyed man, Macias Nguema, won the elections. A shy son of a revered and brutal witchdoctor known as 'His Saintly Father', Macias did badly at Catholic mission schools, but took up jobs as a junior bureaucrat and a coffee farmer, then as a court interpreter and subsequently as mayor of a small town. He became an influential leader within an important subgroup of the Fang, the country's most populous ethnic group, and was groomed for office by a few Spaniards who believed he would serve their interests. They bear some responsibility for what came next.

In power, Macias flattened the economy, destroyed cocoa plantations and killed off a thriving fishing industry. He had two rivals jailed a few months after he took office. Both were murdered: one first had his legs broken and was then starved. That augured ill for everyone else. A bloodthirsty and insecure tyrant, Macias assassinated ministers with zeal, usually after political reshuffles: ten of the dozen cabinet members in his first government were butchered. One survived after militiamen chased him, on foot, through tropical forest. Fishermen's boats were burned and ordinary people banned from the coast to prevent escape. The only road out of the mainland part of the country was mined. Yet fleeing was often the only way to survive. Two thirds of the deputies of the national assembly plus many senior civil servants were driven out, imprisoned or killed. Some 100,000 people – roughly a third of the total population – fled or were killed under Macias. Tens of thousands were massacred.

It was a time of slaughter and misery. Diplomats said Macias ruled through fear alone. Though a charismatic (if incoherent) speaker and able to draw some support, especially among the populous Fang, he launched a war against any possible threat. Most functions of government collapsed. Some 7,000 Spaniards fled, followed later by far more Nigerian labourers. A Swedish researcher who crept in called Equatorial Guinea the 'Dachau of Africa', then got out as quickly as he could. He echoed the name given to the country by travellers a century or so earlier – 'Death's Waiting-room' – when malaria, yellow fever and other diseases took a terrible toll. Macias eventually tried to ban western medicines as 'unAfrican' and many diseases, even leprosy, became prevalent again. The country has yet to recover. The 2004 Lonely Planet travel guide lists a long rollcall of health risks, including rabies, tuberculosis, bilharzia, diphtheria, malaria and typhus. There are also occasional outbreaks of cholera and ebola, plus the widespread menace of AIDS.

But under Macias man struck with most cruelty. At one Christmas mass execution in a sports stadium in the capital, Malabo, palace guards shot 150 victims while music blared. The song: 'Those Were the Days, My Friend'. Other executions took place in the notorious Black Beach prison, usually at night. When it became expensive to use bullets, victims were garrotted or forced to kneel to have their skulls smashed with iron bars. Some died of thirst; others were buried alive or died from gangrene following torture. To spread terror, some were beheaded, their heads left on poles in the streets. Emigrés were kidnapped and dragged home to be killed. Many who survived prison were driven insane.

A witness later recalled: 'No food in the shops, no water, no electricity, no kerosene for the lamps. At night we walked in blackness. Yes, for eleven years we walked in blackness.' Survivors saw relatives and neighbours killed. One man described his family's murder: 'My father was a successful cocoa farmer. In 1974, Macias's troops came. My father and brothers were shot dead and our house was burned to the ground. I fled into the bush ...' Nightclubs and schools closed; missionaries were chased from the country. Macias – like Pol Pot in Cambodia – launched a campaign against the educated and they began to 'disappear'. He banned the word 'intellectual', once fining a minister who used it at a cabinet meeting. He called educated people the 'greatest problem facing Africa today. They are polluting our climate with foreign culture.' He closed newspapers and jailed priests. The ethnic group that dominates the island part of the country, the Bubis, fared particularly badly.

Macias's reign was tragi-comic – and sadly typical of the worst of African leaders. He seemed to compete with Idi Amin of Uganda in acts of bizarre brutality. He declared himself 'president for life', then renamed the island part of the country after himself. He adopted new titles, each more eccentric than the last: 'Major-general of the Armed Forces'; 'Great Maestro of Popular Education, Science and Traditional Culture'; 'The Only Miracle of Equatorial Guinea'. When the national director of statistics gave a population estimate that displeased Macias, the unlucky civil servant was tortured and killed. Former lovers of his mistresses were butchered. Things got so bad Macias's own wife fled into exile.

He ordered teachers and priests to promote his cult of personality. School children chanted that Macias alone had freed the country from imperial Spanish rule. The sanctuary of every church was to show his portrait. Priests read out messages venerating the insecure president, such as: 'God created Equatorial Guinea thanks to Macias. Without Macias, Equatorial Guinea would not exist.' Some 80 per cent of the people were nominally Christian, but he eventually forced churches shut. Builders walled up Malabo's colonial era cathedral.

When he ran short of money Macias took hostages. One author lists prices for prisoners of different nationalities. He collected a generous ransom of nearly $60,000 for a German woman; a Spanish professor earned him $40,000 and a Soviet corpse was released for $6,800; finally, a living Frenchman went for $5,000. In 1976 a Soviet plane crashed into a mountain near Malabo, killing all on board. Macias refused to release any bodies until compensation of $5 million was paid for 'damage to the mountain'. None of this helped his international relations. Spanish and Soviet aid dried up. African governments despised him. Nigeria's rulers planned invading in 1976 after tens of thousands of Nigerian workers were expelled and many were killed. The idea was forgotten only when Nigeria's own military leader, General Murtala Muhammed, was assassinated.

Some say that Macias was a cannibal. It seems likely. The skull of one ancestor, the great-grandfather of the Fang, is revered and held by the leader of the day. Macias held this, and built up a large collection of other skulls. He encouraged the re-emergence of secret societies, like the Bwiti cult, which engage in symbolic ritual consumption of skeletons and sometimes require sacrifices. One expert, Max Liniger-Goumaz, suggests that such societies of powerful men believe eating part of a person is a way to absorb his virtues or strengths. He describes the procedure for obtaining cadavers:

Each member of the society in turn had to provide a corpse. If no corpse was forthcoming by natural means, recourse was had to poison – particularly strophanthus – and the victim was chosen by all the members of the sect. If this process did not succeed, the member responsible was obliged to offer himself for sacrifice.

Others had earlier noticed the habit among the Fang, the dominant ethnic group which Macias now led. Richard Burton, a Victorian traveller and one-time British consul in Fernando Po, had noted 'the average traces of anthropopophagy [cannibalism]'. Mary Kingsley, another Victorian traveller, suggested 'the cannibalism of the Fans [her term for the Fang], although a prevalent habit, is no danger, I think, to white people, except as regards the bother it gives one in preventing one's black companions from getting eaten'. She saw no ritual goal, suggesting of the Fang: 'Man's flesh, he says, is good to eat, very good, and he wishes you would try it.'

Man-eater or not, few dared challenge the ruler of Equatorial Guinea. When a poster of Macias was torn from the front of the vice-president's office, police arrested an opposition leader and killed him. An ex-ambassador, a possible rival to Macias, was immersed repeatedly in a barrel of water for a week until he died. Opposition parties were closed. Terrifying youth militia committed atrocities on the government's behalf.

Given these horrors, why did nobody rise up – or no foreigner intervene? Most outsiders took little notice of the tiny Spanish-speaking ex-colony of no economic or strategic significance. In Africa governments practised self-serving 'African solidarity', which meant not criticising fellow presidents however wicked, as long as trouble did not spill over borders. Macias eventually got so bad that a group of African leaders did suggest, politely, that he stand down, but to no avail. At home, most Equatorial Guineans with power went along with Macias's malevolent ways, while ordinary people struggled to survive and escape. But one effort was made to overthrow the government of Equatorial Guinea – and it would prove to be a model for the Wonga Coup.

3
The Albatross of War

'... BRITISH REGISTERED QUOTE ALBATROSS UNQUOTE ... BRITISH,
CANADIAN AND FRENCH MERCENARIES ... MAY ATTEMPT TO
ASSUME CONTROL OVER FERNANDO PO ...

Foreign Office Cypher, marked 'Secret', 1973

'Knocking off a bank or an armoured truck is merely crude.
Knocking off an entire republic has, I feel, a certain style.'

Character in *The Dogs of War* (1974)

On the third day of the new year a man called Llambias slid
a piece of paper into his typewriter and started punching the
keys. He had a story to tell, one he hardly believed himself.
Doing so, he helped save the dictatorship of Equatorial Guinea.
The year was 1973. Llambias worked for Special Branch, an
investigative part of the British police, in a small patch of
territory on the southern tip of Spain. Gibraltar, a tiny corner
of sovereign Britain, offered little: a large rock, some famous
monkeys and a harbour. But it was a meeting point for gun-
runners, smugglers, mercenaries, terrorists and other shady
characters who passed through the Mediterranean. Llambias's job was to keep an eye on them. He typed a four-page
report for his bosses.

Llambias wrote that the Polish-born British owner of a boat

in the harbour had approached him that day. George Allan owned the *Albatross*, an 'ex-Admiralty MFV' (Motorised Fishing Vessel), a British naval attack and transport ship that he had bought in Britain two years earlier for £11,000. He had made a confession. In October 1972 he was in a nearby Spanish harbour, Fuengirola, when a man called Peter Dean had offered £5,500 plus all expenses to hire the boat and crew for six weeks. It was a good price and a deal was struck. Another man with a Scottish accent then turned up. He used the name Harry Greaves – but was better known as Alexander Ramsay Gay – and was evidently in charge. He ordered the boat to sail for Gibraltar, where it would be fitted for a long voyage – 4000 kilometres (2500 miles) – to the Gulf of Guinea.

In Gibraltar they loaded curious equipment. Gay ordered three 18-foot Seacraft rubber landing boats – also known as rigid inflatable boats (RIBs) – each with a 50-horsepower outboard engine, from Britain. They arrived and were packed into the *Albatross* on 4 November. Provisions and fuel were stored: 2500 litres (550 gallons) of fuel in two large tanks, plus 32 drums of 200 litres (45 gallons) each. That gave the *Albatross* a range of 4800 kilometres (3000 miles). By mid December a small gang of men had gathered, some British and four French. The men soon let slip they were soldiers-of-fortune. Most had fought in the Nigerian civil war, and they had battle anecdotes to share. Gay fought for the Biafran rebels in Nigeria; a Briton called Scott Sanderson plus the four French soldiers had been on the victorious Nigerian government side. Soon more equipment arrived from Tangier, across the Mediterranean in Morocco: 50 jackets, 100 pairs of trousers and sets of military webbing.

By Christmas the boat owner, Allan, had grown suspicious. Gay told him to prepare for the delivery of 106 boxes, each weighing 60 kilos (130 lbs) and containing arms and ammunition of different sorts. The weapons were ordered, said Gay, by 'a German agent', an arms dealer from Hamburg who dealt with the Spanish government. It was done with the 'knowledge of the Spanish foreign minister, Senor Lopez Bravo' and various officials. The Spaniards were first told the arms were destined for Iran, but then a real Iranian delegation appeared in Madrid to buy weapons. So they changed stories: the German said he was really buying guns for a terrorist group, the Black September organisation. When a senior Spanish civil servant questioned the sale, a bribe of $9,000 satisfied him. The arms and ammunition in boxes, it was agreed, would be marked as containing machinery. They would first go to the Spanish port of Malaga, then be put on to a Corsican coaster. The coaster would rendezvous with the *Albatross*, at an unspecified spot, for transhipment.

Llambias's report was dated early January 1973. At that time, said Allan, he had been ordered by Gay to sail on to Olhao, in Portugal, where he expected seven more hired guns to arrive: two more Britons, four more Frenchmen and a Canadian. Then the *Albatross* would sail for the Canary Islands, *en route* to the Gulf of Guinea, where a time and place would be arranged for the weapons to be transhipped. From there the *Albatross* would sail on to Cape Verde, refuel and pick up more provisions. Then, at an unknown point, the boat would collect '50 Negro mercenaries'. Llambias concluded: 'Their final destination will be three miles off Fernando Po where, in conjunction with arrangements already made ashore, they will attempt to take over the island's administration.'

How was Allan sure? 'Under very lengthy interrogation' the boat owner admitted he had carried out a 'clandestine search' of Gay's cabin in the *Albatross*. He found a 'map of the town and port of Fernando Po marked with code names (mainly names of European capitals) showing strategic points'. And why did Allan continue to work for the hired guns? Llambias explained: 'He had no alternative but to carry on with the operation because he knew that if he did not, his life and that of his son and of his wife, would be short ones. He had already been threatened to this effect', by Gay. 'He was therefore carrying on with the operation come what may and if he did survive, would report back.'

Llambias's report is a startling document. Obtained in 2005 from Britain's National Archives it is published here for the first time. It reveals the details of a carefully planned, British-led coup attempt against Equatorial Guinea by a group of hardened soldiers of fortune in 1973. These men had spent the preceding years fighting as mercenaries in a fierce civil war in Nigeria, a neighbour of Equatorial Guinea. In those early days there were many puzzles to answer: the British authorities did not know who financed and organised the plot, nor the reason for it. It was not clear if Spain backed it, and nor was it obvious that anyone should intervene to stop it. Some of these puzzles would eventually be answered, in spectacular fashion.

Freddie's Coup: The 1973 Attempt
Allan, his crew and the band of mercenaries sailed from Portugal on the *Albatross* loaded with fuel, military clothing and other material, heading for the Canary Islands. They planned to rendezvous with the Corsican ship loaded with arms before picking up fifty black African soldiers, probably veterans of the civil war in Nigeria, and sailing to Fernando Po. But Llambias's report triggered a diplomatic response. Soon cyphers and telegrams were whizzing between British diplomats, who could not help seeing the funny side of the

caper. They swapped notes about the dictatorship in west Africa, with one diplomat giggling his heartfelt 'fangs' for a message from a colleague. Another signed off an earnest letter marked 'Confidential' with a quotation from Coleridge's *Rime of the Ancient Mariner*: 'Why look'st thou so? – With my crossbow I shot the Albatross.' The episode was a distraction from the daily tedium of diplomatic life.

A cypher on 4 January, the day after Llambias sent his report, warned extravagantly:

INFORMATION HAS BEEN VOLUNTEERED TO SPECIAL BRANCH HERE OF BRITISH REGISTERED QUOTE ALBATROSS UNQUOTE, A CONVERTED EX/NAVY MFV, TO THE EFFECT THAT BRITISH, CANADIAN AND FRENCH MERCENARIES AND UNSPECIFIED AFRI-CANS EQUIPPED (AT THE EXPENSE OF A QUOTE AFRICAN FINAN-CIER UNQUOTE BUT IN THE FULL KNOWLEDGE OF THE SPANISH AUTHORITIES) WITH SPANISH ARMY MAY ATTEMPT TO ASSUME CONTROL OVER FERNANDO PO SOMETIME AFTER 20 JAN

The British Foreign Office finally concluded that Spain did not know of the planned coup. So the British warned Madrid, though made no effort to tell the awful government of Macias in Equatorial Guinea. British consuls in the Canary Islands, Cape Verde and elsewhere were told to look out for the *Albatross*. Late in January the 64-foot ex-naval craft finally arrived in Arrecife de Lanzarote in the Canary Islands. Spanish police (the islands remain a part of Spain) arrested the mercenaries on 23 January. Under interroga-tion they admitted the coup plot and the plan to 'do away' with Macias. They were deported. Allan and his crew were told to sail away: a Spanish naval craft escorted them to Casablanca in Morocco; a Moroccan naval ship escorted the

Albatross out of its territorial waters; Spain refused it permission to return to its territory.

The news eventually reached Equatorial Guinea. Another cypher, an internal Foreign Office document marked 'Restricted' and dated 30 January 1973, reported: 'Radio Santa Isabel is announcing at regular intervals that the government has been informed that a ship carrying mercenaries and colonialists is on its way to invade Equatoral Guinea.' Macias called a council of ministers and summoned diplomats. Barricades were thrown up in Malabo, especially around the presidential palace. Soldiers were out in force. By the end of the month demonstrations erupted outside embassies.

The plot had been comprehensively foiled. But there remained one big question: who was behind it? Talk of an African financier led to nothing substantial. Alexander Ramsay Gay, who evidently organised much of the groundwork, was sent back to Britain, where he was again arrested and interrogated by British police. There, according to a writer on Equatorial Guinea, Randall Fegley, the police only released him after another Briton intervened on his behalf. This man, according to allegations in the *Sunday Times*, was both the brain and the main financier of the plot. His name: Frederick Forsyth, the well-known novelist.

Frederick Forsyth, by 1973, was reasonably famous. He had reported for the BBC from Nigeria during that country's civil war, then campaigned for the Biafran separatists. He had also made close contacts with mercenaries in that war. Subsequently he wrote a series of very popular novels, including *The Day of the Jackal*, about a plot to kill a French president, and *The Odessa File*. By the early 1970s he was passionate in his support of the deposed Biafran leader, Odumegwu Emeka Ojukwu, wealthy and well-connected in the mercenary world.

After he spoke to the police and helped organise the release of Alexander Gay, Frederick Forsyth sat down and quickly wrote another bestselling novel, *The Dogs of War*. It was published a little more than a year later, in 1974, and proved a great success. It was soon made into a popular film starring Christopher Walken.

Everybody assumed the book was a work of fiction. But, considering the documents obtained from the British National Archives, there is now every reason to believe it was based upon real life. *The Dogs of War* relates many true details of the real life coup attempt the year before, those described in Llambias's report. It describes a plot against a country – 'Zangaro' – all but identical to Equatorial Guinea. A character much like Alexander Gay – 'Cat Shannon' – sets the whole thing up. Guns are bought from Spain through a German agent in Hamburg, then loaded on to a boat. Forsyth even describes a boat – a 74-ton ex-military craft called the *Albatross*, registered in Milford Haven (as was the real *Albatross*), hired in Spain and captained by a 'Mr Allen'. Fuel is loaded in large barrels and RIBs are stored, along with webbing and various military clothing. Some goods are shipped from Britain, some transferred from Tangier in Morocco. A Spanish official approves the arms deal after bribes are paid; front companies transfer money. The boat sails with a group of white mercenaries who have recently fought in an African war. It then picks up some fifty black African veterans, and sails on for the coup. In the book, of course, there is one crucial difference: the coup succeeds.

The official documents in the National Archives for the first time show that Forsyth's bestselling story is based on fact. It is so detailed that one might reasonably assume that Forsyth had been involved. In 1978 a British newspaper, the *Sunday Times*, alleged just that. It claimed that the novelist, rich with his earnings from *The Day of the Jackal*, had financed and plotted a real coup attempt with Gay. The two men apparently planned the coup from Forsyth's Camden flat, using maps, colour slides and a balsa wood model of the landing sites. Forsyth and Gay reportedly even composed a speech to be broadcast after the coup. The newspaper alleged he provided £50,000 for forty former soldiers from Nigeria to overthrow Macias. Another author suggests it was nearer £100,000. The newspaper said that Forsyth – who adopted the name 'Mr Van Cleef' – hoped to replace Macias with his close friend, the regional Biafran leader, Odumegwu Emeka Ojukwu. That made some sense as Equatorial Guinea, in 1973, was still home to thousands of Nigerian Igbo people from Biafra, skilled labourers who worked in the cocoa plantations. They would have backed Ojukwu as the new president. (Forsyth also used Ojukwu as a model for the leader to be imposed in Equatorial Guinea in his fictional tale). They hated Macias for his repressive rule, and for supporting Nigeria's rulers during that country's civil war. Eventually the Igbos were attacked and expelled from Equatorial Guinea, perhaps as an act of punishment, or to prevent others plotting a similar scheme.

Ojukwu flatly denied being part of any coup attempt. Forsyth has long stayed quiet on the subject, but he agreed to be interviewed for this book. He admits he did careful research on how to do a coup in Equatorial Guinea in 1973, but only for the purposes of writing an authentic novel. He suggests Macias was an awful and paranoid dictator, 'so evil, he reduced the place to a hellhole'. Asked if he plotted a coup for real, he first laughs and responds, 'I am certain there was no coup attempt in 1973. But wild rumours circulate in this mercenary world.' His research he admits, was unusually thorough. Over five months, just as the real coup plot was being prepared, he even masqueraded as a South African arms dealer and a coup plotter. He says he travelled to eastern Europe to a secret conference of crooks and arms dealers, where he talked of overthrowing a west African government. 'It could be that the plan of the novel was presumed to be reality,' he says coolly. At one point in Hamburg he believes his cover was blown and a hit man was sent to kill him. He escaped the town, by train.

I originally postulated a question to myself: would it be possible for a group of paid and bought-for mercenaries to topple a republic? I thought, if the republic were weak enough and power concentrated in one tyrant, then, in theory, yes. I looked around and saw Fernando Po, and every story about the country was gruesome. I didn't go there myself, but I met businessmen and others who had been there, and they told me this place was weird. So I decided it could be done ... If you stormed the palace – well, it wasn't really a palace, it was the old Spanish colonial governor's mansion – probably by sunrise you could take over, provided you have a substitute African president and announced it was an internal *coup d'état*.

I began to explore the world of black market arms. Where do you get a shipload of black market weapons? I knew nothing about it, so I dug around. I discovered the capital was either Prague, where Omnipol, the Communist arms dealer was (but for that the client had to be cleared by Moscow), otherwise it was Hamburg. So off I went. I penetrated under subterfuge, using a South African name, and developed my theme. I attended conferences of black market freelance criminals. And I learned about the curious 'end user certificates' [to identify those who are entitled to use and buy weapons], how they were forged or purchased from corrupt African diplomats. One of those attending a conference brought a bodyguard with him, an Alan Murphy, who was a British mercenary. He kept a diary.

Forsyth says Murphy, the mercenary bodyguard, believed his story about a coup in Equatorial Guinea and wrote it in his diary. Later Murphy shot himself and London police found the diary, which was passed to journalists at the *Sunday Times*. In turn, they claimed to have evidence of Forsyth's involvement in a real coup attempt.

Forsyth first suggested he is 'certain there was no coup attempt in 1973', though the British police knew different. They had the benefit of the Special Branch report from Gibraltar and the confessions of the mercenaries arrested in the Canary Islands. They also believed Forsyth had played a central role, according to Forsyth himself. The novelist admits that Scotland Yard contacted him, while he was living in Ireland, and told him never to try it again. Others are convinced, too. An ex-mercenary who fought with Mike Hoare and now lives in South Africa says he received a letter from a person close to Forsyth, Knowle Hamilton, who also confirmed that the novelist had arranged the real plot. Even readers of *The Dogs of War* might have suspected something: though an entertaining novel, much of the story reads like a documentary account.

The evidence suggests Frederick Forsyth did plot a real coup in 1973, which sadly did not succeed. Somehow he lifted details from the real plot, as shown by the newly released documents in the National Archives. Forsyth might have claimed that he was told an insider's account of the real coup plot by others and merely borrowed the information. But then why deny a real coup was ever planned? Perhaps because he also conducted extraordinary 'research' in the same year into carrying out that coup. That reasonably led others – like Murphy – to think he planned a coup for real. It seems that Murphy was right.

Interviewed in April 2006, Forsyth now admits there was a 'stillborn attempt' at a coup. Asked whether he helped plot it, he says his memory is vague: 'I don't know whether I thought of it, or someone else.' As for the relationship between the coup attempt and his novel, he is not sure which came first: 'It was a chicken and egg situation. I'm not sure if the authors of the plot listened to me, or I listened to them … We were sitting around in pubs discussing it … people with a lot of beer in them.'

He also knew Gay – 'a level-headed Scot' – from Biafra, and conceded that the two had co-operated. 'Yes, we were talking, meeting in pubs, over Fernando Po', he says. He admits, too, giving the police a character reference regarding Gay, after a bag with guns was traced to the Scot. And, finally, he admits passing money to the coup plotters: 'Yes, payments were made, always cash.' Though he suggests this was for 'information' only. Asked bluntly if he plotted a coup in Equatorial Guinea he laughed and suggested 'you put in the book what you have found.'

If Forsyth's art imitated real life, it is also clear that life imitated his art. The men of the rent-a-coup mercenary adventures, soldiers like Denard and Hoare, were fond of his novel. They treated it as a useful guide, perhaps because it contained such convincing detail. Forsyth says: 'Denard succeeded, Hoare failed, but in both cases it was remarkable. In Denard's attack, I learned, every mercenary had a copy of Les Chiens de Guerre stuck in his back pocket and in Hoare's attack they all had the English version, The Dogs of War.' The plotters of the

Wonga Coup in 2004 went a step further, apparently repli-
cating Forsyth's work in their own coup attempt. Forsyth
believes the plotters of the 'bizarre' Wonga Coup followed his
book extremely closely.

> It was almost the same, blow by blow, as my novel! There was
> one important difference. I said it cannot be done by airplane.
> A ship can drop over the horizon and be entirely on its own.
> There you can do your training; on board, you can oil and
> grease – or degrease, rather – your guns. You can use inflat-
> able boats for dummy runs. Then you would come ashore in
> RIBs. In my book Cat Shannon, the chief mercenary, had a
> back-up unit of forty black soldiers.
>
> Then thirty years pass and suddenly I hear of this bizarre
> plan in Equatorial Guinea! I've never spoken to Simon Mann.
> But here were the elements of my novel: the British backer;
> there is Severo Moto in exile; an external financier; the lure
> of [mineral] wealth; funding through blind companies; the
> recruitment of an officer to run it all. Then it was a complete
> cock-up, too much chat in bars in South Africa, the intelligence
> soon knew all about it. Yes, it was all taken off the page!

What is remarkable about this episode – apart from the fact
that a prominent British figure was apparently involved in
plotting a coup in Equatorial Guinea, which sadly failed – is
that his exploits were repeated precisely three decades later by
another British figure, Simon Mann. But where the plotters of
the real life first attack had a noble goal – removing a deranged
dictator from power – Mann's scheme was organised for a
more predictable reward. Where the old Equatorial Guinea
was repressive and poor, the modern one is both repressive
and rich – a far more appealing target for a hired gun.

4

Obiang in Charge

'… the Fernando Po people say …[a] ladder reached from earth to heaven so the gods could go up and down it and attend personally to mundane affairs…[But they] threw down the ladder, and have since left humanity severely alone.'

Mary Kingsley, *Travels in West Africa* (1897)

The consequences of the coup's failure in 1973 were not too grave for the plotters. Forsyth profited from *The Dogs of War*; the hired guns avoided jail. But Macias stayed in power for six more years, growing ever more awful. His behaviour also grew increasingly odd. As if performing Shakespeare, he held long conversations with people he had killed, ordering that places be set at dinner for ghosts of particular victims. By 1979, even close family members feared for their lives. He dreaded assassination himself. He was part deaf (which helps explain why he shouted and screamed during speeches), half blind and suffered 'jerky movements', suggesting a serious illness. He could only rule with the support of his immediate family, notably his nephew Obiang Nguema, the commander of the National Guard and the military governor of Fernando Po.

Macias eventually retreated to a fortified villa in his remote home town of Mongomo, on the mainland. When the army stopped receiving wages, a group of officers of the

National Guard visited and asked for money. Macias had them summarily shot. Finally that spurred others to act: the tyrant was removed in a putsch on 3 August 1979, without the help of foreign novelists. Obiang and a group of other senior officers called it a 'freedom coup'. Macias retired with suitcases packed with green banknotes – equeles – bearing his own likeness to his stronghold in Mongomo, where he stuffed the loot in a wooden hut. The exact amount is unknown but estimates vary from $60 million to $150 million. He hunkered down in a bamboo bunker, defended by loyal fighters, with dozens of villagers as hostages.

As soldiers loyal to the new government approached, Macias killed several hostages and a large battle erupted. The hut full of money was set ablaze, destroying the country's entire foreign reserves. A Romanian engineer who hid under a table in a house in Mongomo while fighting raged guessed that hundreds were killed. Eventually Macias fled to the jungle. Racing to the Gabonese border, his car fell into an ambush and the driver was killed. Cornered in thick forest, most of his fighters deserted. A government soldier bragged that Macias was now 'on foot and alone: we shall get him'. Eventually a peasant woman spotted the old dictator clambering out of a roadside ditch, still clutching a small suitcase. He screamed at her: 'You will come under my black magic powers. I don't know why you want to hunt me when I have given you all my money.' An army statement said just one loyal guard stayed with Macias to the end, though he was finally killed. A bullet caught Macias, too, in the left arm, but he was detained alive.

News of the arrest produced 'wild scenes of joy in Malabo', reported Spanish radio. Ordinary people called the old dictator Hitler. He had all but destroyed Equatorial Guinea.

A Reuters journalist who visited shortly afterwards wrote that the 'jungle creeps into cocoa plantations ... The jobless wander about aimlessly and rats dash across hospital wards. Most people live on wild fruit and vegetables, and a packet of cigarettes costs a week's average salary.'

A new regime

But it was not the start of democracy for the country. Macias's nephew and longstanding acolyte, Obiang Nguema, took over as head of a new 'Supreme Military Council'. He anguished over what to do with the old tyrant. His uncle was an important relative, a near father figure, according to custom in this part of Africa. More troubling, Obiang had long supported him. A trial might expose evidence of his own complicity in Macias's misrule, so the nephew wanted to leave his uncle to rot in a psychiatric hospital. But the public demanded prosecution and execution.

A British journalist who visited Macias in jail wrote of him 'cowering in the corner of his cell, crumpled and pathetic ... But those eyes still had that maniacal stare that had sent countless thousands to their death.' A mixed military and civilian tribunal was set up in the largest available building in Malabo, the dilapidated El Marfil cinema, and an estimated 1500 people packed the cinema in awed silence. Frederick Forsyth, who keeps an eye on events in the country, says Macias was put in a cage hung from the ceiling. A handful of close (though mostly unimportant) colleagues joined him to face charges of genocide, mass murder, treason and embezzlement. Prosecutors said it was the first time the head of a genocidal regime, anywhere, had been brought to court.

The chief defendant sat impassively in a casual, short-sleeved shirt as the examining magistrate promised evidence of at least 500 assassinations ordered by the dictator. The court heard an ever-lengthening list of horrors. Some 200 civil servants had been jailed by superiors who wanted their wives as mistresses. One of the accused, the boss of the infamous Playa Negra – Black Beach – prison had set his dog on inmates to feed on their raw flesh. Macias's co-defendants said they carried out atrocities because they feared death themselves at the hands of the despot. Macias said all the misdeeds 'happened behind my back. I was head of state, not a prison chief.' He tried also to blame his nephew Obiang, but the court cut him short.

After four days, Macias and six others were sentenced to death 101 times, whisked off to Black Beach and put before a firing squad. Local soldiers dared not pull the trigger: they were terrified of the old president's magical powers. Sorcery was strong in his family, they knew, passed down from the witchdoctor father. One writer said, 'They feared their bullets were too weak to kill his spirit which "would return as a leopard". ' Instead, members of a new, 80-strong Moroccan presidential guard did the honours. Macias was said to be calm and dignified at his death. At news of it people took to the streets chanting 'Eleven years of Macias, eleven years of small fry'. Over 1000 political prisoners were released. Night-clubs and churches reopened.

Obiang took possession of the Fang ancestral skull and control of the country. But everyone knew of his part in the old horrors. He tried to wriggle out of it, claiming shamelessly that everyone was equally at fault for letting Macias get away with so much murder. 'Who among us can blame others for the errors of the dictatorship ... we were all collaborators of dictatorship, all guilty,' he stated later. But Obiang was Macias's 'leading acolyte' and the 'number two man' in the country, to use the words of one expert. He could be blamed. Some alledged that he supervised the most sadistic interrogation, torture and murder of prisoners in Black Beach. He saw that Macias's punishments were carried out. Forsyth rightly described him as the 'inflicter of many horrors of his uncle'. Replacing one despot with another made only a limited difference.

Obiang did, however, turn to western countries for help, dropping Chinese and Cuban advisers. The old colonial power promptly provided aid and recognition. The king and queen of Spain visited Malabo just before Christmas 1979, when Obiang modestly requested: 'We ask Spain to make Equatorial Guinea the Switzerland of Africa.' While they sat down to a banquet, people rioted outside for a share of a delivery of food parcels. Paranoia continued, but the government spread less terror; rulers ignored the law, but a new constitution was enacted; there were limited economic and political reforms. The small economy, after many years of stagnation, eventually grew: in the best of times the Gross Domestic Product (GDP) expanded by astonishing rates, such as 60 per cent a year by the end of the 1990s when oil exports boomed. Some gave Obiang grudging credit. An African ambassador in Malabo once concluded that 'Obiang is twenty years ahead of any of his ministers', though he added, 'The trouble is, he's twenty years behind the rest of us.'

But these were limited virtues. Obiang looks moderate only when compared with his monstrous predecessor. By 2004, after a quarter century in power, most commentators ranked him as one of the worst leaders anywhere in the world. A British lawyer who is well paid to fight for Obiang's rights later said airily that ordinary people do not need money or good government to be happy. Sitting in a plush district of Paris in 2005, he claimed that Equatorial Guineans were 'happy plucking bananas from trees'. 'They all seem to be smiling,' he noted smugly after a trip there. Perhaps that attitude explains why the government does almost nothing for its desperate citizens. On average, by 2005, each Equatorial Guinean should have been receiving roughly $6,000 a year, an income higher than Poles or Chileans enjoy. But none of this wealth is actually shared out. In 2002 Equatorial Guinea spent the least of any country, bar Iraq, on health (a wretched 1.8 per cent of GDP). No country anywhere spends less on education (a mere 0.5 per cent of GDP). An Equatorial Guinean can expect to live no more than fifty years.

Obiang frequently sounds like a lesser version of Macias. He is known in public as the 'Father Behind the Gates'. A fawning aide on a radio programme in July 2003 called him 'the country's God', who 'can decide to kill anyone without being called to account and without going to hell because it is God himself, with whom he is in permanent contact, and who gives him this strength'. He is not as violent as his uncle, but the catalogue of murder and torture in his prisons, police stations and elsewhere is toe-curling. Amnesty International and Human Rights Watch frequently report on extrajudicial executions, torture and rape by police and soldiers; jurists from the International Bar Association throw their wigs up in horror at the rotten legal system, suggesting torture is common and few in power respect the rule of law. A British judge in April 2005 described Obiang as 'a despot, [who rules] without regard to the rule of law, or democratic institutions (such as free elections), and through a regime which uses torture to procure confessions as a systematic feature of its legal system, and in which the judiciary is not independent but under the control of the President's political party ...'

Black Beach

In Obiang's realm, prisons, especially, are horrific places. Opposition leaders die behind bars with suspicious regularity. Pedro Motu led a small political party preparing to contest an election in 1993. He was arrested and killed by police within days of his returning from exile. Obiang gave an explanation favoured by his monstrous uncle, claiming the opposition leader had killed himself to cause trouble: 'he swallowed some pills that were probably poisoned ... He wanted to create disorder for political reasons.' In fact, he was tortured and murdered. Close watchers of Equatorial Guinea said Motu's liver was removed. A colleague arrested with him also died, after being tortured so badly that he slumped into a coma.

Such events in rat-infested Black Beach prison are common enough. One ex-inmate says the guards 'whipped my hands with electric cables so badly I could not even sign a confession'. Another had his jaw broken when being bundled into the jail. Some were tied to poles in such a way that the bones in their forearms eventually snapped. One said he felt like a chicken in a back yard: 'You never know when they are going to come out and chop your head off.' Such ill treatment is never justified, but it is worth remembering the trivial 'crimes' of some who were detained. Fabian Nsue Nguema, an opposition politician, was arrested in April 2002 for 'insulting' the president. His insult? A lawyer, he dared prepare the defence case for several people accused of plotting Obiang's overthrow. Others – notably the diminutive islanders of the Bubi group, a people under the thumb of the mainland Fang group – were rounded up, beaten, jailed and raped as a means of discouraging political protest or coup attempts. In 1998 a small protest did erupt, dismissed by a foreign journalist as 'four guys, two guns, a pick-up truck and a row at a road block'. He recalls sitting with a minister as they heard the news. The minister – now an ambassador in a western country – immediately warned that 'these people [the Bubis] will be sorry'. Pogroms and attacks on Bubi villages followed and some hundred people were dragged before a military court where fifteen were sentenced to death.

Most outsiders ignored it all unless a foreigner died. Soldiers shot dead a young Spanish missionary as her bus approached their roadblock in July 2003, causing some criticism from Spain. Earlier, a French economist was found dead in his bedroom in Malabo: he had been beaten unconscious and the veins in his neck sliced open, suggesting a professional killing. Some said he was about to expose corruption in an aid programme.

Sometimes, however, outsiders noticed if a rival to Obiang disappeared. Late in December 2003 Obiang's half-brother General Augustin Ndong Ona – seen by some as a rival to the president – was arrested and reportedly tortured.

Equatorial Guinea stages elections and calls itself a 'fledgling democracy', but it is more like the comic-opera dictatorships in Burma or Zimbabwe. Voters know elections are not secret. During campaigns people know to wear Obiang-embossed clothing 'to keep clear of trouble'. 'If you're not seen showing support for the party you can have problems,' said a resident of Malabo during one campaign. The opposition call Obiang and his family 'gangsters with no respect for the law'. The president's son, Teodorin, owns the sole private radio station, Radio Asonga; Obiang owns the only television station. In 2005 the international press freedom group Reporters Without Borders called Equatorial Guinea 'one of the continent's forbidden zones for free expression and an unchanging hell for journalists'.

Few countries have embassies there. The United States

briefly closed its offices in 1995, with officials dismissing Equatorial Guinea as a 'basket case' and 'a nasty little dictatorship in
the middle of nowhere'. When the erstwhile American ambassador, John Bennet, spoke out about the torture of prisoners,
he was accused of witchcraft after police spotted him at a
graveyard during an election 'taking traditional medicine
given to him by election-boycotting opposition parties in
order that the vote would come out badly [for Obiang]'. He
was warned: 'You will go to America as a corpse.'

'An authentic cannibal'

It is hard to imagine what more Obiang could do to be like a B-
movie villain. Environmental activists accuse him of profiting
from large-scale dumping of toxic (and possibly radioactive)
waste on a pristine Atlantic island, Annobon. Others say his
diplomats ship large quantities of drugs around the world. One
was caught at New York's JFK airport trailing cannabis from a
hole in his suitcase as he strolled through the terminal. In 1997
Spanish police arrested and jailed an ex-minister of information from Equatorial Guinea, Santos Pascal Bikomo, for drug-
trafficking. He wrote a public letter describing how Obiang,
his son Teodorin and his brother Armengol distributed drugs
in Europe using shipments of tropical timber, diplomatic bags
and even Obiang's baggage during state trips. Others even
accuse Obiang of cannibalism. Such claims may be made
merely to score political points, but Severo Moto, an exiled
opponent, made his accusation with some elan in 2004. He
warned he would face persecution and certain death in Equatorial Guinea and called Obiang an 'authentic cannibal' who
hungered for his testicles. On Spanish radio he said Obiang
'systematically eats his political rivals' and was a demon. 'He
has just devoured a police commissioner. I say "devoured" as

this commissioner was buried without his testicles and brain.' Moto added: 'We are in the hands of a cannibal.'

Obiang retorted that 'international credibility is not important to us'. In turn, most of the world ignores his speck of territory off Africa's west coast. In most atlases the country lies hidden under the staple. Few outsiders, not even Africa experts, can name a famous Equatorial Guinean. Just one man earned headlines. A 22-year-old swimmer called Eric Moussambani briefly became famous at the Sydney Olympics in 2000. Dubbed 'Eric the Eel', he floundered so slowly in the 100-metre freestyle event that the world's press became enchanted. Eric took nearly two minutes to cross the pool, roughly twice as long as the fastest swimmer. A jellyfish would have moved faster, but sports journalists made him into a star, concocting ever less plausible stories about him. According to some, the first time he completed 100 metres in a single stretch was in Sydney. Others said he trained in the wild. His bemused manager complained: 'Why do they keep printing that he swims with crocodiles? It makes us look like savages. Who would swim in a river with crocodiles?' His own mother said her boy 'liked going to the beach' but he had never been keen on swimming. She said he had merely wanted to see Sydney.

That aside, Equatorial Guinea draws interest from one source: an industry that is notoriously willing to do deals with repressive governments. The oil industry, dominated by big American oil firms like ExxonMobil, flocked to Equatorial Guinea in the late 1990s. The small country proved a remarkably tempting corner for western companies – and an irresistible one for mercenaries, too.

5
The Gushing Prize

'And the place had to have oil. I mean, who's going to do a coup in Zimbabwe?'

Crause Steyl, pilot and plotter

By the turn of the millennium Simon Mann was living in South Africa. He set about getting South African citizenship, as well as his British status, and applied for a passport on the basis of his mother's nationality. According to one source he was removed to a safe house and debriefed thoroughly about his past. The South African government made it clear it opposed mercenaries. The country's tough Foreign Military Assistance act (1998) had forced Executive Outcomes to close. More military escapades would not be welcome. But Mann reportedly had good contacts with some in the African National Congress government. He struck a deal: citizenship and a passport in return for a promise he would lead a quiet life. 'They told him that he must not be involved in any military adventures any more. He agreed,' says a South African with connections in the intelligence world. Mann seemed sincere and, five days before Christmas 2001, he received a South African identity card, number 520626 5294080, followed in August 2002 by a passport, number 436417852.

Mann now had two nationalities and (apparently) his

history of soldiering behind him. Most who met him rather liked the upper-class Briton; women found his old Etonian manners endearing. A South African who met him a few times socially thought him 'quite charming, not too dominating. Physically he is not a hulk, he is not a marine, but smallish, slim-boned.' He wore rimless glasses and was usually quick to smile. Though not overbearing, he had a military presence. 'He is straight-backed and tanned, and talks like an officer ... [he is] a precise interlocutor,' concluded a journalist who interviewed Mann in Britain about his part in a drama about Northern Ireland. 'Equivocation offends him.' As if to remind listeners of his Englishness, Mann peppered conversation with cricketing terms, suggesting that honourable people should always 'play with a straight bat'.

Men generally warmed to him too. His pinstriped London lawyer calls him 'a very likeable chap' who 'loves Africa'. His Zimbabwean lawyer was equally charmed: 'Simon Mann is very intelligent and very sociable. And he is very fit.' An old friend said 'Simon is an entertaining, charming and good chap. He tells a good joke. None of us thought that at age fifty, with all his wealth and a family and with a wife with a bun in the oven, that he'd go on another bloody adventure.' He had a sense of humour. He sometimes called his plot against Equatorial Guinea the 'Patrick O'Brian Appreciation Society Spring Outing', referring to the adventure novelist whose characters sail the oceans to battle foreign foes. A British newspaper once summed up Mann as 'a complex character, part thrillseeker, part businessman, who mined Africa's wars for profit'. Tim Spicer, a colleague in the private military industry, called him a 'good mate ... a great sailor and skier and a thoroughly good sport ...'

A jovial, social animal, part of the affluent South African

suburban scene, Mann had no reason to imperil his newly settled lifestyle. But he was tempted by news of a discovery that rivalled the reason Frederick Forsyth had imagined to justify the coup against Equatorial Guinea in 1973.

Africa, overall, has a handy supply of oil. Its known reserves are small compared with the Middle East: it may have 100 billion barrels of crude, roughly the same as in Kuwait alone. But the continent is poorly explored. As new technology is used to study its land and seabed, known reserves have risen fast. Some western companies hope for big discoveries in dry spots like Madagascar and in parts of east Africa. But they are not only looking for oil. Africa has a useful supply of natural gas. Nigeria alone may have 17 million cubic metres (200 trillion cubic feet) of gas which is barely exploited. Turned into Liquefied Natural Gas (LNG) by 'deep cooling', it is of a quality that suits American consumers. 'You can plug west African gas direct into the North American gas pipeline system,' says an excited hydrocarbon expert. Already large quantities of African gas are being pumped north to Europe. Since poor African countries consume little energy, they are also ready to export almost everything pumped out of the rock. Experts talk of a new 'scramble for Africa', especially for mineral and hydrocarbon resources. Oil firms from rich countries have earmarked hundreds of billions of dollars for 'upstream' African development (that is, finding and pumping out the oil and gas) in the next couple of decades.

The continent has one especially valuable area. The broader west African region is fast increasing output: the most opti- mistic estimates indicate it could export 6 million barrels of oil a day by 2010. This includes one area described by white labcoat-wearing experts, in technical jargon, as 'one of the oiliest patches in the world'. That is, the armpit of the continent, in the Gulf of Guinea in the middle of which is Equatorial Guinea. For years all hoped for a big oil discovery. Spanish prospectors in the 1980s found nothing. Then a tiny Texan outfit, Walter International, struck lucky in 1991. The bonanza began, formally, in October 1996 with a solemn act of inauguration at the first commercial oil field, presided over by Obiang and the executive vice-president of Mobil Corp, Paul Hoenmans. A decade later the country exports some 350,000 barrels of oil a day. At a rate of $50 a barrel, that is worth over $6 billion each year. No one is sure what reserves exist, but there may be another billion barrels of oil to come, plus 4 trillion cubic feet of gas, from Equatorial Guinea.

The country has a tiny population – at a squeeze you could fit everybody into a large football stadium – and lots of oil. Per person, Equatorial Guinea pumps more oil than Saudi Arabia. That should mean good times for all. In 2002 Obiang promised just that: 'Like the Scriptures say when the Pharaoh of Egypt had a dream of lean cows and fat cows, we have passed the time of lean cows that represent hunger, and we are now in the time of fat cows which is prosperity.' Instead, a few at the top take most of the wealth, which – though bad news for most Equatorial Guineans – makes it all the more tempting for others to seize power.

To give an idea what sort of wealth is at stake, consider how Nigeria's leaders have prospered next door. Since 1965, when the black stuff began to flow seriously, Nigeria has earned over $350 billion. That should have helped develop the rest of the economy. Instead, much of the oil revenue has gone straight into the pockets and bank accounts of corrupt civilian and military leaders. Today Nigeria pumps nearly 2 million barrels of oil a day, and is the largest producer in sub Saharan Africa, though its booming population remains one of the poorest anywhere. It is a similar story in Angola, the next largest producer, with roughly half that annual output. Angola's leaders long plundered at least a billion dollars a year from oil revenues, says the International Monetary Fund. Tiny Equatorial Guinea is a more recent player: the oil began to flow in serious quantities only at the end of the 1990s. But already it is the third largest exporter, pumping out nearly a barrel of oil for each of its citizens, every day. 'Equatorial Guinea is run like a family business. It is a micro state, a flea in the armpit of Africa,' explains an African oil consultant. 'But this flea is now getting dimensions. They are aiming for a small Emirates-style country, with a king and his family running it.'

It is astonishingly venal. Obiang is evidently corrupt. Fond of straw hats and playing billiards, his taste is otherwise for the excessively expensive. In 2004 he bought a Boeing 737-700, one of six personal planes, for $55 million. This one has a king-size bed, a state-of-the-art satellite communication centre and – the classic despot touch – a large bathroom with gold-plated fittings and door handles.

Apologists cannot excuse Obiang as a poorly educated man, or as someone with dreadful experience of colonial rule. He studied in the United States at Cranbrook Academy of Art, Bloomfield Hills, Michigan (although Cranbrook would probably rather forget their notorious alumnus). Nor is there an excuse for his eldest son and likely successor, Teodorin. A playboy, Teodorin spent years dabbling as a rap music entrepreneur in California, and then became a government minister. He has a fleet of sports cars in Paris, where he lives in a luxury hotel for much of the year. He once invited French journalists to watch him buy thirty tailored suits and race around the French capital in one of his Lamborghinis.

In June 2005 Obiang blithely told an American journalist that 'one hundred per cent of the oil revenues are being used for programs for the people'. The next month Teodorin bought three luxury cars – another Lamborghini and two Bentleys – to park at his $4-million holiday home in Cape Town. He spent roughly a third of Equatorial Guinea's $13-million-odd annual education budget on a holiday home and some cars.

The family also bought mansions in the United States and stocked other international bank accounts. Land and many businesses became the personal property of the ruling family: these were then leased out, or used to generate contracts, for suspiciously large private payments from American and other oil companies. Almost anybody who has spent time in the country has concluded that graft, from the president down, is deeply embedded. In 2005, Transparency International, the anti-corruption watchdog, said businessmen and other observers found only one African country, Chad, more corrupt. *Tropical Gangsters* – the title of an excellent book on the country by Robert Klitgaard – nicely describes Obiang's ruling clique. Aid groups like Médecins Sans Frontières, and donor organisations such as the World Bank, have long refused to work there because of graft.

Supply is assured. Nor is there any risk that demand will dry up. Chinese buyers are frantic in their search for African oil. They have secured long-term contracts for oil in Angola, Gabon, Sudan and elsewhere. They are buying a rapidly rising share of Equatorial Guinea's output, and the leaders of the two countries are close allies. (While few European countries have an embassy in Malabo, China has a large complex there.) As important, the United States, whose oil firms dominate production in Equatorial Guinea, is increasingly keen on African oil and gas. Whereas the United States was all but self-sufficient in hydrocarbons half a century ago, it depends ever more on imports. But too much comes from the ever-troubled Middle East. Lessening dependence on one region by getting more oil from relatively nearby west Africa (and elsewhere) is a smart policy. It should mean a more secure supply of the black stuff. It also means no shortage of buyers for Equatorial Guinea's oil.

Thus, senior Africa officials in the United States administration talk of Africa, especially the Gulf of Guinea, providing as much as a quarter of all American oil imports within a couple of decades. African supplies of Liquefied Natural Gas will also help to meet rising American demand. Marathon Oil, an American firm in Equatorial Guinea, has invested billions of dollars developing an LNG plant to export 60 million tonnes of gas directly to the south of the United States. A British firm, BG, will ship the refrigerated gas over the Atlantic. That contract alone is thought to be worth $15 billion over some seventeen years. A Marathon executive told an oil conference in Cape Town in 2004 that Europe and North America are increasingly dependent on foreign supplies of gas. The two regions will soon need combined imports of 21 trillion cubic feet of gas a year. West Africa's proximity to both markets makes it an important supplier, and Equatorial Guinea is bidding to become a hub for the region's gas exporters.

Obiang might at least get credit for overseeing the oil boom in his country. For several years Equatorial Guinea's economy grew faster than any other country's – and much faster than the African average. But this hid a big problem. It only grew fast because it was so wretchedly poor in the first place. The oil industry developed twenty years later than in the rest of the region, largely because the government was incompetent. Worse, the terms struck with the oil firms were dreadfully skewed against Equatorial Guinea. At the beginning of the new century Total, a French oil firm, paid Nigeria $8 for each barrel of oil pumped from a field straddling the sea border with Equatorial Guinea. Exxon, exploiting the same field but from the Equatorial Guinean side, paid a mere $3 a barrel. Unsurprisingly, Exxon said that field was one of the most profitable in the world. Exxon enjoyed terms of business, at least in the early years, that were exceedingly generous. Yet the oil firm says it took eight years to recover costs in Equatorial Guinea's large Zafira field, a timespan that looks suspiciously long to some oil experts, given a rising oil price and rapidly rising output.

Though the government had earlier gathered taxes and royalties on oil, it was only in 2004 that it began to get its own direct (and more valuable) share of production. The long delay while Exxon recovered its initial costs ended that year, marking a moment when oil funds would pour especially fast into government coffers. If Equatorial Guinea looked promising to a mercenary as the first oil flowed, by 2004 it seemed to burst with opportunity. You could almost hear exiled politicians and hired guns licking their lips.

PART TWO

The Three Hundred Days

6

Smelly and the Priest

'A good and honest man.'

Simon Mann on Severo Moto

By 2003, ten years after the battles at Soyo and the birth of Executive Outcomes, Mann was restless. He was looking for the main chance. From South Africa he made contact with a suave property developer in London called Gary Hersham. Another old friend and businessman, Greg Wales, was also in touch. The three turned their attention to oil-rich west Africa, in particular to Gabon, a small and relatively wealthy country. In January they arranged to meet President Omar Bongo in Libreville, Gabon's capital. Hersham wanted contracts in construction, Wales offered financial services and Mann thought he might train and support Gabon's military. But Bongo turned them down. Frustrated, Mann flew to London, where Hersham suggested he meet another businessman, a man with excellent contacts in west Africa who could offer some advice. Mann agreed.

Mann met the tycoon Ely Calil roughly a week later. A recluse of Lebanese–Nigerian origin, who says that he has no connection to the coup plot, Calil rarely gives interviews, but an individual who talked to him briefly about the Wonga Coup described him as 'small and quite worn ... [with a]

Levantine look, but he's not a flamboyant character ... He's very sophisticated and quietly spoken.' Born in northern Nigeria, Calil had flourished as a trader, supplying Nigeria's army with basic goods. He later invested in property and then traded oil. In 2004 the *Sunday Times* estimated that Calil had a fortune worth £100 million (roughly $180 million), including a mansion in Chelsea.

Calil's business life is not transparent. In June 2002 he was arrested in Paris while travelling on a Senegalese passport. Investigators were looking into a massive case of corruption that involved the French state oil company Elf-Acquitaine (now part of Total), as well as crooked French and African politicians. Eventually more than thirty people were convicted and jailed in France for using oil company slush funds worth $300 million to bribe African politicians. Calil was questioned about payments in the mid 1990s of millions of pounds from Elf-Acquitaine to the (then) dictator of Nigeria, Sani Abacha. He denied any wrongdoing or involvement in the scandal. The police released him without charge in the absence of any evidence against him.

His political connections are impressive. He is said to be close to one of the most powerful politicians in Nigeria, Ibrahim Babangida, who was president for eight years. And he has cultivated ties with the Senegalese president, Abdoulaye Wade. According to one intelligence source Calil once financed a house for Wade in Paris. He is also well known in London, where he befriended the scandal-prone British novelist, fantasist and lord, Jeffrey Archer, to whom he is said to have given investment advice. Calil also knows the scandal-prone Labour politician Peter Mandelson, now Europe's trade commissioner. In 1999 Mandelson rented a luxury apartment in Holland Park, London, from him and the

Observer newspaper suggested the two men became friends and met several times.

According to one of the plotters of the Wonga Coup, Calil also discussed the affair in Equatorial Guinea with Mandelson while walking in South Kensington near Mandelson's home, in April 2004 – after the coup plot. The plotter says he has a recording of the conversation. The then opposition Conservative spokesman on foreign affairs, Michael Ancram, put down a question in Parliament asking if any ministers or officials had had any discussions with Mandelson about Equatorial Guinea in the previous twelve months. Mandelson repeatedly and vehemently denied any collaboration with Calil, stating that 'I have consistently denied speaking to Mr Calil about this and he has also confirmed that there has not been any discussion between us.'

Mann first met Calil in London, probably late in January 2003. They were likeminded. Each had a long-held interest in Africa and they discussed the politics of the continent, especially war-torn Sudan. Calil, according to Mann, had done careful research and knew a great deal of Mann's background: he was aware of the partnership with Tony Buckingham and how Executive Outcomes was formed in Angola with South African partners; he also knew how it subsequently worked in Sierra Leone. At a second meeting some days later, said Mann, Calil mentioned Equatorial Guinea and Mann confessed he knew nothing of the place. Calil probably described one of his political connections, an exiled politician living in Madrid called Severo Moto Nsa. He knew Moto well: the two men employed the same public relations company in London and shared a fierce dislike of Obiang, the president, though it is not clear why Calil held such a grudge. Calil later told the respected journal *Africa Confidential* that he was giving Moto some 'modest' financial support.

A couple of weeks later Mann and Calil met again, said Mann. At some point Mann gave Calil a nickname: 'Smelly', to rhyme (according to British pronunciation) with Ely, presumably using it only when discussing him with friends. Mann also did his own research. Mann later said that he learned that 'the situation in Equatorial Guinea was very bad' and that Obiang's family ran 'a police state in which they are thought to indulge in cannibalism for medical reasons … murder and rape'. Mann also learned that Obiang was sick with cancer. It was agreed that they travel to Spain to meet the opposition figure he was supporting.

The Priest

Mann learnt quite a lot about Moto, both from Calil and through his own research. Moto is a stolid man, no flash-in-the-pan opposition leader. Short and plump, he has a high brow, a round face and wears glasses. His eyebrows are expressive, each an upward-pointing arrowhead. Like many dapper Africans, he likes formal business suits and sharp ties. Born in 1943 in a village called Acock in the mainland part of the country, he studied first at a missionary school, then spent seven years training for the priesthood in Spain. He took Holy Orders in 1964. Back in Equatorial Guinea he trained as a teacher, took a degree, then worked as a journalist. For much of the 1970s, under Macias, he worked for a loyal radio station and edited a newspaper, *Ebano*. Eventually, like most educated men, he was thrown under house arrest. He was released in 1979 when Obiang ousted his uncle in the 'freedom coup'.

Initially Moto had a good relationship with Obiang. They probably knew each other from Spain when they even pursued the same girlfriend. The new president sent Moto to Cuba for a meeting of 'non-aligned' countries, those which leaned neither east nor west in the Cold War. In 1980 he became technical director in the ministry of information and tourism (a tricky job in a country that sees little of either) and the following year was made minister himself. There the friendship ended. Moto said he wanted media freedom, democracy and other reforms that Obiang would not tolerate. In December 1981 he fled to Spain and founded an opposition group, the Progress Party. 'Obiang is responsible for all the problems in Equatorial Guinea' became his well-worn refrain.

For the next two decades they played a lively game of cat-and-mouse. Moto was occasionally let back into Equatorial Guinea to register his political party or to contest an election. Once there he was often arrested, accused of plotting a coup, convicted and jailed, then somehow released into exile and given an amnesty. After one trip home in 1988 he was sentenced to death. In 1996, he returned to contest a presidential election, but he and other opposition candidates then withdrew, calling it a sham. Eventually – of course – he was arrested, tried (in the same cinema used for Macias in 1979) and convicted of defaming the president, trying to corrupt a policeman and plotting a coup. He got a thirty-year term and was told to stay out of politics. Soon he was out of jail and back in exile.

Perhaps it suited Obiang, as he held sway over factions of the ruling family, to point to Moto as an external threat. Obiang's power-hungry son, Teodorin, and disgruntled brother, Armengol, caused more worries than any opposition figure. If Moto was a credible bogeyman they might be kept in line. In 1997 Moto made his most direct attempt to take power. He went to Angola to recruit a team to overthrow Obiang. Angola seemed an ideal place to do that. The pretty seaside capital, Luanda, bustled with arms traders, smugglers,

scheming politicians, mercenaries and every other stock
character of modern Africa. And though fresh food and water
were in short supply, guns and ammunition were plentiful.
Semi-automatic rifles could be bought for a few dollars in big
public markets, like Roque Santeiro, in rough corners of town.
Moto procured a boat in Luanda harbour and prepared to sail
the short distance to Equatorial Guinea.

Then Angola's police showed up. The country has a decent
spy network and the security forces were probably tipped off.
The head of the Angolan presidential guard detained Moto
and his men and prepared to send them to Equatorial Guinea.
Yet again, Moto and his men slipped the net. They were flown
instead to Spain on the Angolan president's personal plane.
Perhaps the Spanish offered military aid to Angola in return
for Moto, or maybe it suited Obiang to leave his troublesome
priest on the loose. In his absence a court in Equatorial Guinea
handed Moto an impressive – though meaningless – jail term
of 121 years.

The endless game little benefited Moto, but, there again,
life was not too hard. He was comfortable and honoured
in Madrid, where he had a home, a wife and four children.
He sang in church, put on weight, wore his smart suits and
collected human rights awards (he is a 'Knight of the Yuste
Imperial Order', no less). Spain's prime minister, Jose Maria
Aznar, was fond of him. A part of the reason: Spain lacked oil
contracts in its former colony. Other European powers – the
British in Nigeria, or the French in Gabon – have entrenched
national oil firms in their old colonial territories. But Spain
missed out. Its national oil company, Hispanoil, prospected
in the 1980s but failed to spot one of Africa's most lucrative
offshore fields. Instead, American companies prospered.
If Moto one day took office, grateful for Madrid's support,

Spanish oil firms might benefit. But there was no sign of that happening. He could wait to win a free and fair election, but it would snow in Malabo first. To get power, Moto needed to grab it. The ragtag hired guns in Luanda harbour had been useless. He needed professionals.

Madrid

Mann's first meeting with Moto happened in Madrid early in 2003, probably in February or early March. Mann was impressed. He later recalled Moto's studies for the priesthood and thought him a 'good and honest man' who planned to improve the lives of ordinary people. Moto's chief assistant, a General Sargoso, formerly Obiang's head of security, was also present. Mann was struck by Sargoso's story of why he had fled to exile: he had apparently argued with the president, then Obiang had raped his wife and he had been forced to watch. True or not, the tale left a strong impression on the Briton. Moto equally warmed to the visiting former SAS man, asking if he could help arrange a 'military escort' to take him home. He hinted that an internal uprising by soldiers and civilians was due early in 2004. Mann agreed, later calling it a 'necessity [to] try and help the cause'.

Others in the Wonga Coup broadly confirm this version of events. One plotter who met Mann in London shortly after the Madrid trip thinks he was first asked for an escort to guard Moto in elections planned for April 2004. But the elections were not presidential, so quite what Moto planned to do is unclear. According to this version Mann declined, saying, 'It's a nice idea, but it won't work.' Then, some weeks later, he was called to a second meeting with Moto and told of a more daring plan: to grab power. Afterwards Mann reported that 'this is a more serious game than I thought ...[it has] changed scale'.

Another man also confirms the broad account of events in Madrid. Crause Steyl is a tricky character to pin down. He is known as a risk-taker, a dynamic man. 'The human material is good. He's a very nice guy but he's got fire in his arse,' says a farmer friend, adding that Steyl 'has more than the average get up and go'. One of his brothers disapproves, thinking him odd, perhaps 'because he was weaned on goat's milk'. A pilot with minimal formal military experience, Steyl worked with Mann from the early days in Executive Outcomes, both in Angola and Sierra Leone. Steyl frankly admits to playing a major role in the Wonga Coup. Interviewed for this book in 2005 he immediately defended the attempt: 'We didn't see Obiang as a baby catcher. It's not all that wrong to get rid of him. It could have been messy, but millions in the world are dying all the time. Yes, you do something illegal, but if it had worked you would have said it's not a bad thing.'

Mann called Steyl in 2003 and said, in general terms, he had a new 'project' planned. They met at a hotel Mann favoured, the Sandton Towers in Johannesburg, where Mann said, 'The boys have asked me to help them. I've not told Amanda [his wife] anything yet. I want to know if you'll play with', recalls Steyl. He immediately agreed. Mann did not say where in Africa the project would unfold, but he wanted a small group of important men to fly from Spain to Uganda. 'He said I would have to arrange aircraft to do the logistics. He has a team to be picked up in Spain and I must work out a quote to move it at least as far as to Uganda from Spain. He also said it's not necessarily Uganda.' Afterwards Steyl browsed online and soon learned there is only one Spanish-speaking country in tropical Africa. He guessed, too, it would be oil rich: 'And the place had to have oil. I mean, who's going to do a coup in Zimbabwe?' He found a country that is roughly the same distance from Spain as Uganda. 'Until that moment I hadn't ever heard of Equatorial Guinea,' he admits.

Steyl, a man fond of bravado, claims he did not hesitate over the plot. 'I calculated we had a 30 per cent chance of success, but most coups are family feuds. That makes our one, this one, the poshest of all coup attempts. If you're not killed in the first week, the most chance would be two years in jail. That's all.' And the chance of financial gain was enormous: 'It's better to live like a lion for one day than as a sheep for a hundred days.' He pauses to elaborate. 'In fact, it is better to live like a lion for a hundred days! All the projects I've done with Simon have been successful: in Angola; in Sierra Leone; Papua New Guinea; and in other things like equipping Angolan aircraft with spy cameras. Everything we've touched has turned to gold. Simon is full of ideas. He finds profitable solutions.' Just how profitable Mann would later spell out in detail.

7

Assembling the Wongamen

'Another bloody Moustache, that's all we need.'

Nigel Morgan

Johann Smith is no angel; nor does he claim to be one. A veteran of 32 Battalion, he fought covertly in Angola (where he was twice shot) and formed close ties with Unita leader Jonas Savimbi. He worked as a liaison officer for the South Africans, gathering intelligence on the Unita leader for many years. He says that he once saved Savimbi's life by smuggling him out of Luanda, Angola's capital, in a diplomatic car. Smith, who now walks with a pronounced limp because of bullet wounds (and thus is called Peg Leg by some friends), eventually quit the army in the early 1990s suffering post-traumatic stress. He did not work with Executive Outcomes, now saying he was reluctant to turn against Savimbi. But he kept in touch with other veterans. The old officers (mostly white) formed a social club in Pretoria. The footsoldiers (mostly black) made a habit of visiting him, seeking work or small amounts of money, notably after Executive Outcomes closed shop. Smith helped them where he could, and in return picked up information on their activities.

He also developed another line of interest, in Equatorial Guinea. From 1996 he visited the oil rich country regularly, forming close ties with the regime, offering information and advice. After a decade of friendly relations, the rulers in Malabo trusted white South Africans, and Smith fashioned himself as a freelance intelligence operative. He helped Obiang organise early (and badly flawed) multi-party elections and advised on political matters. He took up a trade that is popular in Africa, as a freelance intelligence man. Just as rag-and-bone merchants worked in Britain a century ago, pottering around streets on a cart pulled by a horse, loaded with junk, trading as they went, the modern intelligence dealer darts about Africa with a laptop and satellite phone, lingering in hotel bars, picking up scraps of information where he can, selling them on to willing buyers, whether corporate or government. The more sophisticated use electronic, online or other surveillance.

Smith specialised in warning of threats to Obiang's security, especially coup attempts. Equatorial Guinea became 'his patch', he says, which he guarded against other intelligence merchants. He spent time in Malabo, having made some forty visits by 2004, sometimes for months on end. He had good access to Obiang and others in the government and even became a godfather to one minister's child. In 2000, long before the Wonga Coup was launched, he produced a report alleging that ex-mercenaries from Executive Outcomes plotted to put the exiled politician Severo Moto in office. That made some sense: Moto had been caught red-handed trying to launch a coup in 1997 and everybody expected him to try again. Another time Smith alleged that Russian special forces had sleepers in the country and were ready to seize power.

By 2000, however, a new business opportunity arose. Several other freelance intelligence men were interested in west Africa, including a jovial and sandy-haired individual called Nigel Morgan. A Briton of Irish descent, Morgan is a former member of the Irish Guards (he calls them the Micks) where he worked in military intelligence. His character is one that the novelist Graham Greene might relish. He trained briefly as a Jesuit priest, shortly after working for a thinktank that advised Margaret Thatcher in the 1980s. Known by friends and neighbours as Nosher or Captain Pig, he has a startlingly red face, the sort that glows in a dark room, having spent years under the African sun while swallowing pints of pink gin and tumblers of whisky. His love of hearty English food, rich cheese and cigars is matched only by the pleasure he takes in spinning yarns and arguing about politics.

By the turn of the century Morgan had met Smith and, along with a couple of others, they formed a small firm, Cogito. The goal was to sell intelligence services to Equatorial Guinea and to foreign firms that worked there. But Cogito got nowhere. Much depended on Smith producing the right introductions and, he says, a 'sixth sense' warned him to hold back. There was ample time, however, for all involved to learn that Equatorial Guinea lacked a serious defence force. Soldiers were often drunk, equipment was kept in poor repair, and levels of training were low. Smith reflects that 'maybe even then the plan was started for a coup'. Smith was also approached directly by Greg Wales, the accountant with ties to Mann and Executive Outcomes who touted for business in Equatorial Guinea. Smith refused, unwilling to trust Wales.

Cogito folded after another brief foray, this time to Angola. Morgan moved on, hired by a Belgian diamond mining company to end chronic theft at its operations in Congo. He recruited some ex-32 Battalion soldiers, through Smith, to be his guards. Among them was a man called Victor Dracula, an

Angolan of fierce fighting pedigree, although not considered particularly bright. Once asked, outside a South African court, why he had the name Dracula, he replied, 'I can only say this: I took blood!' Another was Sergio Cardoso, from Sao Tome and Principe, who is described admiringly by a fellow fighter as 'a thug, very ugly, a mulatto built like a brick shit house. But quite friendly if he doesn't want to kill you.' Morgan also hired a young South African communications expert, James Kershaw, as his personal assistant. A taciturn man in his early twenties with a snub nose and pale skin, Kershaw proved unusually skilled at radio, online and advanced forms of electronic communication. He and Morgan operated closely together until the anti-corruption project collapsed in 2003. All these men would later have their parts to play in the story of the Wonga Coup.

Then, in 2003, another freelance man appeared on the scene. Servaaf Nicolaas (shortened to Nic, Niek, Nick or Nicky) du Toit was considered a 'legend' in the ranks of South African special forces. 'He was a brilliant soldier, brilliant officer,' says Smith, though the two men are not close. Another mercenary and veteran calls him 'a good man, a gentle person, a good soldier. He was a hero in Angola.' A lawyer who later interviewed him concludes: 'He's very composed, calm. He answers the bare minimum of what you ask. He is very philosophical.' His long army career, in the special forces and fighting in Angola, was followed by a brief spell with Executive Outcomes. In 1996 he became a site manager for a mining company, Namco Diamonds, in Angola, at roughly the time Mann developed the diamond interests of Executive Outcomes there. The two got to know each other about this time.

Du Toit's main business appears to have been arms trading. He founded a company called Military Technical Services incorporated (MTS), based in Pretoria, and became a familiar face among traders, striking deals with various suppliers of small arms, including a state-run company called Zimbabwe Defence Industries (ZDI). He worked with another South African, Henry van der Westhuizen. The two were heard boasting they would somehow 'change the face of Africa'. A British journalist who travelled with du Toit in Liberia in 2002 describes him as 'an arms dealer, mercenary, chaperone'. Pictures at this time show him to be middle-aged, sporting a grey beard and dark hair. His hands are unusually large and he looks like a typical Afrikaner farmer: a bronzed and careworn Boer who has spent long days at outdoor work.

Du Toit and Mann apparently considered investing in and running a diamond mine in Liberia early in 2003, but decided that was too risky. Instead, by the middle of that year they were collaborating on plans for a coup – often called 'the project' – in Equatorial Guinea. Mann later recalled he contacted du Toit 'who was an old acquaintance and friends of a good friend of mine' as early as May or June 2003. 'I talked through the project with him. He also thought it was a good idea. We agreed to try and set up legitimate businesses in Equatorial Guinea. If the project went ahead, these would be useful. If the project did not go ahead, then hopefully they would make money.'

(There are allegations that du Toit was also involved in dubious activities with rebels elsewhere. A document of unproven veracity suggests he struck a deal with some rebel soldiers in southern Congo who called themselves the PDD, for 'Peace, Development and Democracy', on 15 May 2003. It stated that the he would supply 'military and financial support to the PDD', to enable it to launch a coup in Congo. In return, du Toit would get access to mineral riches. The Congolese rebel leader was named 'K. S. Nyembo', but his group – if it even existed – was insignificant in that massive country.)

Thus, by mid 2003 – some months after Mann and Moto had first met – du Toit was in Malabo, Equatorial Guinea. His cover story was that he was working for a South African security firm called Omega which was investing in new businesses. In fact he was establishing himself, and a team of front men, as the forward group for the Wonga Coup. Lucie Bourthoumieux, a French lawyer who worked for the government of Equatorial Guinea, recalls how warmly du Toit was received at the time. 'He had been welcomed by the authorities ... Malabo is a small village. It had just two or three hotels. He came saying he had money to invest, an easy way to be accepted. The authorities ... they took him as their friend.' Du Toit recruited two old military colleagues to work for him. One was Sergio Cardoso (who had worked with Morgan in Congo), the other Abel Augusto. They were allegedly there to investigate the fishing industry. They met advisers close to Obiang and the president's younger brother, Armengol Nguema. Others followed. None were hired for their knowledge of the fishing industry, for none had any inkling of that sort of work. Du Toit hired ex-soldiers and fierce fighters with histories of performing well in battles. But their only experience of tuna was eating it.

Du Toit also met the president's brother Armengol and they discussed agriculture and fishing. Dealing with Armengol, who has a fierce reputation as head of security in the country, meant playing for high stakes. The American State Department has described him as a torturer whose 'minions urinated on their victims, sliced their ears and rubbed oil on their bodies to lure stinging ants'. He is barely literate (his signature on documents confirming a business relationship with du Toit is shaky, like that of a very old man), but he is not stupid.

Even those close to the regime say Armengol is 'not known as a mild-mannered man or a man that can be crossed without consequences', and confirm he presides over a 'heavy-handed intelligence service'.

But du Toit's actions soon rang alarm bells. Smith, with an eye on Equatorial Guinea and the veterans of 32 Battalion, felt a greater urge than ever to warn of a coup. He noted du Toit and his companions 'throwing around' money in Malabo. Though he was often rubbished, Peg Leg said evidence of future trouble was building up. If none of that were enough, an event unfolded that should have given a dazzlingly clear warning.

In July 2003, Sao Tome and Principe, a tiny former colony of Portugal that pokes out of the Atlantic near Equatorial Guinea, saw its government toppled. The poor country is famous for nothing but, after years of searching, experts now say it has every chance of striking huge deposits of oil. Locals long knew of oil seeping from rocks in the jungle. In the 1990s American companies started looking for oil and gas fields deep offshore. Predictably – for Sao Tome suffered coup attempts – soldiers made a grab for power. They succeeded while the president, Fradique de Menezes, was abroad. They secured ministries, a radio station, the airport and other typical targets and claimed to be opposing 'tyranny and injustice'. A few shots were fired and some grenades exploded, but no one was hurt.

That attack by the self-proclaimed Junta of National Salvation sent a stark warning because some of the Sao Tomeans involved were 'Buffalo Soldiers', that is men who had fought as part of apartheid South Africa's army, in 32 Battalion. At least one man, Alercio Costa, had also served in Executive Outcomes. And though the Sao Tomean coup was reversed in a few days, thanks to fierce political pressure from Nigeria and the United States, the putsch set a precedent for the region: hired guns could snatch power in an oil rich country. In Sao Tome the Buffalo Soldiers had a near mythical reputation. To this day they gather behind the red door of a building known as the House of Buffaloes, described by one journalist as a 'frat house for mercenaries', where they reminisce over old battles and plot new ones.

The event inevitably concerned Smith. In the following weeks, using contacts with veterans of 32 Battalion, he learned that the old Buffalo Soldiers had not hung up their boots after the coup in Sao Tome. Costa, one of the three leaders, subsequently contacted other 32 Battalion and Executive Outcomes veterans living in Pretoria, South Africa. He also repeatedly met Sergio Cardoso, the man who had been with Morgan at the diamond mines in Congo and who now worked in Equatorial Guinea with du Toit. Cardoso met others who had been part of the coup in Sao Tome. He was learning how they did it. Then several other ex-members of 32 Battalion met Cardoso: Domingo Passaco, a former staff sergeant and special forces operative (4 Reconnaissance); Georges Allerson, a former sergeant and member of another special forces unit; Neves Matias, a specialist Small Team Operator and another veteran of the special forces. These men included some du Toit recruited to work in Equatorial Guinea, while others were recruited by Mann in South Africa. They were getting advice from colleagues who had conducted the (briefly) successful coup in Sao Tome.

As the year moved on, Smith knew the veterans were meeting frequently and shuttling around west Africa to share information. In November, he heard a tip from a former Buffalo Soldier. A veteran called Netu came to his home in Pretoria. He had been at a hotel in Pretoria where he had heard that veterans of 32 Battalion were being recruited for a well-paid job. He had arrived too late and missed recruitment for it. Frustrated, he told Smith what he knew: soldiers were being recruited for a coup in Equatorial Guinea. Smith was unamused. 'Yes, I was angry', he says. 'Others were pissing on my patch.' He resolved to stop it.

8

Plans and Documents

'Beware, beware the Bight of Benin,
For few come out though many go in.'

Old slavers' rhyme in west Africa

Throughout the planning of the coup, Mann and the other plotters faced a dilemma. On the one hand, those conspiring in a secret plot should not leave lying around many documents and contracts that might be used as evidence against them if things go wrong. On the other, mercenaries and crooked politicians are a treacherous lot. It is imprudent to leave terms of a contract unspecified and unsigned, or to trust that verbal agreements will be kept later without papers to back them up. Those who hired the coup plotters – the men who did nothing to risk their own skins or freedom, but who were willing to finance the scheme – were not inclined to keep (or show) any documents about the case. But Mann and the others wanted some guarantee of the rewards they would get. That explains why there exists a startling variety of contracts, documents, plans and dreams that the plotters committed to paper. This thickly strewn paper trail, written between July 2003 and the date of the coup attempt, gives a clear idea of their hopes, fears and ambitions.

The first pair of contracts were sketched out on 22 July 2003, between Mann and Moto. The timing is intriguing: a few days after the coup in Sao Tome, and a few months after Mann and Moto first met and discussed the idea of a coup in Equatorial Guinea. The two documents show a formal relationship has been established between the two men. Moto is the client without much ready cash; Mann is the professional hired to make his customer president of a small oil rich country. Once in power, Moto would be wealthy and powerful. So it is at this stage, when Mann had relatively more clout, that he haggled for a good reward.

Copies of these documents, in the author's possession, are signed and initialled by Mann (though not by Moto). In these the melodramatic Mann calls himself 'Captain F': it was said that he is fond of code-names. Moto is declared – a little prematurely – as president of Equatorial Guinea. Juicy rewards are promised for Mann and his party: $1 million dollars each for Mann and three other plot leaders (whom Mann would name). For six other junior officers, some $50,000 each; for seventy-five footsoldiers, $25,000 each. In total Mann wanted over $7 million in cash for overthrowing the government of Equatorial Guinea. He and his men would be named citizens of the little country and would be made immune from prosecution for any killing or nastiness they inflicted; they would also be protected against any foreign government that tried to extradite them to face justice elsewhere. Finally, Mann would have the job of providing Moto's personal bodyguard, in the style of the French mercenary Bob Denard in the Comoros, who controlled presidents by controlling their guards.

But the second contract, also marked 22 July 2003, promised Mann greater riches. It seems he kept this contract secret (it is marked confidential) from the other coup plotters – perhaps he learned a tough lesson in Executive Outcomes when others, like Tony Buckingham, prospered more from the corporate army than he did. In this contract Mann is brazen. He demands a minimum of $15 million for himself, within days of installing Moto as president. In addition, all his costs are to be covered (indeed twice over) by the client, and anything Mann has bought for the mission – planes, boats, weapons, champagne – is to be repurchased by the client. Any late payments by Moto would incur high rates of interest, while Mann would get a diplomatic passport and an honorary rank in the military 'as deemed appropriate'.

That is just the beginning. This secret second deal orders that, immediately on taking office, the new government must begin a 'phased programme of military procurement and build up'. This must happen 'as quickly and as aggressively as possible'. Arms buying might even begin before the coup, and Mann expects generous pay for conducting it. Mann, through a company he would form, would be the sole provider of a range of military services. He would also recover money – hundreds of millions of dollars – stuffed in foreign bank accounts by corrupt politicians. He would control private security operations and supply consultancy, procurement and outsourcing services to the government. The men of his presidential guard, a hundred of them, would each get a salary of $6,000 a month, with an upfront payment of $1.8 million 'required immediately on our arrival'.

These secondary business opportunities would make Mann and his cronies extremely rich. The second document sets out in black and white what a modern mercenary expects for overthrowing a small government. But it also shows the sort of thievery that many African politicians are routinely found to commit – the only difference would be the colour of Mann's skin. And while Moto would appear to run the new government, Mann intended to keep as much control as possible. Crause Steyl believed that an admirable goal: 'Simon is a smart person. He would have made a good shadow president.' Equatorial Guinea's new wealth would be milked as furiously as possible. Mann was not just being greedy – his pay would simply reflect the huge risks in doing the job. But it is a damning document, undermining any idea of him as a hero involved in a caper to help ordinary Africans.

While Mann was busy calculating what he would get paid, another plotter, Greg Wales, was (almost certainly) drafting the first of a pair of remarkable political documents. Wales, the accountant and close friend of Mann who once worked with Executive Outcomes, considers himself a businessman, an academic, a wheelerdealer, a friend of mercenaries (though not a gun-toter himself) and a writer. He likes to meet in London cellar wine bars, usually over several bottles of chardonnay. He wears black-rimmed, half-moon spectacles with a string attached, and frowns frequently when trying to look serious. He usually dons the near-uniform of English expatriates in Africa: crinkled linen suit and pale blue shirt. Like most who were connected to the Wonga Coup, the ex-accountant is prone to rambling lectures.

He had the job of thinking out the political consequences of attempting a coup in Equatorial Guinea. It was up to him – along with a few others with good political contacts in Africa, Europe or America – to consider the reactions of governments and businesses with interests in Equatorial Guinea. Wales specifically asked the author that he get credit for using the old rhyme 'Beware, beware, the Bight of Benin' in connection with the Equatorial Guinea coup plot. He makes no bones about his desire to see Obiang overthrown and Moto installed. He says he wishes the 'game' had succeeded. He believes Spain supported it. Wales says he met Moto in Spain in 2003, along with someone from Spain's then ruling party and an American lobbyist from Washington DC. He found Moto both friendly and ready to 'talk the talk' of democracy and economic reform for Equatorial Guinea. Everyone present at the meeting assumed Moto would be president within three months and Wales made it his business to stay close to him. He denies he planned any military operations and he threatened to sue a British newspaper that suggested he helped finance the plot. However, there is no doubt he was involved in the political side of the affair. He says he thought his job was to 'keep Moto in line' for the first thirty days of the new president's rule, and he sees no reason to apologise for it.

Wales produced two long documents, among several memos, that sketched out his thoughts. The first he wrote in July 2003 (it is dated the same day as Mann's contract with Moto), and subsequently distributed to others involved in the Wonga Coup – for example, Nigel Morgan recalls Wales giving him a copy later that year. It carries a gracious title, 'Assisted Regime Change', which implies some gentle and measured reform. It is the sort of beguiling public relations term that hints at something trivial: a new bus timetable, more assisted care in an old people's home. But of course it means a violent *coup d'état*. He passes over the military aspects of the mission, for he is not a military expert, and suggests ways that the new government of Moto (supported by Mann and his plotters) should run the country. Foreign investors are to be reassured. Nearby countries that might be tempted to invade in the 'immediate aftermath' of the coup must be discouraged. Diplomats, businessmen, aid workers and journalists are to be briefed about the coup soon after it happens, as part of a determined public relations campaign. Rival foreign-based 'pretenders' to leadership, in other words those opposition leaders who competed with Moto, had to be identified and 'neutralised'.

Wales runs through several suggestions of how to do this. He thinks organising a coup on a Thursday or Friday 'may well be ideal', as ministers would be in the capital and could be rounded up. The weekend would be a useful time for new rulers to consolidate their grip on power, in time to open the doors of government for business on a Monday morning. The press would be organised 'to be unanimously supporting the new leadership', he suggests. International flights and phone calls would be blocked. Wales considers it important the new rulers should seem legitimate, so they would announce 'impressive plans for social, political, medical and economic improvements for the general population' while in fact milking the country for all they could.

Wales's recurrent point, in conversation with plotters and in his documents, is that taking power is quite a different matter from keeping it. Projecting a good image to the world is necessary to discourage an invasion or counter coup. The example of the reversed putsch in Sao Tome was obviously fresh in his mind. Crause Steyl recalls: 'The guys who did that coup, we spoke to them. They said it [the military bit] was pretty easy, but we were supposed to look at the politics. That was Greg's job.' And Wales made a serious point: the soldiering team, led by Mann, had also to think beyond military affairs. That is a recurring theme in the Wonga Coup. Mann, Nick du Toit and others had the military means and experience for a successful coup, but also they needed to consider the politics of modern Africa.

Wales worked hard on this theme throughout 2003. Mann's bank statements showed he passed money to Wales (and to a foundation that Wales controlled), paying him to travel to the United States to gauge reaction of American officials to a coup. He made some sort of contact, probably at a conference on military companies, with Theresa Whelan from the Pentagon and with representatives of an industrial lobby group for private military firms. Wales also considered taking Moto to Washington DC to introduce him to officials, academics and the media. He approached an American lobbyist called Joe Sala, who said a four day programme of such introductions could be arranged for $40,000. Phone records later showed that Wales constantly phoned American contacts in these months, for example logging more than thirty calls to Sala in the year to February 2004 (when the phone calls abruptly stopped).

Wales boasted to all who would listen that the CIA had paid him to do a survey of Equatorial Guinea in the middle of 2003, and he endlessly claimed (though it is never possible to tell what was bluff and what might be true) to have secret and important contacts in the American administration. One South African security consultant later complained that Wales hired him to conduct an 'intelligence survey' of Equatorial Guinea, to see what size ships could enter the harbour in Malabo and to see how carefully cargo was monitored on those ships. He said that Wales owed him $28,000 for the survey and, when pressed for money, the South African was told to contact Mann. Wales would later brag, usually after a bottle or two of chardonnay, of having contacts with Scott Fisher from the State Department, Herb Howe from the National Security Agency, as well as assorted lobbyists and public relations people in Washington.

By the turn of the year, Wales's ideas (and presumably Mann's, too) had expanded to something grander in Equatorial Guinea. He proposed forming a company, controlled by Mann and his closest plotters, to run Equatorial Guinea with Moto as a puppet leader. The English accountant had long liked to dream up plans and models for how to run failing countries. He says he has written other proposals for other companies modelled on the old buccaneering firms that underwrote British imperial expansion in India and Africa. He thinks Somalia and Gabon should be run by boards of directors, not by governments or warlords. So he wrote a lengthy document, the Bight of Benin Company document, describing how such a company could take power and run the oil-rich west African state. Johann Smith believes the document shows the coup plot 'was pure neo-colonialism, to put Moto in place so they can remove him at any time. Simon would have been the president's security adviser and his company, the Bight of Benin Company, would have controlled it all.'

Wales was following old models. Much of Africa, at least the British-run parts, was colonised by private companies. The first, as early as 1618, was a 'Company of Adventurers of London Trading to the Ports of Africa', also known as the Guinea Company, that dominated British trade with the continent. By the eighteenth century the Sierra Leone Company was founded with the part-philanthropic goal of snatching a corner of west Africa and repatriating ex-slaves from London. And in the Victorian era it was profit-seeking firms whose employees wielded machine guns and conquered land and people all over Africa. In the south, Cecil Rhodes' British South Africa Company – and its mercenary army – overwhelmed much of what is now Zimbabwe and Zambia. In east Africa Frederick Lugard (a soldier-of-fortune turned colonialist) of the Imperial British East Africa Company conquered territory, then moved to west Africa to help another British firm colonise land along the Niger river.

The plotters of the Wonga Coup evidently hoped to follow in this long tradition of procuring wealth in Africa through the barrel of a gun. The Bight of Benin Company document – which Wales admits he wrote – along with memos from plotters' meetings, show a preoccupation with oil firms, the untrustworthiness of fellow plotters and the risk of counter-invasion, perhaps from Nigeria, after the coup. It is dated January 2004 and one copy (a version now in the author's possession) was found in Mann's South African office later that year.

The Bight of Benin Company document shows the plotters fretting that oil firms may not play ball after the coup. If the oil revenues stopped flowing, what was the point of taking control of Equatorial Guinea? They knew that regular, direct flights existed between Malabo and Houston – an indication of the growing American interest in Equatorial Guinea's oil as so many American workers needed to shuttle across the Atlantic. They pondered which firms owned which blocks (areas where each firm works) in the sea around the island country. And even if the oil continued to flow, how could they squeeze more revenue? They knew any attempt to renegotiate deals with oil firms would be difficult: such haggling is heavily frowned on once production is underway. An earlier effort by Obiang to do just that, over the productive Zafira oil field, 'went down very badly in the industry', says an oil expert. But 'the coup makers would have thought they would allocate new blocks, or would form little oil companies of their own, then trade them or farm out rights to other firms', he suggests.

The plotters knew not to provoke American displeasure. Messing with the superpower's oil interests might be 'what gets the Marines coming in', hints a note on one agenda. Reassuring the American government would be necessary early on. The Americans might be assuaged if lucrative jobs were offered to American private security firms. In one document, the plotters suggest the firm Military Professional Resources, Incorporated (MPRI) might get the job of guarding the new president. Wales reported to his colleagues that the Pentagon's Whelan had been enthusiastic at their meeting in 2003, at least about the general idea of American security firms getting more business in Africa.

The Bight of Benin Company document makes clear that the plotters hoped to control Moto as a puppet leader, even taking charge of who has access to the new president and what official contracts he was allowed to sign. But keeping such control would be difficult, especially given the likely divisions that would appear between the plotters themselves. The two, colourful opening paragraphs of the document illustrate that point:

> The 2 most potent general threats are:
> 1) as it is potentially a very lucrative game, we should expect bad behaviour; disloyalty; rampant individual greed; irrational behaviour (kids in toyshop style); back-stabbing, bum-fucking, and similar ungentlemanly activities.
> 2) if the result is not seen by the outside world as noticeably better than the current situation, our position there in other than the very short term, will be hard to sustain; and our involvement will be much more likely to be the subject of unfavourable scrutiny.

They did not trust Moto, even though he was their client. Once he was in power, the men who led the coup would become relatively weak. Moto might think 'whoever puts him in power can be a disposable syringe'. So he needed to be kept weak enough to depend on those who put him in office, but strong enough to keep away others who wanted power. It would be a difficult balance to strike. Moto might denounce his mercenaries as 'a threat to him, re-writing history to claim that we were working for the previous mob (our current strategy making that easier)'. Mann, Wales and others had good reason to worry. Angola's government had eventually turned against Executive Outcomes in the late 1990s. Its president, Eduardo dos Santos, privately asked the American president, Bill Clinton, to call him publicly to throw the mercenaries out of Angola. Dos Santos complied while appearing to do so regretfully. In similar fashion, Moto might try 'getting oil co's (eg) to pressure USG [United States Government] to push for our removal'.

Moto might be kept weak, however, if he were unpopular. So there should be no elections for the new president, according to the Bight of Benin Company document: Moto 'needs to achieve power by coup or putsch; not by public acclamation on return, or by political dealing after it'. The mercenaries would monopolise violent force (the definition of the modern state), making sure they paid and controlled all important military men including the 'Army/Navy/Air Force, Military Equipment, Intelligence, Palace Guard ... Customs, airport and port security; maritime security ...' They would also try to take charge of government finances and foreign policy. As they plundered they would nonetheless seek 'the moral high ground' by seeming to promote open government and fighting corruption. And if Moto eventually proved too troublesome, they would groom a successor-in-waiting who could be imposed on the country by the mercenaries' military might.

The document lists many other threats to the plotters. Would 'EK' be a problem once the coup was over, given his excellent political contacts in west Africa? He might be in league with Nigerians who might consider invasion to reduce Equatorial Guinea to 'vassal status'. Could Nick du Toit really be trusted, or might he develop his own military strength after the coup was completed? The French or South Africans could protest against the coup, cause trouble at the African Union and possibly stir up an international campaign against the new government.

This is the closest the plotters came to realising that their scheme to steal a country would not be tolerated. But the author of the document then dreams up some remedies. If the United States (and Spain) backed Moto, Nigeria might hold back. The Nigerians should talk to the Americans about the plot. The intelligence man Nigel Morgan, a close friend of Mann, might help. He had a useful contact in the Nigerian government and might supply 'very good intelligence' on Nigeria's reaction. Nigeria might be 'the biggest threat of all, a massively revised plan would be needed ... The NM intelligence function is vital'.

For students of coup plots, ridiculous African adventures, high jinks in the tropics, and for anyone interested in the nether world of freelance spies and shady oil company activities the assembled documents relating to the Wonga Coup make fascinating reading. A more complete list of documents and contracts is noted in the epilogue to this book, but it is worth recording here that few coup attempts in recent years – at least those not plotted by governments and bureaucrats – can be so well documented as this one. The reader might draw various conclusions from the abundant paperwork. The plotters were careless, leaving their paths so heavily strewn with evidence. Or the plotters were canny, creating a baffling mix of evidence to be seen alongside intelligence reports, genuine business contracts and emails, that together would confuse any investigator or prosecutor. Or the plotters were dreamers, fantasising about their wealthy futures and making it all the more real, all the closer, by writing down the details on paper.

9
Future Moto

'Obiang wants me to go back ... [so he can] eat my testicles.'

Severo Moto

From mid 2003 the planning of the Wonga Coup picked up speed. Exiled in Madrid, Severo Moto had few tasks beyond asserting some authority. Immediate support in Equatorial Guinea was not essential. But to sustain his eventual rule, Moto needed more than mercenaries. Was he popular? He said he was, and Mann and others believed him. They talked of Moto 'winning' an election in the mid 1990s, though officials usually assign Obiang at least 97 per cent of any vote. Moto did briefly contest a presidential election but he, and other candidates, then withdrew. The truth was, nobody knew if Moto was popular or not.

Two other constituencies worried Moto. He needed international acceptance. Spain he could rely on, as prime minister Aznar signalled support for him and hostility to Obiang. In turn Spain could expect a favour or two from the United States, after stalwart support for the invasion of Iraq that year. With some lobbying on Moto's behalf in Washington, organised by Greg Wales, that might be arranged. Support from Africa might be trickier.

Finally, the exiles, mainly in Madrid, needed persuading.

All despised Obiang, but there was fierce rivalry between camps. Some said Moto had no right to pose as their leader as others had taken greater risks defying the despot. Some had suffered more in jail. But by August 2003 Moto had united three opposition groups as a 'government-in-exile' in Madrid, with him as leader. He issued solemn statements, set up a website and condemned Obiang. He drew up a constitution and economic policies. All of which lent him pomp and seriousness. By September 2003 Moto promised to be in power in Equatorial Guinea within nine months. He told a press conference that Obiang would fall due to 'illness of the dictator, the internal struggles in the palace, the sufferings of the population and international discredit'. He seemed, really, to believe that Mann's military skill would do the trick. By the end of the year Moto was heard boasting he would be in office within weeks.

Meanwhile Nick du Toit was active in Malabo, courting friendships and setting up his front companies. At the end of August he met the president's brother, Armengol Nguema, and discussed a fishing business using an imported boat. The ocean around Equatorial Guinea was stocked with valuable fish. Foreign trawlers, notably Spanish and Asian ones, already took great advantage in the Gulf of Guinea. Pirate fishing, when unlicensed boats exploit the waters of a poorly organised state, is common in west Africa. Few countries have a strong enough navy to deter intruders. Thus it was natural for du Toit to be interested in this industry. Du Toit later explained to a film crew that he 'joined a joint venture company with Mr Armengol, one of the ministers of the country, Antonio Javier, and a third guy, and we called the business Triple Options Trading, Equatorial Guinea'. There was also talk of agricultural work. The ruling family remembered South Africans had done a good job farming cattle and poultry on the volcano during the apartheid years. Perhaps this South African, too, could make good use of the land.

Du Toit split his time between developing businesses in Equatorial Guinea and reporting back to Mann in South Africa. An agricultural consultant was recruited to draw up plans for a farming business. Du Toit later claimed he was setting up legitimate companies at this time, not fronts for the coup plot. In fact he did both: the firms could prove lucrative whether or not the coup went ahead. But there was no doubt in other plotters' minds that du Toit was there as the forward team. Crause Steyl says, 'Simon Mann sent Nick du Toit up to Equatorial Guinea. Nick wouldn't have gone otherwise. It was all a smokescreen.' 'Lots of people have front businesses,' he adds. Du Toit was 'not really a spy or anything like that, but if the opportunity comes around, well. Nick didn't think it would happen within months. Sometimes you start a business and you tell investors [coup plotters] the time is not ready. You might wait years. There are these businesses all over the place.' Perhaps du Toit believed the coup might never be attempted, or at least not soon. If so, he would take Mann's money and set up businesses. Late in 2003 he met Wales in Pretoria to discuss Mann's investment. It was the first of at least two meetings between the two men.

Du Toit's business steamed ahead. On 25 August 2003 he registered a South African company in Pretoria as Triple Options Trading 610 CC. This was a sister firm of the one registered with a similar name in Equatorial Guinea (the joint venture with Armengol, the president's brother). By October he had found a fishing trawler in South Africa that could be used in Equatorial Guinea. The crew for the trawler, made up largely of old Buffalo Soldiers, would raise suspicion, however.

Du Toit later told investigators: 'I bought a boat called *Roslyn Joy* in South Africa, which sailed to Equatorial Guinea in December 2003 with Captain J.P. Domingo, Engineer Americo Ribeiro and deck hand Georges Allerson.' It seems likely that Mann paid for it.

By the end of 2003 du Toit had a useful network, a bundle of contracts signed with the Equatorial Guinea government and growing interests in fishing, aviation, agriculture and security. He arranged for planes for his aviation business. He met President Obiang in December 2003. He signed contracts thick and fast. On 23 January he signed a joint venture deal with a local company, Sonage, to provide more airline and marine services. And though du Toit's wife, Belinda, later told journalists that her husband was threatened by Mann and forced to go along with the coup plot (she recalls Mann shouting at her husband one day at their home in Pretoria), it seems that he was a willing participant from early on. Du Toit played a large and prolonged role. He would help to buy weapons and recruit men. His tasks included taking control of the airport in Malabo and delivering mercenaries to 'positions of strategic importance in the capital city' – probably including military bases, the police station and two entrances to the president's palace – during the coup.

All the while, Mann bankrolled du Toit's firms. Du Toit's accounts for his business in Malabo from July to November show he received $112,000 from a benefactor, probably Mann. One of Mann's bank accounts shows he paid du Toit $15,000 in October, and transferred $11,417 to 'Eleanor Fishing CC', perhaps for du Toit's fishing trawler, the *Roslyn Joy*. On 1 December Mann guaranteed $2 million for du Toit's firm. His bank records show four more transfers from Mann's companies in 2004 (on 5 and 16 January, 17 February and

2 March) totalling some $220,000. Du Toit was at various plotters' meetings in 2003, for example at one meeting near Pretoria and again in the coastal town of George just before Christmas. Du Toit later recalled meeting Greg Wales, David Tremain and a number of others involved in the coup.

By late 2003 Johann Smith, the rag-and-bone intelligence man, heard ever more insistent rumours of a coup. He was not alone. Other intelligence networks were starting to hum. By October the British government, for example, picked up foreign language news reports of a pending coup. A British individual once connected to Executive Outcomes, with close contacts in the British government, Tim Spicer, was rumoured to have visited Malabo late in 2003. Public discussion of a coup was rising. Towards the end of the year Nigel Morgan had heard of a plan for mercenary action in west Africa and suspected Mann, a close friend, was involved. Morgan resolved to get close to the action. He was interested for two contradictory reasons. On one hand, as a freelance intelligence man, he wanted a chance to make money. This could be a moment to resurrect his Cogito firm and finally do business in Equatorial Guinea, where his friend Mann would be running things. On the other, as many knew, Morgan had close ties with the South African authorities and would be expected to pass on what he knew to them.

So when Mann said he needed a personal assistant who could manage computers and understand finance, Morgan put forward James Kershaw, his friend who had worked in Congo. The young South African was a capable administrator and had various skills, notably in electronic communication. Mann hired him. He sat at the centre of Mann's operations, arranging meetings, keeping track of his bank acounts and liaising with several others. Many of those recruited, or otherwise involved, recall dealing with him. And though Kershaw says he had no idea what was going on, suggesting he thought a mining operation was planned in Congo, others recall he showed a great interest in Equatorial Guinea at this time. Smith, for example, was badgered by Kershaw for copies of his intelligence reports on Equatorial Guinea. Kershaw was also present at many meetings of those involved in the plot.

Morgan relied on Kershaw to relay information of Mann's movements and meetings. Kershaw effectively became a mole within the operation. Mann probably knew, but he did not mind, that old Nosher got some information from Kershaw. It is likely he also suspected Morgan relayed some of that to the South African authorities, assuming intelligence traders are obliged to debrief government contacts to some degree. But Mann could not know how much of substance would reach his South African hosts. Nor could he be sure what reaction the South African authorities would have to his scheme. He might have hoped that the government, if it severely disapproved, would pass a message of discouragement back to him. That, apparently, did not happen.

Crause Steyl also became actively involved. He recalls agreeing to take part in the Wonga Coup in mid 2003, but he had little to do with it before October. He visited Mann at his luxurious home in Cape Town. There was talk of code words (apparently the phrase 'the pictures have arrived' would be used at some point to indicate plans were going as expected; the men would also take different names – for example, Mann would be 'Frank'). Steyl was told that a front man called Nick was in the target country setting up front companies. Then Steyl joined Mann to inspect the fishing trawler – the *Roslyn Joy* – that would soon leave for Equatorial Guinea. Finally Mann said he had a specific task for the pilot.

It was a pleasant task. Steyl was to undertake reconnaissance at a tourist haven, the Canary Islands. Mann made it clear that he intended a coup. Steyl's task was to fly a group of important people from the Canary Islands to the target country (the idea that Moto would go via Uganda having been dropped). This group would include the opposition leader Moto, who would be installed as the new president. Naturally it would be a clandestine operation. Steyl's instructions were clear. As he should not go through customs or immigration when Moto was aboard, he should establish how to leave the Canary Islands secretly. He must report back at the end of October. Steyl leapt to it.

Though he ran a successful air ambulance business in South Africa, Steyl was thrilled by the idea of a military exploit. Like many, he still yearned for the adrenalin-filled days of Executive Outcomes. He asked for $15,000 and travelled, via Madrid, on a commercial airliner on 20 October. Four days later, Mann paid the agreed fee into the pilot's account. Steyl returned the next day and the two discussed what he had seen. The Canary Islands, roughly halfway between mainland Spain and Equatorial Guinea, would be an ideal launch pad. As they are a part of Spain, Moto would arrive using an internal flight. Also, the Canaries are large enough for a group of foreigners to pose as tourists, but sleepy enough that flying out unauthorised would be possible. Steyl would prepare transport, as he once organised flights for Executive Outcomes to Angola. He would hire a Beechcraft King Air propeller plane, registration number ZS-NBJ, from a small company in Pretoria, from December 2003 until the end of March 2004. When the time came, Moto would fly from Madrid to Las Palmas on Gran Canaria. Steyl would ferry him onwards.

Enthused, Steyl suggested others who might help. He

also agreed to meet a man called Harry Carlse – formerly of
Executive Outcomes, then serving as a hired gun in Iraq – to
explain the project. Steyl was convinced it could succeed: 'You
ask what is the military backing? You see sixteen people and
a bread wagon take over Sao Tome. Equatorial Guinea would
have been a walk in the park. Simon said that never has a shot
been fired in anger in that country. And we are going there
with 32 Battalion, a generation of real warmongers. We would
have walked all over it.'

Back in tropical Equatorial Guinea, the political temperature
was rising. Just one family had ruled since independence in
1968: first bloodthirsty Uncle Macias, then Obiang from 1979.
It was an extremely rare example of dynastic rule in Africa,
where political power almost never passes from one relation
to another. The Fang dominated, and within that a subgroup
from Mongomo town, which in turn was presided over by the
ruling family. The family had grown accustomed to power
and the administration was stocked with Obiang's cousins,
half-brothers and uncles, none with any special skills to offer.
Obiang knew his relatives, and took to heart the advice to
keep your friends close but your enemies – your rivals in the
ruling clan – even closer.

   There were always fears of plots and skulduggery,
warnings of foreign meddling, all compounded by suspicions
of internal splits. While Equatorial Guinea remained dirt poor
and sleepy, Obiang knew everything that happened, because
little did. But as oil money flowed in the late 1990s two things
changed. Firstly, it became more obvious that holding power
meant getting rich. The trappings of corruption – luxury cars,

overstuffed foreign bank accounts, shopping sprees in Paris – made high office more tempting. Second, the extended ruling family proved unable to deal smartly with oil companies, complicated contracts and tough negotiations in order to get the best from oil and gas stocks. Obiang needed new blood in the government, technocrats who knew what to do. And that meant squeezing out the men who traditionally held power.

So by late 2003, heckles were up. As oil wealth grew, loyalty became less predictable. Decisions were taken in the shadows. As more power and wealth were invested in one man, Obiang, it grew more tempting for others to kill him. And by 2003 Obiang grew frail. A deadly competition to succeed arose. Though simplified, one could see the domestic battle as one between two brothers, Obiang's two sons. On one side Teodorin, the playboy elder brother, an arrogant and power-hungry man. Few liked him. He once ran a recording studio in California, then took charge of tropical timber exports from Equatorial Guinea. His power in government steadily grew. Oil companies were said not to trust him. He was quick to argue. He threatened his father. Backed by his powerful mother, Obiang's first wife, he knew he was favourite to succeed, if only Obiang relinquished his grip. By September 2003, said Johann Smith (who was close to the ruling family), relations with Obiang were fraught. After one confrontation a furious Teodorin stormed out of the country. There were whispers he had plotted against others in the ruling clan. In private discussions he said he would be president soon and would renegotiate oil contracts struck by American firms.

The second son, Gabriel, represented another part of the ruling family, opposed to Teodorin, who feared that if he took power they would be pushed aside, possibly killed. Gabriel was considered an outsider because his mother, Obiang's second wife, was from Sao Tome. But younger, educated in America, less obnoxious and more capable than Teodorin he was favoured by foreign oil firms. This second faction of the ruling family included some powerful men. One was called Augustin Ona, an uncle of Obiang, who would crack from the strain, apparently attempt suicide and be arrested later that year. Another was Armengol, Obiang's brother, the man who struck a business deal and joint venture agreement with Nick du Toit.

10

Filthy Lucre

*'It sounds to me like a gentleman's plot from the eighteenth
century. You each put in 100,000, then try to get it back tenfold.'*
Henry Page on the financiers

One Monday in 1985 a group of white men wearing crumpled
business suits and carrying suitcases arrived at Hammond
airport, near New Orleans, USA. They expected to board a
charter flight to Suriname, a small former Dutch colony in
South America. Their cases were stuffed with semi-automatic
weapons. They also carried revolvers, compasses, walkie-
talkie radios, shotguns and commando face-blackening cream.
Packed in bags were thousands of rounds of ammunition and a
book – *Ambush and Counter Ambush* – for last-minute revision.
Once in Suriname, they planned to pose as bankers, arrange a
meeting with the president, overpower him and take charge
of the country. Somehow, they believed, Suriname's military
would accept the *fait accompli* and let them get away with it.

In the annals of ridiculous coup attempts, the one by
Tommy Lynn Denley, an American former customs agent and
one-time policeman in Panama, must count as one of the most
stupid. Homer Simpson could have done a better job. Denley
recruited thirteen others from small American towns like
Sugar Tree, Tennessee and Oak Forest, Illinois. He apparently

hated left-wing rule in Latin America. But money was also a big concern. There were rumours that a Dutch foundation would pay 'hundreds of millions' of dollars for the removal of Suriname's Marxist regime. Financiers were apparently pledged tenfold returns. That rate seems to be the standard to lure investors to coup plots. But whatever the fantasy of reward, operational funds were short. An original plan had called for thirty hardened fighters to fly via Nicaragua. That was later dropped in favour of a smaller group flying direct from the United States.

But the FBI infiltrated the plot early on. Undercover agents even chartered the plane and arranged other transport for the hard-up conspirators. Just before departure, Denley and his men were separated from their guns and arrested. They later pleaded guilty to various federal offences. *Newsweek* magazine noted in 1986: 'Amateur mercenaries have a well-established tendency to fall for crazy plots and get in over their heads ... in the course of recruiting, seeking financial backing and buying munitions for the coup, Denley made so many waves that he picked up almost as many federal infiltrators as genuine recruits ...'

Denley perhaps got his idea from a similar plot four years earlier, also in the United States. In 1981, ten white supremacists from Canada and the United States vowed to take over the Caribbean island of Dominica. A man called Michael Perdue dreamt up 'Operation Red Dog', to sail a team of hired guns 3,200 km (2,000 miles) from New Orleans on a yacht, the *Manana*. A former head of the Ku Klux Klan in Canada took the code name 'Red Dog 3' and served as a forward agent, to guide the mercenaries to a darkened dock with a flashlight. But, vain and careless, they bragged of their plans to a Canadian radio station. One explained: 'I consider myself a little bit of a rebel in society ... And I'm also, of course, going to benefit financially from it, which will afford me a good life ... I hope I'll be fixed for the rest of my life after Dominica.' They also gave documents and more interviews to a Canadian woman who planned to write a book about the escapade. They said they would use assault rifles, 12-gauge shotguns and sticks of dynamite wrapped with roofing nails to 'blast' police guards and seize the local radio station and government. They expected little resistance from the ninety-nine men of Dominica's army.

But the working budget was small. An ex-minister of Dominica who wanted his old job back may have pledged funds, perhaps $150,000. The island would be used as a base to promote white supremacist views and the mercenaries would make money, too, by selling false passports, running guns and logging trees. There were elaborate plans for an airport, a casino, hotels, off-shore banking and – an imaginative touch – a holiday playground and money-laundering venue for American mobsters. One Canadian mafioso paid $10,000 upfront. In return he expected to become a major in the defence force. But police heard of the plot, infiltrated the loose-tongued gang and arrested Perdue and the rest before they boarded the *Manana*. They were tried and jailed.

These two cases tell an obvious story: low-cost rent-a-coups rarely work. It is much the same in Africa. Toppling someone else's government is tricky and expensive. Frederick Forsyth was alleged by the *Sunday Times* to have put £100,000 (the equivalent of roughly ten times that today) into the 1973 plot against Equatorial Guinea. (He now admits giving some cash, but claims it was only for information.) Three years on, Bob Denard – as mentioned earlier – had a budget of roughly $1 million, probably from the French government, to seize power in Benin with ninety men. He failed, but succeeded in the Comoros a couple of years later with a smaller team, a fishing trawler and a crate of good champagne. Mike Hoare originally budgeted $5 million for his coup attempt in the Seychelles, though that dropped as his plans for 200 soldiers were reduced to a few dozen and a shoestring budget. Hoare concluded that coups 'cannot be carried out on the cheap. The unexpected beats you. It is horrifyingly expensive.'

As lessons in failure, these attempts might have been useful for the Wonga Coup plotters. Doing the job well required money. If you lack funds, you are more vulnerable to other problems. There is the need to recruit, train, accommodate and sustain a fighting force that is loyal only to cash. The bigger the army and the more training needed, the greater the cost. Reconnaissance trips to the target country are essential. More elaborate efforts entail setting up a front company, or some other cover.

Then there is transport. Amateur rent-a-coups are more likely in small countries (Benin, Suriname) and island ones (the Comoros, the Seychelles, Dominica, Equatorial Guinea). That means crossing the sea. Hoare's cheap ruse – disguising his fighters as rugby-playing tourists and buying plane tickets to the Seychelles – meant he lacked a means of escape when things went sour. As Forsyth said in 2005, attackers should approach by sea: 'A ship can drop over the horizon and be entirely on its own.' There are no controls on the waves, but there is time to test weapons and give late orders. Bob Denard, in the Comoros, and the Dominica plotters of Operation Red Dog favoured that method. But finding and buying a suitable craft is not easy. Fishing trawlers were initially preferred by Hoare, though he later dropped the idea. Mann and du Toit bought at least one trawler, too. Flying your own plane is the other option, and a few aircraft – DC3s in the past, the Boeing 727 more recently – are popular among hired guns.

Weapons are moderately costly. In Forsyth's meticulously researched novel he said an attack force should overthrow the government in Equatorial Guinea, then a larger army would keep power: 'The [attack] force should not be less than a dozen men, armed with mortars, bazookas and grenades, and all carrying as well submachine carbines for close-quarters use.' Attackers expect to use surprise and limited force, not to engage in many battles or prolonged fighting. Plots usually involve elements of an invasion, but should unfold quickly and quietly. Each soldier needs a rifle, plus ammunition. One can be bought almost anywhere in Africa for the price of a good restaurant meal. A machine gun or two, and some grenades, might be thrown in. If you are French, champagne is essential. Even cut-price attackers are likely to need radios, first aid kits and other basics, plus appropriate clothing. Bigger spenders add items like a helicopter gunship. All attackers expect to be better trained, organised and led than any defenders. In order to keep power, the army will need heavier weapons, but these might be seized in the country of occupation.

There are incidental costs. Some information comes from the advance guard, but other material is bought from rag-and-bone intelligence men. There are bribes to pay, perhaps so no one interferes when the mercenaries depart for the attack. While a scheme is prepared, there are costs of entertaining contacts, communications and other sundry items. Then money goes astray. After all, this is about plotting a big, if international, crime. Ordinary bankrobbers swindle each other, or pocket funds that should have paid for the getaway car. Coup plotters are no different. No one audits the finances. No one can run to the police if their investment is stolen. Only the fabled honour among gentlemen thieves, plus a shared hunger for success, keep conspirators in line. Many of those even loosely involved in the Wonga Coup were afterwards quick to talk, somewhat bitterly, of money owed them.

Nobody, perhaps not even the organisers of the Wonga Coup, is exactly sure of its budget. Estimates range from $3 million to $20 million. James Kershaw kept the closest eye on Mann's finances, but claims he thought the money was for a mining project in Congo. He refuses to talk in detail. Mann was usually involved in several different business schemes at once and was casual about his accounts. Money flowed between his companies, serving different ends. So it is hard to prove that a particular deposit was intended for a coup plot rather than, say, for a legitimate gold mining project in South America.

But the plotters used at least $3 million, probably more. Where did they find it? The best source of funding, as Bob Denard knew, is a friendly government. For his Seychelles attack Hoare got limited aid – weapons and training grounds – from apartheid South Africa. But few freelance plotters enjoy such backing. A rich plotter might fund everything himself. But with risky projects it is natural to share the gamble. Some treat it as a business. Entrepreneurs raise capital with bank loans, by mortgaging property, selling shares or getting venture capitalists involved. Business-minded buccaneers do the same. Francis Drake used some of his own money to fund fleets to plunder Spanish gold. But he also promised good returns to individuals – including his sovereign, Queen Elizabeth – who put up matching funds. Henry Morton Stanley, the nineteenth-century explorer-conqueror, funded his trips to Africa with sponsorship from British and American newspapers. Later, a single investor, Belgium's King Leopold, paid him to stake out a massive private empire in central Africa, now the Democratic Republic of Congo.

Mann followed Drake: he put in funds himself, used savings, possibly having taken a loan against shares in a diamond mining firm in Angola and – he claimed to other plotters – having raised a mortgage on his London home. As an investor he could claim a large share of the riches afterwards. But he also asked friends and colleagues – very private investors – to help. An inner circle were also plotters. Equatorial Guinea accused Ely Calil, the wealthy Lebanese–Nigerian oil trader, of being the lead financier of this sort, though he stoutly denied it. David Tremain faces arrest in South Africa, where investigators say he helped finance the plot, but also attended planning meetings and more. He has stayed silent on the matter, issuing no comment or denial. A South African charge sheet, which explains what they would be charged with if arrested, accuses him and Greg Wales of 'raising funds to finance' mercenary activities, conspiring with Mann and making plans to install a new government in Equatorial Guinea. (As of April 2006 there was no indication that this had been withdrawn.) Then a second circle of financiers, with less precise – if any – knowledge of the scheme, were promised an excellent rate of return, perhaps tenfold, if they asked few questions. Henry Page, a lawyer acting for Equatorial Guinea's government, later suggested: 'It sounds to me like a gentleman's plot from the eighteenth century. You each put in 100,000, then try to get it back tenfold.' This circle included a fascinating cast of investors.

A Chain of Investors

Mann wrote a detailed confession in March 2004 giving useful information about money. He – and his lawyers – say this document should be ignored. It was obtained under duress and perhaps after torture. It was not used in court against Mann, presumably for these problems, though a lawyer acting against him in Britain denied torture took place. He noted the free-flowing handwriting did not suggest 'someone treated like Guy Fawkes'. Though obtained under dubious circumstances, none suggested the confession was fabricated.

It shows Mann preoccupied with a 'shortage of funds' and costly payments during his preparations. He wrote of meeting Moto and the plan to 'escort' him home: 'my role was to be concerned chiefly with the military and security aspects'. He recalled that, by June 2003, 'The whole programme, in terms of my part, then stalled through lack of funds.'

Yet later that year the money worries eased. Mann signed two investment agreements in mid November on behalf of his company, Logo Logistics Limited. Logo had registered offices in the British Virgin Islands, but operated from an address in Guernsey, a tax haven in the English Channel. The two deals are similar, each five pages long with a dozen bland articles of agreement. The interesting bit is the short preamble (identical in each) which specifies that each investor will pay $5 million to Logo Logistics – 'The Company' – to chase intriguing but ill-defined schemes in west Africa:

The Company has identified potential projects in the fields of mining exploration, commercial sea fishing, aviation (cargo and PAX [passengers]), helicopter charter and commercial security, in the following countries: Guinea Republic [a separate country], Sierra Leone, Liberia and Angola.

An initial investment of USD 5,000,000.00 (American Dollars Five Million) is required from The Investor by The Company to evaluate and initiate the above mentioned projects, which have been identified by the company.

There was no mention of a coup, though 'commercial security' and the other operations were precisely what Mann planned once Moto became president of Equatorial Guinea, as mentioned in the July contracts. 'Mining exploration' might refer to the oil industry. Du Toit was already setting up the fishing and aviation firms. The timing was intriguing: just when Mann was scrabbling for investors in his coup attempt, he signed two deals worth a total of $10 million. Though care was taken not to leave an obvious paper trail – there is no specific mention of Equatorial Guinea – these funds would have gone to Mann's firm and would have been used in the businesses that du Toit and Mann were creating.

Who agreed to invest? Crause Steyl, the pilot and plotter, recalls Mann saying he 'was approached, I think, by a Lebanese consortium. They promised him money.' The names on the investor agreements gave clues. One was signed on behalf of Verona Holdings Limited, registered and based in Vaud, Switzerland. The other was signed on behalf of Asian Trading and Investment Group SAL, registered in Beirut, Lebanon. For those seeking a Lebanese connection to the Wonga Coup, this firm became the centre of investigation. One man, Karim Fallaha, appears here. Records of a meeting of Asian Trading on 27 June 2003 show Fallaha held a post in the company. Other plotters later made references to him. He eventually showed up in person in the Canary Islands in February and March. Calil and Fallaha are said to be acquaintances, though Calil denies any links to Asian Trading.

Soon after signing these agreements Mann passed money down the chain to du Toit. On 5 December he guaranteed a loan of $2 million to du Toit's firm, Triple Options Trading, for unspecified 'projects in the fields of commercial sea fishing, and commercial safety, in the Republic of Equatorial Guinea ...'

The deal was signed by both men. Repayments would begin on 1 May 2004, when both Mann and du Toit expected to be much richer. In the mean time Mann repeatedly provided du Toit with cash. In December the fishing trawler, the *Roslyn Joy*, left Cape Town and sailed up the Atlantic coast of Africa. Ten days later it arrived in Equatorial Guinea. Early in December, du Toit agreed to provide various 'integrated risk, agriculture and fishing' services to the government. The same month he arranged with a German businessman called Gerhard Merz to broker two cargo aircraft, an Ilyushin Il-76 from Ukraine and an Antonov.

Du Toit needed the planes urgently. On 27 November he had struck a deal with the Equatorial Guinea government to form an air transport cargo firm. His business proposal said Pan African Airlines and Trading Company, or PANAC, would provide much-needed links with nearby countries, using huge Russian aircraft, notably the Iluyshin Il-76 (with an Armenian crew). Based in Bata, on the mainland bit of the country, customers could rent the aircraft for $6,000 per hour. But the PANAC business document had a curious conclusion. After explaining the aviation business and the use of the Iluyshin, it offered:

> 10. Triple Options Trading 610 GE SA will make a proposal towards the president concerning security. Part of the proposal will include the donation of 6 (six) Toyota Land Cruiser pick-up trucks by the SA partners, to be utilized by either the police or the military. These vehicles can be transported with the IL-76 directly to EG, pending the approval of the security proposal.

Why give the president six Land Cruisers? It appeared to be a gesture of goodwill, or perhaps a bribe. In fact, it was an early plan for the Wonga Coup.

On 13 December at Wonderboom airport, near Pretoria, Mann met du Toit, Greg Wales and Crause Steyl. They moved to a holiday resort east of Pretoria where – probably over beers and steaks – they discussed the coup. Steyl recalls the plan they discussed at the time. It explains why du Toit had offered six cars to the president. The luxury vehicles would be loaded into the hold of the Ilyushin and flown to Malabo, with some weapons (bought in Uganda) hidden on the same plane. Obiang would be lured to the airport by the cars and, as he inspected them, the second plane, the Antonov, would land in Malabo. It would be packed with combat-ready mercenaries, also flown over from Uganda, who would rush the apron, guns trained on the president and his guard. Those on the Ilyushin would pull out their own weapons and 'apply violent measures', snatch Obiang and install Moto. Steyl explains: 'We had this plan for Obiang. We would take him cars, but first pick up our guys from Uganda. Then at the airport we would grab Obiang, and Moto could come in and have a few cars.' Obiang's life expectancy would be short. 'If the Moroccan guard had resisted, and if he had come in the line of fire, then as sure as fuck he'd have been killed. Like any buffalo, there is a time to shove him out. Then Moto would come in.'

The plan had much to recommend it. It was bold and simple. Obiang would be vulnerable out of his palace, protected only by bodyguards. The attacking soldiers and their weapons could easily reach the point of use, at the airport. A helicopter would also be useful as an air ambulance or as a gunship. Mann said a financier was already lined up for that. With planes and a helicopter, the attackers would be mobile, heavily armed and could escape if things went wrong. But there were drawbacks, too. It would happen by day, in the open, watched by anyone who happened to be there. Obiang's Moroccan guards were notoriously twitchy on the move. And, although the plotters probably did not know this, plans to kill Obiang at the airport had been exposed at least once before.

A World Bank adviser, Robert Klitgaard, watched Obiang arrive at Malabo late in the 1980s when Moroccan soldiers patrolled the apron. One had 'a submachine gun ... wrinkled fatigues and an olive-drab baseball hat', he noted. Others lined the fence of the airport, ready for an assault from a nearby forest. There was no attack that day, but a plan was exposed 'to assassinate the President as he deplaned, in full view of the honor guard, the Moroccan soldiers, all the ministers and military men, and the television camera'. Some forty high-ranking officials were arrested, tortured and jailed for (supposedly) dreaming up the idea. Nearly two decades on, paranoid Obiang might have been suspicious of a trip to the airport, and indifferent to the bait of six Land Cruisers. It was more likely he would send his brother, Armengol, or playboy son, Teodorin, both of whom like luxury cars.

But the plotters knew little of this. They thought the idea was sound, and set an attack date of 25 January, just over a month later. There remained much to do. Early recruitment of soldiers had begun, and some finance had been promised. Du Toit's friend and business partner, Henry van der Westhuizen, had approached a highly placed man in Uganda to discuss weapons. But a deal was not assured. Nor were travel arrangements fixed. Steyl was to organise both Moto's arrival from Spain and transport for the main attacking force from South Africa. Now he said he could not deliver. He recalled: 'By late in 2003 I was supposed to be ready to get troops up there [as well as Moto's team]. But around November I said I can't do both.' Mann was unamused. Steyl suggested that an Ivan Pienaar could arrange planes for the footsoldiers, leaving him to deal with Moto. Mann, though not pleased, agreed.

And the helicopter? Obiang had two MI-24 helicopter gunships. The attackers wanted something, too. In the days of Executive Outcomes, and earlier when 32 Battalion fought in Angola, helicopters were essential kit. Mann and the others knew one could tip the outcome of a battle. The idea of using a helicopter for this attack had been floating around for months. 'In military operations you have lots of things: cannons, pistols and other stuff,' said Steyl. 'A helicopter? It wasn't essential, but a luxury item. We would use it when we were there. We never discussed exactly what we'd do. We discussed having hard points [where a machine gun could be fixed] on it. But you could also have a guy in the door with an AK-47 ... Had things gone down successfully it would have been a mystery bonus. It would make us look powerful.' As another bonus, Mann had someone ready to fund it.

11

Enter Scratcher

'Some are always willing to surrender morals for profits.'

British businessman, 2005

Mann, though rich himself, always sought money from elsewhere for his new project. He had promises of $10 million set out in the two investor agreements in November 2003, but wanted more. His hunger for funds led to one of his bigger blunders: involving the famous son of a former British prime minister. Mann had been friendly with Mark Thatcher in Cape Town since they met in 1997. They had a mutual friend in Nigel Morgan, whom they affectionately called Nosher or Pig, and both had visited the intelligence-gatherer's remote country home. Thatcher had worked also with Morgan and Smith on the Cogito idea (selling business intelligence to companies or the government) in Equatorial Guinea. It was Thatcher who provided the capital for Cogito to be formed in the first place, and he had earlier helped Morgan through a difficult patch in his life in South Africa by providing him with a home for a spell. Both Thatcher and Morgan developed a steady interest in Mann's obscure west African scheme.

Like a man waving a golf club in a thunderstorm, Mark Thatcher invites intense and unwelcome attention. For a quarter of a century, since his mother became prime minister,

Mark (Sir Mark after his father, Denis, died) has drawn the interest of British journalists. Intelligence agencies probably keep an eye on him, too, intrigued by his range of business contacts. And though Morgan later claimed that Thatcher was never more than 'peripheral', a mere 'voyeur' of Mann's plot, he knew the British press and others would find his involvement in a coup plot to be momentous news.

Thatcher's life had been one of unhappy privilege. Born in 1953, he struggled as a child. Some teachers recall he was a quiet boy, overshadowed by his twin sister, Carol. Others at his snobbish public school, Harrow, thought him dim-witted and lowerclass. His mother was a rising star in the Conservative party, but for cruel schoolboys that was something to be teased about. He did poorly at exams and was sometimes called 'Thicky Mork' as others laughed at his accent. But he was attracted to adventure and often pored over Frederick Forsyth novels, presumably including *The Dogs of War*. He tried different careers, including selling jewellery then racing cars, travelling to South Africa for races in the early 1970s. After his mother became prime minister in 1979 – the same year Obiang took office – he drew constant media attention to himself, usually for gaffes.

On New Year's Day 1982, while taking part in the Paris–Dakar off-road car race, Mark Thatcher and his female co-driver disappeared in the Sahara. They were lost for six days, bringing the prime minister to public tears. When the two drivers were eventually found unharmed beside Mark's car, he shrugged off the incident, showing no gratitude to those – including his father – who had organised a massive search. His unofficial biographers, Paul Halloran and Mark Hollingsworth, say in *Thatcher's Fortunes*, that he was later an unofficial agent for David Bayley, who 'set up a private office in

Muscatar [as] an arms dealer' and who subsequently sacked him, saying, 'Mark is useful but a complete idiot. He is so incompetent.' Thatcher became known as arrogant and ready to exploit his mother's famous name for private gain. In conversation he can be affable enough, though aggressive, too. In the course of three interviews for this book he joked that any unflattering comments published about him would lead to this author needing 'a new dental surgeon', and if I dared identify him with the Equatorial Guinea plot I would end up 'as Mr Stumpy', that is, walking around on stumps for legs. In larger groups, perhaps because he grows nervous, he can be unpleasant, hurling threats at waiters and drivers, friends and strangers alike. But he is at least conscious of this. For a time he introduced himself saying: 'Hello, I'm charmless Mark.'

He made most of his early money, said Halloran and Hollingsworth in *Thatcher's Fortunes*, 'facilitating' trade in military equipment, though he said he personally never sold as much as a penknife. When Britain supplied a huge arms package to Saudi Arabia while Mrs Thatcher was prime minister, her son collected a 'fixing fee' of at least £12 million, claim his biographers. The British public never warmed to him. He was told to keep out of sight during his mother's re-election campaigns. He moved to the United States and met his future wife, Diane, in Texas. But by the early 1990s the American tax revenue service (IRS) launched proceedings against six former directors and investors in a firm called Emergency Networks, one of whom was Thatcher. He responded by saying he was not responsible and the case was eventually settled out of court, with Thatcher incurring no penalties. But, with Diane and their two children, he moved on again. They opted for a reclusive expatriate life in Cape Town, South Africa.

There Thatcher ran a trading business, focused on finished

oil products, in part with Sasol, a big South African oil company. His expertise, he says, is in logistics. He struck up a friendship with Mann, the two sharing an enthusiasm for business all over Africa in mining, oil, security and aviation. Thatcher was well travelled. But where many outsiders fall in love with the continent, despite its manifold problems, he grew fiercely pessimistic about it. 'Africa is dead, it's dying of cancer,' he concluded later. South Africa, his adopted home, he saw as having a dismal future. He blamed venal presidents for most of Africa's woes. 'In Africa a corrupt politician is practically a sequitur.' Most decent investors were shy of the continent, he argued, because of instability and poor leadership. That left only exploiters, those keen to make a quick, unethical profit – as some are always willing to surrender morals for profits.

Mann was fond of Thatcher, but few others liked him. One plotter later concluded: 'I put up with him, largely because I admired his mother. He put up with me because I was friends with Simon and he is an SAS groupie. He's a pain in the arse in large doses. He is heavily insecure, probably because he is the son of two bright parents ... he is not the sharpest pebble on the beach.' Crause Steyl dealt with Thatcher but did not like him. 'He was not the kind of personality I'd warm up to. I wasn't going to have tea with his mother. He's got lots of issues. I don't need any more issues in my life. The way he spoke to his driver, I didn't like that. Luckily, the only thing I had to take was his money.'

Thatcher, at least in early interviews for this book, made it clear he disliked the government of Equatorial Guinea and suggested outside powers had a duty to tackle the corruption and misrule there.

But he denies he ever supported a coup. Thatcher – when thinking hard he puffs out his cheeks and glares – doubts that violent 'third party intervention' would be right. He suggests a coup plot is little different from terrorism. 'Bearing in mind my family has been subject to an actual terror attack in Brighton, I'd never knowingly be involved in something like that,' he explains. And he adds that coups do nothing to benefit ordinary folk. 'It would have been bad because coup attempts only breed others.'

And yet, Thatcher was said to be eager to become involved in Mann's affair even while other plotters kept him at arm's length. Steyl says Thatcher 'was keen to be part of the game. But Simon thought that could be a problem. He feared Mark's inferiority complex might lead to the British press having a field day.' Greg Wales, writing in his Bight of Benin Company document, warned that if Thatcher's involvement in the coup plot were known then the 'rest of us, and project, likely to be screwed as a side issue to people screwing him. Would particularly add to a campaign, post-event, to remove us.' Short of excluding Thatcher from the scheme, Wales emphasised that his role should be kept hidden. There was no remedy if Thatcher's part were suspected, so 'Ensure doesn't happen'.

And Mann was willing to involve Thatcher. The reason was simple, says Steyl. 'The money. He brought us nearly $280,000.' Mann squeezed Thatcher for money, though he may have kept some of the details of the coup plot secret. The idea was to get Thatcher to fund a helicopter that would be used in the airport attack against Obiang. Steyl continues: 'The only thing Mark actually did was lease a helicopter. Apart from that, nothing. We never discussed Equatorial Guinea with him. We said we wanted to take an airplane to west Africa. But it was clear to me he was suspicious.'

Thatcher was associated with the plotters from the early days of their operations. In June or July 2003 Thatcher met

Nick du Toit to talk about hiring a helicopter. Thatcher later told a court in South Africa:

> The purpose of that meeting was to discuss with Nick du Toit the possibility and practicalities of the renovation of two civilian helicopters which Mr du Toit had for sale, or knew were for sale. The purpose was to express to Simon Mann my opinion whether renovation was economically viable. These helicopters were civilian helicopters. My recollection is that Simon Mann advised me their intended use was for support of a mining operation in Sudan.

Du Toit also recalled the meeting. He later told a BBC film crew:

> I had a business in South Africa called Military Technical Services which is a middle man business between governments and military installations to sell arms and ammunition, mainly in Africa. He [Thatcher] approached me to find out if I can help him to buy helicopters and I had some helicopters available so we discussed helicopters ... He told me that he wanted to use it in gold exploration in Sudan ... Simon Mann introduced me to him and said that this guy wanted to buy helicopters and he knew that it was my line of business so he introduced him to me and we discussed helicopters ... He's a very nice guy, straightforward, I didn't have a lot of dealings with him ... I knew that he was in the arms business ... He came to me with a request for helicopters and I could help him.

They met at an interesting moment. By June 2003 Mann said (in his disputed confession) he had already discussed the coup plot with du Toit. Various documents – contracts between Mann and Moto, the proposal for 'assisted regime change' – suggest active plotting had begun by mid year. Perhaps by now Mann had in mind the idea of using a helicopter for an airport attack. He chose this same moment to involve Thatcher in discussions about a helicopter, though supposedly for use in Sudan. For whatever reason, however, nothing came of the first meeting.

Instead, a few months later, Mann again asked Thatcher for help and advice on renting a helicopter. In November 2003, just as Mann signed the two investor agreements for projects in west Africa, he saw Thatcher again. The pair met in Cape Town. Thatcher later recalled that Mann said he was getting involved in a transport venture in west Africa, and possibly a mining deal in Guinea Bissau. Mann wanted Thatcher to help charter a helicopter. Thatcher agreed. They discussed types of helicopters and concluded that a Bell Jet Ranger III might be suitable.

Such is Thatcher's recollection of why Mann had first asked for his help. First, mid year, he had thought a helicopter would be used in Sudan (in east Africa) for a mining job. Then, by November, the story had changed. A helicopter would be needed in west Africa to transport executives or possibly for a mining job. Yet a third version was also put about. Ron Wheeldon, a friend, lawyer and an amateur pilot who likes to fly jet planes, says Thatcher explained the prospect to him.

> I think he had no idea what was going on. He thought he was investing in an air ambulance to operate in west Africa, including Equatorial Guinea. Crause Steyl proposed to Mark Thatcher a workable project. You have to remember that both Mark and I know a man called Simon Everett in Kenya, he's

a mutual friend. Simon Everett runs an air ambulance in east Africa and does well. Crause Steyl came along and said, 'There is no air ambulance in west Africa, I have the licences to operate a business there, but I need money to lease a helicopter.' The deal would have given Mark 60 per cent of the earnings. It would have been good business.

This third version of events – that the helicopter would be used as an air ambulance in a deal with Steyl – was current by December 2003. Crause Steyl became closely involved and suggested they rent an Alouette helicopter. Thatcher learned that a pair of Alouette II helicopters were for sale in Wellington, a town in South Africa. An Alouette is a French, jet-powered helicopter, made in the late 1950s. He called Steyl to discuss what he had found. The two men met at an airport, Lanseria, near Johannesburg in December. '[We] discusssed the cost options with reference to the Alouette II helicopters, as well as the other options that may be available,' Thatcher later testified. In one of the interviews for this book, Thatcher recalls the discussions: 'The Alouette was to be used as a medi-evac aircraft. All have quick change capability. It can be converted into an executive's helicopter.' Might it also have been used as a gunship? He believes not. 'But you can't just mount hard points. In order to have a pukka gun mount you need to fix a steel plate, a heavy plate, into the floor. You look at the huge mounting on the floor. And on a helicopter it's all about weight. Were such modifications to be made to this type of helicopter it would have been too heavy to be used for this purpose as it could not take off!'

Perhaps for this reason, Steyl and Mann turned down the helicopters that Thatcher had found. Mann phoned Thatcher to tell him so. But a later version of the Alouette, the Alouette III, would be suitable, he said. The Alouette III is more powerful and can seat up to seven people, or take two stretchers inside – it was used by the Rhodesian and South African air forces in military operations. Later, in December, Mann told Thatcher he had found such a helicopter. It could be chartered for a three month period. Thatcher agreed to help fund it.

Cape Town is popular at Christmas. From mid December to mid January residents decamp from Johannesburg, Pretoria and other landlocked cities and head for the beaches, cafés and hotels of the 'Mother City'. The southern hemisphere summer also lures foreign tourists. Most years Mark Thatcher threw a house party. He was not especially popular with his neighbours in Constantia, however. One man describes him as having 'an ego the size of a herd of elephants and attention span of a gnat'. He was said to be rude to waiters, and imperious to everyone. His parties were well-attended, especially when – as became increasingly frequent after her husband died – Baroness Thatcher was present. But the neighbours and guests were hardly grateful: 'If it wasn't for his mother, he'd be an East End barrow boy,' said one.

Greg Wales recalls leaving Johannesburg with Mann, shortly before Christmas, in a plane flown by Crause Steyl. They headed for Cape Town for Thatcher's party. Wales thought Steyl an exciting pilot. They flew first over Johannesburg, low over the city, well below the tops of the skyscrapers, he recalls, then on to Bethlehem, in the centre of South Africa, and through a narrow gorge in the Drakensberg mountains called the Golden Gate national park. Wales talks of his exhilaration as Steyl raced low inside the yellow stone canyon, twisting the plane sideways to bring them through. On arrival in Cape Town, Steyl, who had not been invited, amused himself while Mann and Wales attended Thatcher's elite party.

Other characters gathered that Christmas. Morgan was his guest recalled Thatcher: 'I have known Mr Morgan for more than seven years. I have met him on numerous occasions. Indeed, he has stayed at my residence in Cape Town many times. Most recently in 2003/2004 as a house guest.' Their usual 'topics of discussion were wideranging and included cigars'. A well-connected American lawyer and close friend of Mann's family, Rebecca Gaskin, also stayed at Thatcher's home at this time. She had worked in Congo, apparently for a bank, at the same time as Morgan. Wheeldon was at the party, too. He notes it was the last time he saw Mann, who was talking of a 'mining adventure in South America'.

Although everyone else recalls the party, Thatcher himself, oddly, later denied he threw one that Christmas. He says that neither Mann nor Wales attended a Christmas party, though he did have a celebration on New Year's Eve. Mann was busy in his own large rented house, with sixteen guests, says Thatcher. None the less, several characters of the Wonga Coup did spend Christmas together in the Mother City just weeks before launching their plot.

Thatcher had contact with other interesting individuals. Ely Calil was not in Cape Town that month, but Thatcher met him earlier in 2003. He says he also attended lunch with Mann at Calil's home, but left soon after arriving. He was most interested in the décor of the millionaire's Chelsea home: 'I met Calil only twice, firstly in 1979 as a guest in his house and again a second time in mid 2003, for only the second time in twenty years, for tea at his London house. I left soon after arriving. I just wanted to see the house again. He has supremely good taste.' In London Thatcher also knew Jeffrey Archer, the British novelist, and David Hart, a former adviser to his mother, who were both to be dragged into the story later on. In Cape Town he knew David Tremain 'distantly'. He had met James Kershaw several times, he admitted, though he called these meetings 'brief encounters' and he did not consider Kershaw a friend.

As for du Toit, he was in South Africa that Christmas, but did not mix with the high society of Cape Town. In George, a coastal resort nearby, however, another meeting was held. Steyl later told investigators that: 'On landing in Cape Town and moving on to George, I saw Mark Thatcher again for the second time very briefly. We flew across to George where we met Nick du Toit.' Steyl, Mann and du Toit went to a coffee shop in George, on 23 December, to discuss preparations for the coup. Du Toit warned that too many details were leaking. He had friends inside the South African Secret Service (SASS) who were telling him that his activities were under scrutiny. Johann Smith's intelligence reports warning of a coup in Equatorial Guinea were circulating faster than Christmas cards.

But du Toit's worries were pushed aside. There was some discussion that the base of operations might be moved from South Africa. The mood should have been upbeat. Mann later recalled that 'At Christmas 2003 funds were made available to me to go ahead. $400,000 of this money was my own.' Perhaps the extra cash, partly, was courtesy of the two investor agreements signed in November between Logo Logistics (Mann's company) and a Swiss company and a Lebanese one. Thatcher had also promised to fund a helicopter. So, for now, money woes were eased. But time was short. The idea of launching a coup in late January was dropped, but a new target date of mid February looked possible.

Interviewed for this book, Thatcher suggests that even in January he still had no idea the helicopter he agreed to fund was to be used for mercenary activity. He believed, he repeats, that it was intended for an air ambulance business, or possibly to move executives around in west Africa. Steyl operated an air ambulance company in South Africa. Thatcher noted that Steyl had 'warranted as a pre-condition to the investment that he had licences to operate in west Africa as an air ambulance company when, in fact, he had none'. Thatcher later considered suing Steyl for this lie.

But according to Thatcher's court documents, in December he 'began to doubt Mann's true intentions and suspected that Mann might be planning to become involved in mercenary activity in the west African region'. Despite his 'misgivings' he decided to invest. In early January, Thatcher deposited $20,000 into a bank account controlled by Steyl's company, AAA Aviation, at a branch in Bethlehem. A few days later, on 16 January, he paid in another $255,000. Why did he do so, despite his suspicions? Presumably because he thought working with Mann might produce an adventure as well as a profit. 'He thought he'd put his bum in the butter,' says someone who knew him well.

Steyl then used Thatcher's money to charter a civilian helicopter that was owned, ultimately, by the South African government (which was therefore partly responsible for its use, argues Thatcher). It was flown from another coastal town, East London, to Walvis Bay in Namibia. This might have been the first stage of a trip to Equatorial Guinea, following the coastal route of the fishing trawler. And perhaps, by late January, Mann seriously thought of moving the base of operations to Namibia. Wales flew to Namibia soon afterwards, presumably to check that out. But the helicopter sat idle, and the plan of the coup plot changed. 'In the end we decided it was too complicated and said, "Take it back",' recalls Crause

Steyl. The idea of overthrowing Obiang at Malabo airport was dropped. After three weeks, the helicopter flew back to South Africa. None of Thatcher's money was returned to him. Instead, early in March, $100,000 was transferred from Steyl's AAA Aviation account to Mann's Logo account. The helicopter Thatcher had helped to charter was, effectively, unused and some of his money had been appropriated. But those facts would not keep the former prime minister's son out of trouble.

12

Money and Recruits

'… a little tumult, now and then, is an agreeable quickener of sensation; such as a revolution, a battle, or an adventure of any lively description.'

Lord Byron

The month of January may be icy and miserable in New York, London or Madrid, but those smart and rich enough to spend it in Cape Town enjoy balmy days. It is a time to bask on the beach. At Simon Mann's luxurious home the pool was in use. Mann threw at least one big garden party in January 2004, as usual mixing business and pleasure. He did it to raise money. A look at his bank accounts for this time show great activity. Some funding had become available in December, but he faced cash flow problems soon after. He spent money as quickly as it appeared. Mark Thatcher provided one source of funds. Thatcher admitted in court in South Africa that he suspected 'Mann might be planning to become involved in mercenary activity in the west African region' and that the helicopter he helped hire 'might in fact be intended for use in such mercenary activity'. But he paid $275,000 to Crause Steyl for that helicopter, none the less. Around the same time Mann deposited $150,000 from one of his firms, Systems Design Limited, into Steyl's account.

Thatcher's payments helped fill the kitty, but more was needed. So Mann took the risky step of appealing to other friends and even neighbours in his well-heeled neighbourhood. At the drinks party staff pottered with trays of champagne while Mann chatted up his guests. To some he asked a pointed question. Would they be interested in a good deal, a very good deal? In 2004 one visitor to Mann's home told the *Sunday Telegraph*:

> It was a casual conversation at a drinks party around a swimming pool in January this year about 'a security project' at an African mine ... It was all very casual and vague, but the hook was the quick profit. If you showed interest then you were invited to another meeting and given more details. Once Equatorial Guinea was mentioned, I declined and heard no more about it.

Anyone keen was asked for $100,000, for which some were apparently promised a remarkable $1 million within ten weeks. Such a generous rate of return – tenfold in ten weeks – should have made most people suspicious. Mann could not generate such wealth by guarding a mine in Congo, so he explained some of his Equatorial Guinea plan to relative strangers. It was the sort of too-good-to-be-true opportunity that Nigerian con artists offer the gullible, often by email. When ordinary crooks do it, police call it an advance fee fraud, or a 419 scam. But it is also the sort of return coup plotters and financiers have long used. In this case there was the added temptation of oil concessions. There are all sorts of rumours about who invested. South African investigators thought a syndicate of smaller investors was arranged. They later issued charge sheets, yet to be withdrawn, against two British businessmen for helping fund the coup plot. A Chinese man living in Cape Town reportedly put in $50,000.

James Kershaw, running Mann's office, oversaw Mann's accounts. He also let slip useful information to Nigel Morgan. In the first four months of the year Morgan produced ten intelligence reports about a coup – or, as he termed it, a 'catalyst for regime change' – in Equatorial Guinea. These were read by South African intelligence.

Morgan gleaned more information from the inside, from Mann himself. They dined together twenty-two times in the months before the coup. On a typical night Mann proposed dinner at the Butcher Shop and Grill in Sandton, Johannesburg. After large tumblers of pink gin they moved on to steaks and heavy red wine, while chatting lightly and cracking jokes. Next they moved to cigars, port and whisky, staying late as the restaurateur tried to close. One moment it was trivial, then Mann would slip in serious questions. A thinly disguised discussion of his plot followed. Mann half-jokingly threatened to kill Morgan if he leaked a word. The next minute, however, he was asking more advice. It was, recalls Morgan, as if Mann were writing a film script and discussing fictional characters, not plotting a real event.

Others compiled intelligence, too. Johann Smith had sighed with relief at the new year. He first feared an attack during New Year's Eve, when drunken soldiers and politicians could not defend themselves against a mosquito let alone against an invasion force. But the big night passed with no more fireworks than usual. Yet Smith still sensed the pending coup. A document he produced, dated January 2004, described the ex-32 Battalion soldiers he thought part of the advance guard. Sergio Cardoso, who had worked with du Toit for months, had twice met a group of other veterans, including Victor Dracula, in Pretoria. They talked of Equatorial Guinea and the departure of a second fishing trawler. Ex-soldiers were flitting about west Africa, wrote Smith. One was 'definitely acting as a "runner" for the Group of former 32 Bn members'. Smith gave a prescient warning. 'Cardoso would, on his return, recruit a total of seventy-five ex-SADF [South African Defence Force] members, mainly from within the former 32 Bns and Special Forces ranks.' They would later launch a coup. 'These actions are planned to take place in mid March 2004' and: 'Knowing the individuals as well as I do, this timeline is very realistic and will provide for ample time to plan, mobilise, equip and deploy the force.'

Enter the German
The cast of the Wonga Coup is so heavily stocked with rogues and eccentrics there seems little room for more. But one character deserves attention. Gerhard Eugen Merz managed an airline called Central Asian Logistics GmbH. A middle-aged German from Frankfurt, he had spent some of his youth in Israel, then had moved back to Germany. By the early 1990s the American government had identified him as a dangerous individual. In 1994 President Bill Clinton signed an executive order saying Merz and two others had promoted 'proliferation of nuclear, biological and chemical weapons'. The Americans said he had arranged sales of materials from China to Iran, between 1991 and 1993, for use in making chemical weapons. With two accomplices and various companies he was blacklisted. Americans were barred from doing business with him.

Such people often retreat to remote corners like Equatorial Guinea. Merz and du Toit grew to know each other and Merz helped supply planes and air crew for du Toit's aviation company, PANAC. Central Asian Logistics provided an Antonov and an Ilyushin 76. Merz also contracted an Armenian flight crew through a firm called Tiga-Eiri. Du Toit later recalled: 'These agreements were brokered by Mr Gerhard Merz on my behalf sometime in December 2003. The two aircraft were brought to Malabo on the 8 and 10 January 2004 respectively.' On 12 February Mann, through his Logo Logistics, paid Merz's air company nearly $125,000. Investigators later concluded that Merz had joined the plotters as their 'transportation officer'. He would pay a heavy price.

One oil executive recalls bumping into du Toit's group, including Merz, at Nautica, one of Malabo's few restaurants. Nautica is in a picturesque spot by the harbour, near the presidential palace. On the evening of 19 January the oil worker dined near a table of thirty-five drunken expatriates who roared in Afrikaans. Asked why they were in Malabo, the foreigners gave differing answers. One said they were pilots hired by the government, another said he was setting up a fishing business. A third, an Angolan, looked scared and would not talk. A fourth said they were 'working on a very big project, and that the boss would be here'. Then du Toit walked in, a tall and striking figure, who promptly joined the boisterous crowd.

Later the executive bumped into a smaller group of the same men at a hotel, and was invited by Merz to join them for a drink. 'Merz was the most friendly of them all,' recalls the executive. 'He had a big beard, a smallish face, he was hefty but not hugely overweight.' The men were obviously in the middle of a meeting, but paused to hand out their business cards. Malabo is a small place, and the identity of outsiders is soon known to all. But they were making it laughably easy for strangers – this executive happened to be close to the presidents of both Equatorial Guinea and South Africa – to gather information on them.

Du Toit was busy. He shuttled to South Africa for frequent meetings with Mann. It was in January, he said, that he first heard about 'Ely' the Lebanese. Around the same time Mann dropped the idea of snatching Obiang at Malabo airport, so needed a new plan. One was for a team of soldiers to be deployed to Annobon island, a remote speck of land in the Atlantic, as a base for launching a raid on Malabo. But Annobon is tiny and its runway is inadequate for long-range planes. And there were two outstanding practical concerns, aside from the ever-tiresome funding, of guns and soldiers. The need for weapons was to grow acute in February, and will be discussed in the next chapter. But what of the footsoldiers?

Mercenaries are most easily recruited from the ranks of men who have recently left regular armies. Mann and the others knew where to recruit officers and men. Johann Smith says a battalion of fighters can be raised in South Africa with a few phone calls. Early in 2004 a plentiful supply of soldiers existed, especially among black veterans who were not in demand in Iraq. Mann wanted to draw on the 32 Battalion and special forces men who had earlier fought for Executive Outcomes. Some had also worked in Morgan's non-military operation at mines in Congo. Morgan says at least six of these went on to be part of the Wonga Coup.

The first round of recruitment happened late in 2003. Now more soldiers were needed. Smith was right that seventy-five men were sought. Mann later told investigators he also hoped a local force might turn on Obiang. If not, his group would have been sufficient anyway:

Nick du Toit started to put a team of seventy-five men together. This team was to stay in present employment and was to hold

itself ready. Nick du Toit and I judged that seventy-five men
was the minimum number to safely escort Severo Moto when
he returned and should things not go to plan and should the
mutiny/uprising not take place.

In an effort to cover their tracks, a false paper trail was made.
On 14 January, Mann's company, Logo Logistics, signed a
contract with du Toit's aviation firm, PANAC, to provide
seventy-five expatriate security guards to Equatorial Guinea.
Logo would supposedly earn $525,000 a month and the guards
would arrive in February. The document, signed by Mann and
du Toit, was to show to anyone who grew suspicious about
their collaboration over Equatorial Guinea. Mann passed a
bundle of such documents to Morgan early in 2004, hoping
– but failing – to allay his suspicions.

On 18 January at a meeting in South Africa Mann told du
Toit to complete recruitment. He acted quickly. Du Toit later
told interrogators: 'I started asking around for people to be
used on a security job ... Within five days I had approximately
fifty-five people available. Included in this group were also
the white members ... who would lead the teams. I handed
all the details over to James Kershaw, who was to administer
the group from then on ...' Eventually du Toit's efforts were
put on a more formal footing. On 12 February Mann (through
Logo) and du Toit (through his Military Technical Services)
signed a deal setting the men's wages. It is yet another piece of
a heavily strewn – if rather confusing – paper trail. This time
du Toit's firm was to supply 'trained and competent professionals' for 'projects in the fields of security and logistics'. Du
Toit would get 3 per cent of all the salaries paid, or a minimum
of $5,000 a month.

Naturally du Toit sought men who could recruit others.

He asked Neves Tomas Matias, a former special forces soldier of Angolan origin, to help find Buffalo Soldiers who wanted work. One of the accused, Harry Carlse (Jacob Hermanus Albertus Carlse), admitted he also helped recruit the team leaders for the operation. He said Neves pulled in some sixty footsoldiers, offering them a salary of $1,500 a month each. Team leaders would each get $5,000, he said. But a copy of a payroll document, with the names and bank account details of most of those hired for the coup, suggests each footsoldier was promised an upfront payment worth double that. Others sources give different figures. Whatever the exact amount, it tempted ex-soldiers who otherwise earned pitiful wages. Kashama Mazanga, a veteran, recalls: 'When you get another job offering a bit more money ... you have to accept it.' Mazanga was trained as a special forces soldier and had worked for Executive Outcomes as a translator.

Another footsoldier, who has asked not to be identified, was hired early in 2004. 'My cousin was involved, that is how I was recruited. If he had known about any coup plot he would never have got me involved ... In February my cousin said they were recruiting for DRC, to work at a mine. We were to meet at a McDonald's in Pretoria. Then we were taken to the 224 hotel, where we met the first white guys: Loutjkie Horn [another plot leader] and Carlse. They said, "We need security guards in Congo and will pay $6,000 a month." The wage seemed high. 'But it was a bit risky in eastern Congo. I asked around, so it all made sense to me. Companies they pay a lot, so you do not steal the money, or the diamonds. They rather not recruit natives [Congolese] because they steal so much, but then pay more for foreigners.' He claims nobody mentioned Equatorial Guinea or a coup.

Another veteran says he was asked to take part as an

officer, but chose instead to fight in Iraq. 'I had heard about and was approached for the EG plot a few months before it was planned to go down. I know two of the people involved very well, but the presence of some other individuals made me decide not to get involved in this fiasco ... I have a high regard for two of the individuals I know very well and think that they should never have involved themselves in this coup, but I do not know the stakes involved that made them continue nevertheless. Like they say, "money talks". I guess the fact that this was supposed to be a quick buck in an area that all these individuals know well, was one of the reasons they opted for this option, rather than work in Iraq. The whole Iraq operation was also not as streamlined as it is today.' Johann Smith also saw the attraction: 'You can see why this is tempting. It's fun, it could work, you trust the leaders. Some of the guys did it for the kicks, because life is boring.'

The most pitiful stories of recruitment are to be heard in Pomfret, the asbestos-ridden ex-military base that was home to many 32 Battalion soldiers. Families told of husbands and fathers who scrabbled at the chance of well-paid work, no questions asked. At one house a wooden carving on the wall shows a lion eating a man with a gun. Cecilia Tchimuishi says her father, Eduardo, fought as a Buffalo Soldier for the South Africans for nearly two decades. He received a small army pension and took a job as a security guard in Pretoria, leaving his family behind. 'Because there's no jobs in Pomfret. Pomfret is only full of humans, there's no jobs.'

'He was working in Pretoria, his contract had finished and he came home for Christmas and New Year. When he returned to Pretoria he met a guy at an association for people who were in Battalion 32, a hostel. If you have no family in Pretoria, you stay there. Then he phoned us and told us he was going to

Congo.' Like many, he was recruited at the small house where former mercenaries and veteran soldiers always stay. 'He said he was going to Congo to work on a mine as a security guard. He gave us a cell phone contact number to call if there was a problem. It was the first time he had gone abroad to work.' Viviana, Eduardo's Portuguese-speaking wife, interrupts, 'He was happy, he had a job.'

A neighbour tells a similar tale. At the home of Augusto Fernando a black banner of 32 Battalion, showing a buffalo head, hangs on the sitting-room wall. Christina Fernando says her husband worked at a game reserve near Pretoria in January 2004. 'He phoned home and said somebody had offered him a job that paid better, as it requires going to Congo and working as a guard for a diamond mine. He didn't know the pay and didn't say how long he would be away. He had never been there before. He said a friend working for another company was going, too.' Similar accounts, repeated throughout Pomfret and in Pretoria, tell of relatively poor men hungry for better-paid and more satisfying work. Many lived at the same hostel in Pretoria, and kept in close touch with other veterans. Friends recruited each other. Cousins urged relatives to join, hoping to bring more wages into the family.

The signs of misery in Pomfret – broken windows, sandy streets strewn with litter – all help explain the readiness of men to board a plane for an ill-defined military job. Many of the footsoldiers, and their families, later claimed ignorance of the coup plot. Perhaps they were not told, at least not early on. But if they were ordered to fight in a coup, at short notice, the footsoldiers would surely have complied. They were well used to taking orders to fight from white bosses.

13

Spain

'The Spanish PM has met Severo Moto three times. He has, I am told, informed SM that as soon as he is established in EG he will send 3000 Guardia Civil.'

Simon Mann, confession

While recruiting was underway in South Africa, others took on different tasks. Greg Wales arranged for a lobbyist to promote Moto in Washington DC. Mann shuttled back and forth to London, meeting Ely Calil and others. He also signed new contracts, again helping create a false paper trail. One deal said Logo, Mann's firm, would provide logistical support and security services to a company called YKA Mining, supposedly registered in Kinshasa, Congo.

Mann also signed a deal for Crause Steyl's aviation company to provide air services for 'projects' in west Africa. This apparently assured Steyl a lucrative business after the coup. Steyl grew busier. At a dinner in Johannesburg – once more at the Butcher Shop and Grill – a group of men gathered to discuss a 'dry run' for the coup. Mann, Kershaw, Steyl and another pilot called Linde were present. At a neighbouring table sat Henry van der Westhuizen and du Toit. The popular restaurant had become an open office for coup plotters – and an ideal place for anyone who cared to listen in on their plans. Nobody was discreet. Excited plotters puffed on cigars and boasted to anyone who would listen of being 'on the inside of a very big game'.

It was agreed that a practice run from the Canary Islands to Equatorial Guinea would be useful, to judge the time needed, to identify refuelling stops and the likely reception at Malabo airport. Steyl took a King Air plane to the Canary Islands. Then, on 15 January, he flew to Malabo before returning to South Africa. Steyl would later fly back up to Malabo, to bring du Toit and another member of the forward team back into position.

By late January some practical tasks were done and a new date in mid February was chosen for the attack. But there were worrying developments. It was clear that the secrecy of the operation was laughable. Few could keep their mouths shut. Mann himself had chattered to neighbours and friends in Cape Town about a fabulous opportunity in Equatorial Guinea. Morgan gathered documents and information from his friends, then produced intelligence reports every few days. These were read by South Africa's authorities. In January he said Calil planned to send Karim Fallaha, his Lebanese associate, with Moto to Equatorial Guinea. He described how Calil 'boasts privately that he has Moto in his pocket' and called the businessman a 'prime mover' behind the planned coup. 'When will it happen? The answer is – soon or it will be too late. Obiang has got wind that there is trouble brewing and is tightening his personal security ...'

Smith's warnings also continued. The writer and film-maker James Brabazon says he was invited by du Toit to accompany him on a coup plot. Like many mercenaries, they evidently wanted someone to record their deeds. Many others learned of the pending coup. Heavy-drinking recruits talked in Pretoria's bars. The leaders held forth in Johannesburg's hotel lobbies and restaurants as if the coup was already complete. Men who were approached to join, but who turned down the offer, also chatted. The forward team in Malabo drew attention to itself. And Wales talked to oil companies, canvassing their views on regime change, helping spread rumours, too. Oil men starting gossiping that Equatorial Guinea was 'about to change dramatically' and several journalists picked up on the rumour.

Even the clumsy government in Equatorial Guinea might have suspected something by now. Smith's reports were doing the rounds and the president's brother and intelligence chief, Armengol, could have gathered information on his business partner du Toit. By the last days of January, the British Foreign Office had intelligence of the plot, too, passed on by another government. The foreign secretary, Jack Straw, asked his officials to discuss matters with someone in a British private military company. The latter was probably Tim Spicer, formerly of Executive Outcomes and a friend of Mann. But Straw saw no reason to warn the dictatorship in Malabo.

Most remarkable, the plot was debated at a semi-public meeting in London. Early in February, academics, businessmen, journalists and Africaphiles met at Chatham House – home of the Royal Institute of International Affairs – to discuss the future of Equatorial Guinea. A foreign policy adviser to South Africa's government interrupted the meeting. She asked why they debated internal splits in the ruling family when many knew mercenaries planned to invade. Some in the audience thought she was talking nonsense. But her warning, based on Smith's intelligence reports, was accurate enough.

Mann's whole operation was riddled with informers. Other coup plots show that is almost impossible to avoid. Even if recruits are not already working for an intelligence service, some will trade information about the plot for money or government protection. One investigator in South Africa admits 'a lot of people have been asking for the *impimpi*, the informer. Everyone is looking for them. But I've always been amazed what people believe. Simon Mann and Nick du Toit were aware that the South African intelligence knew what was going on. Henry van der Westhuizen had given them a report, Johann Smith's report, while they were meeting in George [in December]. So why did they proceed? Perhaps because of the Sao Tome thing. Or they had the perception it had been given the OK. You should ask Simon Mann why they went ahead. Maybe he was conceited.'

Mann, a respected soldier and member of the SAS, allowed wide indiscretion. Worse, once he was aware of the lack of secrecy, he pushed ahead. He had let military standards slip partly out of arrogance: he believed a tinpot republic like Equatorial Guinea could not stop his invaders. Crause Steyl concluded that even if Obiang knew of the plot they might still succeed. 'They can't guard themselves twenty-four hours from air, sea and land. Intelligence always leaks. If you're on the offence you can still determine when to hit.'

But, more important, Mann and others believed the plot had outside support. He and other leaders told the footsoldiers and junior officers that the project was cleared by the South African authorities. Niel Steyl, a pilot who became involved, later said: 'The problem is when the [South African] intelligence department didn't know what they were doing. We were cleared by some, but the others were not informed.' He continued: 'There was ill-feeling from the military guys [recruits], mostly against Simon Mann. They felt he had given an assurance that all this was cleared with the South African government and there was nothing to worry about. I don't blame Simon for anything at all. Maybe he was lied to. He really thought things were OK. I felt comfortable doing this knowing he was coming …'

Mann thought he had support, or at least tacit backing, from lower-level sources in South Africa's government. Morgan's reports were being read by South African officials throughout the first months of 2004, yet no effort was made to discourage the plotters from going ahead. Mann might have believed that by talking so closely with Morgan the African response was squared. However, Morgan now denies ever giving – or even being in a position to give – the impression that South Africa approved of the scheme. But the plotters had some contacts with the authorities in Pretoria. Alwyn Griebenow, a lawyer in South Africa, says many of the plotters believed a senior South African official had 'okayed the whole mission. They were told that Thabo Mbeki was looking forward to meeting the new president. They were told this by Simon Mann and Harry Carlse. The whole story had been okayed, the operation was given the green light … The number one in National Intelligence had talks with Simon Mann. These men were told that Spain, America, Britain and South Africa knew of all this from Simon Mann and Harry Carlse … The bottom line is that these guys were brought in under the impression it was legal.' A South African prosecutor did not deny that a senior official had met at least one of those involved in the coup, but suggested the purpose of the meeting was 'only [for] seeking more information on what the plotters intended'.

There were also leaks back from South African intelligence suggesting a blind eye would be turned. Du Toit's colleague, van der Westhuizen, thought he had been given some sort of permission for the plotters to proceed. And the South African government is rumoured to have sent a diplomat – perhaps a man who used the name Holmes – from Lisbon to meet Moto in Madrid. 'In the South African government you had some on Simon's side and some on Obiang's side,' concludes a plotter. Some old hands still in the government bureaucracy, veterans of the days when whites ran things, perhaps reassured Mann that the coup would be acceptable. But as more senior South African officials learned what was happening, sympathy for the plotters presumably evaporated. The result: South Africa's canny government conducted its intelligence operation, read Morgan's reports and let the plotters proceed, for now.

The plotters were also confident of some level of support from Britain and America, the latter because of Wales's assiduous lobbying, notably with oil companies. And then there was Spain. The old colonial power was ready to offer more than a blind eye. At the end of January there was public discussion of a pending coup in Equatorial Guinea in Madrid. Newspapers *El Pais* and *El Mundo*, as well as Spanish radio, talked openly of it. Spanish naval vessels set sail to the Gulf of Guinea. It was widely known that 'Moto was very friendly with the Spanish government', says an oil executive who spent a great deal of time in Equatorial Guinea. An unverified intelligence document suggests Moto met senior representatives of the Spanish government in January and February. If various plotters are to be believed, he also spent time with an official from Spain's ruling party. The plotters expected the Spanish prime minister, Jose Maria Aznar, who was due to leave office in March, to deliver a speech in support of Moto (and offering recognition) once he was installed. Moto may have met Aznar at this time. More important, the plotters believed several hundred Spanish paramilitary police on board ships would, when requested by the newly installed Moto, arrive in

Equatorial Guinea to 'keep order'. Which would help prevent military intervention from Nigeria or others.

Simon Mann later wrote that Aznar was directly involved himself. Point 12 of his confession is published for the first time here and provides strong evidence that Spain's government, under Aznar, was deeply involved in the coup and that South Africa, at the least, was forewarned about it. Mann wrote:

> 12. The Spanish PM has met Severo Moto three times. He has, I am told, informed SM [Moto] that as soon as he is established in EG he will send 3000 Guardia Civil.
>
> I have been repeatedly told that the Spanish Govt will support the return of SM immediately and strongly.
>
> They will, however, deny that they are aware of any operation of this sort.
>
> The South African government have recently last week contacted SM stating their support for him and inviting him to meet the President of South Africa.

Another plotter says Mann explained that Aznar and Moto met three times in the months before the coup. Crause Steyl also recalls: 'We were all along told that Aznar was supporting us in this.'

Aznar's office later, inevitably, denied involvement and challenged journalists to provide proof of any direct or indirect role by the Spanish government. There is, however, circumstantial evidence and off-the-record testimony to suggest Moto would have received such support. In January Spain did deploy two ships to the Gulf of Guinea, and sought permission to dock in Malabo. They were refused. They then sought permission to 'exercise' in Equatorial Guinea's waters. Again they were refused and Obiang called the deployment 'provocative'.

A lawyer for the Equatorial Guinean government, Lucie Bourthoumieux, explains what happened early in 2004: 'The Spanish government proposed to Equatorial Guinea to send two military boats with marines inside. The president of Equatorial Guinea asked why. They said "We propose to protect you because of the problem of Gabon." The president said, "No and No." The president sent a letter of protest. He said, "I don't want them." And he informed the United Nations secretary-general that "we don't accept Spanish marines to solve pretended problems".' Despite that letter and protest, the Spanish sent the ships a few days before the attempted coup. The Equatorial Guinea government wondered why the ships still came. It could be an obvious conclusion: the Spanish could have been behind the coup. It's very important. The spirit of colonialism of the Spanish is similar to the French. There is a kind of paternalism in the relationship.' A national security adviser in Equatorial Guinea, Ruben Maye, says bluntly that Spain's security services backed the plot. He blames Aznar's government and concludes that, 'All the threats Equatorial Guinea is facing come from Spain'.

On 2 February 2004 the Spanish ministry of foreign affairs confirmed that two Spanish warships had departed a few days earlier from La Coruna harbour, bound for Equatorial Guinea. The foreign minister, Ana Palacio, called it a 'mission of co-operation', while the defence ministry contradicted her, claiming the ships were only exercising in the Atlantic. The plotters certainly believed support was forthcoming. That helps explain why some were so cavalier about secrecy.

Yet du Toit still worried. He was at the sharp end if things went wrong. He and others told Mann of their concerns at several meetings. Wales, Crause Steyl and others were present and they knew that Smith's intelligence reports, for once, were on the mark. Du Toit and his colleagues were vulnerable. The plotters should reduce the public discussion of the plot, they agreed. They might also move operations out of South Africa, where it was illegal to recruit men as mercenaries. The first cases of soldiers arrested for such activities, including one who had been fighting in Côte d'Ivoire, were then in the news. The plotters might move operations to a quieter spot, perhaps Namibia or Congo, both of which were closer to Equatorial Guinea.

From Namibia troops could be airlifted to some other point nearer to Equatorial Guinea, perhaps even to Annobon island, a remote part of the country itself. They would use two DC3 planes for this. Weapons could be sourced from Cyprus, in the Mediterranean. Around now the helicopter funded by Thatcher was in Namibia. Wales admits he went to Namibia, too, in late January. Perhaps he checked if Windhoek, its capital, could serve as a new base for operations. However, for some reason – perhaps lack of time – the base of operations did not move. It was yet another mistake. How many more could the project survive?

14

Get your Guns

'Five tons of small arms.'

Simon Mann

Time was short. The plotters were worried about two elections: one in April in Equatorial Guinea which could help legitimise Moto's grasp on power; the other in March in Spain marking the retirement of sympathetic prime minister Aznar. So February was the month to launch the plot. Spanish ships and marines were powering into position. Nearly seventy footsoldiers had been recruited. Despite public discussion of a coup, it seemed Equatorial Guinea had no comprehensive warning. The attackers still enjoyed limited surprise. Aircraft were arranged: the Thatcher helicopter was dropped, but Steyl had done a dry run with a King Air plane from the Canary Islands to Malabo, and a man called Ivan Pienaar had helped hire two DC3 planes. Many believed Pienaar had contacts with South Africa's authorities, so his presence might have reassured Mann and others. Back in Equatorial Guinea, du Toit and his forward team moved into position.

Mann still needed more officers. Two South Africans took large roles here. Jacob Hermanus Albertus Carlse (widely known as Harry) and Lourens Jacobus Horn (shortened to Loutjkie, Hecky and other nicknames) are typical 'moustaches', a term coined by Nigel Morgan to describe tough South Africans. Of Afrikaner stock and proud, hard soldiers, they are the sort you want to have on your side in a fight. Carlse is one of four brothers. A family friend calls him 'a very tough guy' and says he was known as 'The Enforcer' after breaking a debtor's arm over a restaurant table. Having served in South Africa's army and in a special forces regiment (1 Reconnaissance), he met Mann in 1993 and fought in Executive Outcomes' first battle, at Soyo in Angola. Later Carlse became a nightclub bouncer in Johannesburg, where he met Horn. Horn had a similar past, serving first with South Africa's police and then with special forces (4 Reconnaissance Regiment), though not in Executive Outcomes.

Carlse and Horn then worked as guards, forming a company called Meteoric Tactical Solutions (taking a similar name to du Toit's firm, Military Technical Services). In 2003 the firm won security work in Iraq. Among other contracts it struck a £250,000 deal with Britain's international development agency to guard staff in Iraq. The firm also helped train Iraqi police. In October Carlse was back in South Africa briefly and met Crause Steyl, who offered him work of the Executive Outcomes type. By February 2004 both he and Horn were ready in South Africa. Horn told some colleagues he was taking a holiday to 'chill out on a hunting farm', though he boasted to others of going back to Africa for a quick 'security job' that would pay extremely well.

The two met du Toit at a Wimpy burger bar in Pretoria and heard details of the coup plan. Their company would be rewarded with security contracts in the new Equatorial Guinea. Horn later testified that Mann, Neves Tomas, Kershaw and another former soldier, Simon Witherspoon, joined them at the Wimpy. Witherspoon, yet another veteran of South African special forces (5 Reconnaissance), calls himself a professional hunter and 'security consultant' for foreign governments. He says he was invited by a 'James' (presumably Kershaw) to join the operation at the last minute. Witherspoon – like most involved in the Wonga Coup – is affable and friendly when you meet him, though he has an intimidating past as a soldier.

At the Wimpy du Toit gave out pay-as-you-go mobile phones, while Kershaw collected bank details so he could handle financial arrangements. Horn took an administrative role, paying for hotel rooms for the footsoldiers (most stayed at Hotel 224, a sad-looking spot in the centre of Pretoria). He checked contracts for the footsoldiers to sign when out of the country and beyond the reach of anti-mercenary laws. He was also supposed to organise transport to the airport for most of the men. Carlse became a direct assistant to Mann. He was to join his old boss on the day of the coup.

A few others signed up. Errol Harris, a huge man with cropped blond hair, said Mann approached him and suggested he join. He quit his job as a prison warder, said his lawyer, 'because he was told he would have a job to start a new prison in Equatorial Guinea'. His military background was less impressive than the others' and he had never left South Africa before, but he had a useful connection to the plotters – du Toit had married his sister, Belinda. Yet Harris later claimed (on South African television) he had no idea what du Toit planned: 'I knew he was in the special forces, but he never told me himself.' Asked if he was a hired gun, he replied: 'No, I don't even know what mercenary means.'

Du Toit now supplied more information about the target. Though Malabo is small, the city is divided into several districts, some of which are poorly lit and/or are not clearly named. The presidential palace, the main target, is on the farthest side of town away from the airport. For the plotters, knowing the local geography would be vital. Du Toit later told investigators:

> Sometime in February 2004 ... I found a map of the town of Malabo pinned on the walls of one of the offices of Murray and Roberts, a South African construction company. I asked for a copy of the map ... which I later gave to Harry Carlse on my return to South Africa. It was to be used after landing in Malabo on the day of the 'Coup deTat'. The map was unmarked except for the Pizza Place restaurant, which was already marked when I obtained the map. I indicated the positions which were to be taken over to Harry Carlse ...

One vexing task remained: buying weapons. At first glance, that looks easy enough. Used AK-47 assault rifles are traded all over Africa. Foreign journalists occasionally try to buy one in a Kenyan slum or in a dangerous part of Johannesburg for the sake of a story. Various factors affect supply and price. At the end of a war soldiers sell their old weapons and the price drops: after Uganda's civil war you could trade a chicken for an AK-47. Otherwise there is a well-developed black market for guns. In Soweto, in South Africa, criminals rent out weapons and ammunition for the night. Elsewhere a used assault rifle – one that might have been traded between wars, buried for a while, perhaps used by child soldiers – could sell for well under $100. In Mozambique, where artists break up rifles to make impressive sculptures with the pieces, it may be cheaper to buy the working model than the art.

But the plotters of the Wonga Coup wanted more than a few bent rifles. In war zones larger consignments of arms are sometimes available. Africa fell relatively quiet in 2004, but wars spluttered on in Sudan, on Uganda's borders, in eastern Congo and in Côte d'Ivoire. Arms producers, especially in eastern Europe, continued to export assault rifles, mortars and other weapons that helped sustain African conflict. Many deals were brokered by shady British, Israeli or east European traders, with cargo sent through Cyprus, Malta or other relay points in southern Europe. Given the right connections, tapping into this supply network is said to be quite possible. Questions about paperwork – end user certificates – may be ignored. What counts is money.

The plotters of the Wonga Coup, however, seemed unsure how to find a supplier. Previously Mann had worked for governments and acquired weapons legally. Du Toit, with some experience of trading arms himself, said he knew where to go. They first relied on du Toit's associate Henry van der Westhuizen, who had contacts in Uganda. 'As of December 2003 we expected the guns to come from Uganda, the likelihood was good,' recalls Crause Steyl. 'Henry van der Westhuizen is an arms trader ... Henry and Nick are partners. Henry was supposed to buy arms from Salim Saleh [the head of the military] in Uganda. Henry said the deal was on.' But by 2004 there was a problem. Steyl continues: 'Salim Saleh then pulled out. I'm not sure why. I think Oxfam were investigating him or something.'

This, Steyl believes, was a devastating setback: 'When Salim Saleh refused to do the deal, by then we were beyond the point of no return. The troops were hired, the aircraft hired; Nick was running the front businesses. As a private individual foreigner, to organise a coup is difficult. It's easy to shoot your uncle ... At that moment we should have said, "It's over." But you can't pull out. Those guys have given you money. You can't walk away. Nick didn't get out of it, though I think he wanted to ...' Mann later elaborated: 'We applied to the source of weapons that we had previously contacted. This contact had been indirect and was via Henry van der Westhuizen. At this stage this contact failed.' Which created a 'difficult position', although 'other options' included 'a military source in Zambia, one in Kenya, one in Bujumbura – and ZDI [Zimbabwe Defence Industries]'.

Zimbabwe Defence Industries, like many companies that make or trade military equipment, is owned by the state and has close ties with the armed forces. A Colonel Tshinga Dube ran it. Though Zimbabwe's small and fast-shrinking economy produced little, ZDI was kept busy trading weapons that others made, selling them on to dealers like du Toit. In theory, they could only sell to licensed traders with the right documentation, notably the end user certificate. In fact, staff at ZDI – like many – had few scruples and would sell, if the price was right, precisely what Mann and his co-plotters wanted.

From a distance, however, it is astounding that Mann and du Toit chose to do such a sensitive deal in Robert Mugabe's Zimbabwe. As Mugabe aged – he was well over eighty by the time of the Wonga Coup – he presided over a collapsing economy and grew ever more isolated in office. He attacked his opposition, then launched a populist campaign against Britain and whites. He regularly accused the old colonial power – 'Tony Blair and his gang of gay gangsters', as Mugabe alliterated – of planning evil schemes. British journalists were arrested merely for visiting Zimbabwe. Tourists, businessmen and others mostly stayed away. Zimbabwe's intelligence agency, the Central Intelligence Organisation, grew ever stronger. It was said that one in five adults in Zimbabwe worked for it. Mann and du Toit were sure to draw its attention.

There was a greater risk of being arrested and denounced in Zimbabwe, for the sake of a propaganda attack on Britain, than anywhere else.

Mann saw some danger. He and du Toit told few people about their approach to ZDI. Wales claims he was shocked to hear Mann had done a deal there. But Mann later said ZDI was widely recommended. It had a reputation as a reliable and efficient supplier of smaller weapons. Mann recalled du Toit said that its officials 'would ask few if any questions' and he had 'done several deals with ZDI previously. Some or all of these had been without proper paperwork.' Mann also thought he had the backing of senior people in government, a misjudgement he repeated elsewhere. 'Naively I believed that by dealing with ZDI, I was dealing with a very high level and would be fully "covered" in terms of what we had to do,' he later explained.

Mann and du Toit flew the short distance from South Africa to Harare on 8 February. The Zimbabwean capital is a pleasant city if you have fuel and food, and if you can avoid the truncheon-wielding policemen. Most Zimbabweans are articulate, confident and welcoming. Mann later told a Zimbabwean lawyer, Jonathan Samukange, they received 'the red carpet treatment' on this trip. '[We] didn't go through immigration but were taken through by ZDI officials. We were treated like diplomats.' They might have checked into Harare's Wild Geese Lodge, where photos of Mike Hoare, the mercenary, and Roger Moore and Richard Burton (who starred in the film *The Wild Geese*) adorn the walls. Instead Mann pitched up at Cresta Lodge, a hotel chain popular with businessmen. Its bar served dreadful coffee and snacks such as a 'jungleman's platter' of chicken drumsticks, beef kebabs, samosas and chipolata sausages (for the urban jungleman).

The barman, Paul Tembo, found Mann a 'good customer ... Yes, I still remember his face. He liked to sit here in this lounge.' Mann, says Tembo, was both fond of the local Bollingers Beer and generous with tips.

Mann and du Toit met a man from ZDI called Martin Bird and explained their cover story: they needed weapons to guard a mine near Isiro, a town in north east Congo, near the border with Uganda. Bird's wife was present at the meeting, which Mann found offputting. They had a precise shopping list. Du Toit's notebook shows jottings for '7.62 x 39 x 50 Box', '7.62 x 54 x 50 Box', 'PG 7 x 100' and 'Mort x 60mm x 200'. These refer to rifle ammunition, propelled grenades and mortar bombs. A complete list of rifles, mortars, pistols and more was dictated to the Zimbabwean official. Then, to Mann's surprise, du Toit added a second, larger order of weaponry. He explained it was for rebels in Congo.

Mann was puzzled. He recalled that du Toit 'said that it would help the EG order, the one I was worried about, in two ways. One: the EG order was very small beer for ZDI. Two: the second order was for [Congolese] rebels.' Du Toit believed that the Zimbabweans 'would be very interested in making friendly contact with [Congolese] rebels. I asked him why and he replied that Zimbabwe had a major ongoing interest in DRC [Congo] in various ways and in some mining.' Du Toit had contacts in a rebel group in Congo, he said. Though Mann was obliged to pay for all the military goods, the bigger deal would mean he got his weapons fast. Zimbabwe did have a strong interest in Congo, as powerful individuals exploited mineral riches for private gain, backing various groups as occasion arose. Selling guns to rebels, though illegal and destructive, clearly tempted ZDI. Du Toit claimed there were 'about 1000 rebels in the Katanga region of the DRC who wanted to fight the Kabila government'. He was evidently referring to the group he (apparently) struck a deal with in 2003, the PDD.

Next they met Colonel Dube, the disdainful boss of ZDI, who showed little interest. He 'seemed negative', Mann said later. 'We met in his office. When I tried to explain the cover story as to why we wanted these weapons (we did not feel we could tell the truth) he was not interested. When I tried to show him where the mine was on the map he didn't look.' They were told to return to meet a junior officer, Group Captain Hope Mutize. But du Toit spent some time alone with Colonel Dube. He emerged 'very pleased', said Mann. 'He was sure everything would go smoothly. When I asked why he replied that, as he had suggested earlier, Col Dumbe [sic] was very pleased that ZDI and ... [the] Zimbabwe intelligence services would gain a direct and positive link to the new DRC rebel grouping.' Mann now felt certain that 'a) [he was] dealing with the highest possible authorities in Zimbabwe, b) we would get good products and a good service'.

Hope Mutize of ZDI later said: 'They told me that they did not want any paperwork involved in the transactions', but he insisted. Mutize, du Toit and Mann signed the quotation for the original order of arms the same day. Only du Toit and Mutize signed the other, the shipment for Congolese rebels. Mann's order would cost just over $80,000. That paid for 10 Browning pistols, a supply of 9mm ammunition, 61 Kalashnikov rifles and 45,000 rounds of ammunition. In addition, he would get 20 machine guns, with ammunition, 7 rocket-propelled grenade launchers, plus attack projectiles, and 2 mortar launchers with 80 mortar bombs with high explosives. Finally, 150 offensive hand grenades would be included and 20 Icarus flares. A handwritten note on one copy of the quotation, apparently by du Toit, estimated the weight of the goods: 'Kit 1' at 4255 kg

(9400 lbs), 'kit 2' at 6000 kg (13,000 lbs) and unspecified 'packs' would weigh another 4800 kg (10,600 lbs). Mann later boasted over dinner with Nigel Morgan that he was buying 'five tons of small-arms to be used for the operation'.

Mann's arsenal was hardly suitable for guards at a mine. Attack grenades, mortar bombs, high explosives and rocket-propelled grenades are assault weapons, while machine guns and rifles can be used for either attack or defence. The Congo mine story deceived nobody. But Mann expected little interest in his shipment, with officials lured by the bigger deal with Congolese rebels. Mann and du Toit promised to return to inspect and collect the cargo a few days later. The total cost of the two orders would be nearly $200,000. A down payment of roughly half that was made soon afterwards by James Kershaw, Mann's assistant, who flew to Harare. The money was not banked (to evade Zimbabwe's strict foreign currency laws) but was placed in a safe.

Investigators in South Africa were later horrified by the arms firm's deal, condemning Zimbabwe's government for being ready to sell to rebels and mercenaries. European arms exporters, African governments and state-owned arms dealers all help fuel wars on the continent. A senior South African investigator says: 'ZDI were willing to provide this type of weapon to a private individual. Shit. You don't sell that sort of gun [the assault weaponry] to private entrepreneurs. We need to crack down on this sort of deal if we are to stop wars in Africa. Why is ZDI selling this stuff to private individuals? Everyone is closing their eyes to what is happening in Zimbabwe with ZDI. If you want to clean up Africa look at the list of weapons, mortars, rocket propelled grenades, AK-47s. In a democracy you ask that type of question, what will these weapons be used for?'

Mann and du Toit flew on to neighbouring Zambia, to prepare the final details of the coup. They went north to Ndola, a town in a copper-mining region that borders Congo, and met a man 'who was apparently leader of the Katanga uprising shortly to occur'. Perhaps he represented the PDD rebel group. He was told to expect the weapons du Toit ordered. In exchange his rebels would secure a 2-kilometre/ mile-long airstrip at Kolwezi, just over the border in Congo, where Mann and his team could gather to prepare the assault on Equatorial Guinea. The rebel 'was told he must secure the airstrip at Kolwezi for twenty-four hours so that his equipment could be delivered to him', Mann said later.

PART THREE

The Big Push

15
Strike One

'Pull off a coup and you're a national hero, fail and you're an evil criminal; in business it's the same difference between bankruptcy and making a fortune.'

Jeffrey Archer, 'The Coup' (1980)

The launch date loomed. Rather than grab Obiang at Malabo airport, the plotters decided to unleash a more conventional attack. Before a bullet could be fired, however, a complicated manoeuvre had to be completed, getting several teams, the weapons and the planes to the right positions. Mann's description to his fellow plotters would have been something like this:

The German, Merz, brings his Antonov from Equatorial Guinea and flies south to Zimbabwe. Harry and I wait in Harare for him, where we load the cargo, turn around and fly north. We aim for the airstrip at Kolwezi. It's a thousand miles from anywhere, in the south of Congo. Nick has an arrangement with a group of rebels in Congo. His pals will secure the landing zone for us at Kolwezi. Now the two DC3s take off in South Africa. Each one takes half the guys and the team leaders. They clear immigration at Polokwane, then fly north and head to the same Congo airstrip in Kolwezi, where we rendezvous. There we split the weapons into two piles.

One lot is for Nick's rebels to play with; we keep the other half for Malabo. Maybe there'll be time to test them. At dusk we all take our Russian bird to the target. We fly overnight and it's game on by dawn ...

The final days were ticking down. Mann was in Johannesburg for the last preparations. At some point in February a small celebration was held at the Butcher Shop and Grill, Mann's favourite. Among others, Mark Thatcher was present: it was the last time he saw Mann. He later told a court: 'The last meeting was in February 2004 at a restaurant in Sandton Square in Johannesburg. He [Mann] had recently been advised that his wife was pregnant and we met to celebrate the news.' It seems a safe bet that the news of the pregnancy was not the main topic of conversation that night, as the plot was due to be launched within days. Asked if he and Mann had ever discussed Equatorial Guinea, Thatcher produced an unconvincing reply. Speaking in a thin, nasal voice, he claimed: 'To my recollection I discussed Equatorial Guinea with Simon Mann twice. I discussed Equatorial Guinea in the context of the west African region. I have no recollection of talking about anyone in Equatorial Guinea or any Equatorial Guinean.'

Another meeting took place, probably on 17 or 18 February. Various sources say that Henry van der Westhuizen met a man called Bulelani Ngcuka, the head of South Africa's national prosecuting authority (and thus chief of a crack investigative team called the Scorpions), who was known to be close to President Thabo Mbeki. He explained something about the plan in Equatorial Guinea. Ngcuka listened but said little, possibly indicating that any official response would have to come from another part of government. But van der Westhuizen believed he got no warning to stop. Applying the logic that anything not forbidden is therefore permitted, du Toit and Mann went ahead.

This was the prime moment to attack. Steyl left for the Canary Islands in the King Air, ready to escort Severo Moto to his new job. Next he flew via Equatorial Guinea, dropping off du Toit and a young assistant, Mark Schmidt, in Malabo, then refuelling in Mali. On board, he recalls, were Wales and David Tremain, the quiet accomplice, as well as Alex Molteno, a stunt pilot. They eventually arrived in the Canary Islands on 17 February and checked into the Steigenberger hotel on Gran Canaria. There they met Karim Fallaha, the Lebanese businessman from Asian Trading – the firm that apparently had agreed in November to invest $5 million in Mann's Logo firm. The same day Mann went to Harare, Zimbabwe, intending to inspect his weapons. He told ZDI he would soon collect his order. The officers and footsoldiers in South Africa prepared to board the DC3 planes. All were poised and ready.

At first, the complicated plan worked. Groups took position. Du Toit was in Malabo. Moto reached the Canary Islands. Mann was in Harare. They communicated by satellite and mobile phone. Before dawn on 19 February the footsoldiers, who had been sleeping at Hotel 224, climbed on to buses and drove to Wonderboom airport, near Pretoria. They boarded the two DC3 Dakota planes and flew over the dry veld of northern South Africa to a small airport at Polokwane. They cleared emigration (a flight registration ZS-OJM was used), then aimed for Congo and the Kolwezi rendezvous. The same day the Antonov left Malabo and began its long trip south. Merz was in charge, but the captain of the plane was an Armenian, Ashot Karpetyan.

Now problems arose. Cheap, second-hand and poorly maintained east European aircraft are popular all over Africa.

The problem? They are cheap, second-hand and poorly maintained. The Antonov was soon struggling. It broke a nosewheel while landing in Douala, Cameroon. That was fixed and the Antonov flew a short distance further, this time to Brazzaville in Congo Republic (the smaller of the two Congos). There it suffered again, sucking a bird into an engine. If any of the Armenian crew were superstitious, these mishaps should have made them uneasy. But the battered plane limped on, well behind schedule.

Then came the second blow. Mann had sent a small team to liaise with the Congolese rebels. This group was possibly the PDD, the rebel group with whom du Toit had apparently signed an agreement in May 2003 to provide military goods and advice. South African investigators say Mazanga Kashama, Simon Witherspoon and perhaps a third man 'were in Kolwezi with the rebels for the first attempt'. They were to tell Mann when the airstrip was ready. But the rebels' bravado did not mean they would really act. There are two versions of what happened next. One holds that the rebels failed to show, leaving Mann's group with nothing to do but report that the airstrip was not secure. Another version holds that some rebels appeared, failed to take the airstrip, then became angry when they heard their weapons were not coming. South African investigators prefer the latter, saying Mazanga and Witherspoon 'had to run from there, they had to move, the rebels might *moer* them, get cross, because they didn't get their goods'. The Antonov never made it to Harare; instead, it landed in southern Congo, in Lubumbashi, a short distance from Kolwezi and close to the Zambian border.

Mann later summed up his dismal day in a confession: 'The AN12 was *en route* to Harare and the pick was to take place. The aircraft broke a nosewheel in Douala and had a bird

strike in Brazzaville. It ended up in Lubumbashi, then eventually flew back to Equatorial Guinea empty. In the mean time
the rebels had not secured Kolwezi and the whole operation
was cancelled.' He postponed plans to collect the weapons in
Harare, and told the pilots of the two DC3s to forget Kolwezi.
Instead, they flew to Ndola, a Zambian border town close to
Lubumbashi. Mann flew up to pay for yet more repairs and
fuel for the stricken Antonov. The footsoldiers on the DC3s
were told of problems in Congo. They waited three hours at
Ndola, only to be sent home. Some perhaps still do not know,
even now, of the plan to attack Equatorial Guinea. One recalls:
'We were told there was a problem that the rebels had attacked
the mine, so we are going back until it is peaceful again. I
believed it.' They returned the same evening to Hotel 224.

On the Canary Islands, the force that was to escort Moto
had the least to do. They posed as holidaymakers and waited.
First they heard the attempt was postponed by a day, then
by several days. Wales, Tremain, Steyl, Molteno and Fallaha
passed their time sunbathing. Steyl recalls, 'We tanned at the
hotel. David Tremain was a brilliant chess player, a really
good guy. He gave me a book on Alan Bond' (Tremain once
worked for the Australian tycoon). Moto was also on the
island, but kept away from the plotters. For several days they
drank, dined and waited. Eventually Steyl paid the hotel bills
with cash and returned to South Africa on a commercial flight
via Zurich. Others went on to London or Madrid. They left
behind the King Air for later use.

Mann was furious. The failure now meant all sorts of new
problems. The Spanish frigates in the Gulf of Guinea would not
remain there for long. Then came reports of a small uprising
in Equatorial Guinea and the arrest of conspirators, including
a Brigadier Antonio Nchuema Nguema. This appeared to be

the effort Mann and Moto hoped would coincide with the invasion. Another uprising was extremely unlikely. Next time the invaders, plus du Toit's forward team, would have to do everything themselves. Mann also had to reassure ZDI, his weapon suppliers. Back in Harare, on 20 February he handed the balance of money owed to ZDI – some $90,800 – wrapped in a bundle and stuffed inside a magazine (the newspaper sort, perhaps the *Economist*, not the military sort). At a later meeting at a well-known meeting point called the News Café in Harare, with du Toit present, he agreed to pay a surcharge of $10,000, 'to compensate ZDI for the inconvenience we had caused them by failing to collect the first time'. At this meeting du Toit irritated Mann by asking the ZDI representative, Martin Bird, to add another pair of items to the shopping list of weapons. Du Toit wanted two missiles added to the order. Mann complained later, 'This seemed unnecessary but, more importantly, dangerous, because to ask for such sensitive items might raise the alarm and compromise the whole deal.'

By now everybody's blood pressure was up. Morgan, the red-faced freelance intelligence man, recalls he felt physically sick soon after the February attempt. He had missed the big event. Though he had given South Africa's authorities several warnings in January and February that a coup attempt was imminent in Equatorial Guinea, he had failed to notice when the DC3 planes set off. He had dined many times with Mann in this period, mostly in Johannesburg, and had monitored events from his hideaway on a remote South African moor. Yet he had not spotted the launch. He could not bring himself, at first, to admit the attempt had really been made. Mann had set off without triggering any alarms and had every chance to fly on to Equatorial Guinea. It was a golden opportunity. Morgan, for one, resolved not to let it happen again.

But Mann was also disheartened. He had slipped from South Africa without problems, but he could not be sure of that again. There was no time to rebase his operations in Namibia. Then there was the question of money. Keeping over sixty men in a hotel in Pretoria drained resources. Arranging for planes was costly, too. And, though Mann did not know it, there were signs that Equatorial Guinea was receiving better intelligence of a plot. When a King Air plane similar to the one used by Steyl landed at Malabo, its crew were hauled aside by officials and subjected to fierce questioning. The arrest of local plotters also suggested Malabo was on higher alert.

Those near Mann noticed his mood darken. The affable aristocrat grew ill-tempered. Like other coup plotters before him, he found that costs mounted and funding was never quite adequate. He still chased money, the dribs and drabs promised – but not delivered – by friends and investors. It is possible he misled other plotters over how much he had invested himself. He was 'visibly uneasy' by late February. 'He looked under huge emotional pressure,' recalls one who saw him regularly. Matters were not helped by Amanda, his free-spending wife. On one occasion, he 'lost it'. 'He threw the phone ten metres at a wall and it smashed into a thousand bits,' says somebody who worked in his office. The reason? On top of the stress of finding cash for his coup, he had to provide ever more dollars to his wife. Mann could afford it in the longer term, but he lacked ready cash. His wife and children, used to luxury, were running up bills just as he needed every dollar. Another man might have thrown down his cards, said he was beaten and retired to think up another plot. But under pressure, determined to recoup his losses, repay his investors and produce another military success, Mann vowed to push on. 'Simon got cavalier because he was worried about money,' says the colleague. 'And there was his pride.'

He had to continue – in part, because so many people were involved. Looking back, Crause Steyl complains the Wonga Coup was immensely complicated. He recalls Mann talking a few years earlier as they sat together in his English country house. Mann spun a tale about Drake, who lived in a similar old house in the south of England, says Steyl. 'In the days of British pirateers plundering Spanish ships in the Atlantic, the Spanish would do all sorts of things to protect the gold they brought back from the New World. They would put ships in a convoy, or camouflage them. Once in a hundred years the pirates would get it right and plunder a ship full of gold,' laughs Steyl. And like them, 'We were going for a once-in-a-hundred-years deal.'

But there were difficulties. Mann's plot was grand and unwieldy. 'The problem is the scale. Simon was doing this when acting with a hundred guys. You're almost like a semi government, and much less flexible,' concluded Steyl. By late February, after the first coup attempt failed, many were disheartened. Du Toit, eager to keep his business interests, again wanted out. He called his journalist friend Brabazon to say he had 'withdrawn from the operation' and was 'walking away from it'. Steyl, too, had his doubts and thought of withdrawing. But Mann saw no option. Crause concludes: 'Simon had put so much money into it, he had to see it through to rescue his money.'

Morgan also heard, through Kershaw, that Mann was under great strain. He was shouting and swearing. Mann was driven on by a mixture of vanity, the need to recoup his losses and by the love of adventure. But the plotters, who had done much in good humour early on, were falling out. Du Toit saw no reason to keep trying. Steyl was out of Mann's favour – the two spoke less and less. Investors were pushing for their money. After years of success with Executive Outcomes, Mann now battled just to keep his team together. Yet somehow, from his luxurious enclave in Constantia, Cape Town, he conjured up a feeling of power. He lived in an 'unreal world', says Morgan. He ignored those who told him to scrap his plot. 'Essentially he said, "Fuck it, let's just go,"' believes Morgan. His spirit pushed him to try again. 'Simon Mann was taking a major chance,' concludes another friend. But that, after all, is what adventurers do.

A New Plan, a New Steyl

A resourceful British soldier, trained to think around problems, Mann decided to simplify his plan. The unreliable Congolese rebels and shoddy aircraft were dropped. He needed reliable allies and equipment, so he turned to the trusty Boeing 727 that had done so well in Angola for Executive Outcomes. Its three noisy engines guzzled fuel, but it was powerful, able to reach 30,000 feet from take-off in fifteen minutes if lightly loaded. A single plane could take the men from South Africa, then stop to pick up the weapons in Zimbabwe. With a top speed of 900 km (560 miles) an hour, it could travel to Malabo in six hours, refuelling on the way. One could easily be found. There are 'so many aircraft standing around in desert locations, refugees from the scrap heap', says one aviation expert. Though expensive to maintain in the longer term, Mann wanted it for a single journey. Then it could be left to rust beside a runway.

Steyl recalls sitting with Mann and David Tremain at the end of February in a hotel lobby in Sandton, Johannesburg. They set a new date for the coup attempt, choosing 6 March, a Saturday. Mann clearly expected to move fast. He said he had already arranged to buy a 727 in Mena, a small town near Kansas in the United States. Suspicion as to the source would naturally point at Steyl, who bought 727s for his early aviation business, Capricorn Systems, in the days of Executive Outcomes. But he denies organising the purchase, pointing to Ivan Pienaar, whose role grew as Steyl fell from favour.

One Robert Dodson Sr, president of Dodson Aviation Inc. in Ottawa, Canada, had offered to sell a Boeing 727-100 for $400,000. He also promised to buy it back six months later for $300,000 if its vital parts, especially the engines, were undamaged. Dodson specialised in selling planes for the US government. He would see it delivered to Wonderboom airport, near Pretoria, by 6 March at the latest. It would remain in Dodson's name while it cleared the United States. It had a white fuselage and a blue line along the length of it. The registration number, N4610, was painted just below the starboard engine at the rear.

In fact, N4610 is a remarkable aircraft, one of very few such Boeing 727-100s in use, and almost designed for the needs of a modern mercenary. The plane, according to an American researcher, was formerly used by the 201 Airlift Squadron of the American National Guard to transport personnel, but was equipped with special devices that allow manual control of the steering mechanism in case of hydraulic failure, while special tanks allowed rapid dumping of fuel in case of emergency. The baggage compartments were both heated and pressurised, allowing access to at least one of them while the craft was in the air. Perhaps most important, the wing flaps used for landing and take-off had been adapted so that the Boeing could approach a runway at low speeds, and thus make use of a shorter landing strip – such as those found in the more remote bits of Africa. The timing is striking: Mann managed to get hold of a specialist plane from the United States extremely quickly after his first, failed attempt to overthrow the government of Equatorial Guinea. And he did so through a company, Dodson, that had offices in the United States and a subsidiary based, conveniently, in Pretoria, at Wonderboom airport. No doubt some will ask whether Greg Wales's special lobbying in Washington DC might, somehow, have helped obtain this semi-official aircraft.

Now all Mann needed was someone to fly it. Niel Steyl could pose as the ageing pop crooner Rod Stewart in a lookalike competition. Like any 1970s rocker, he drives an open-top red sports car, has a mullet of grey hair down to his shoulders and dresses in a denim jacket and jeans. But he is no singer; he is a pilot. He is engaging, easygoing and is probably the least bitter of any involved in the Wonga Coup.

Life, he suggests, has generally been good. Like many in his family he loves planes and adrenalin. With his two brothers, Crause and Johann, he flew for Executive Outcomes in the 1990s. He was a 'tanker jockey', a pilot with the dangerous job of flying diesel and other fuel to remote airstrips in Angola's jungle. Rebel soldiers sometimes took potshots at him with heat-seeking missiles. He enjoyed that. Then he found a better career as a pilot for an Indian tycoon, the owner of Kingfisher breweries, Dr V. J. Malya. 'I flew his personal Boeing 727. It was an awesome job. We followed the Grand Prix circuit. We went to the Monaco Grand Prix and watched the race from the balcony of his apartment, then went for a huge party on his yacht moored in the harbour there.' They waltzed around the world, partying hard. Steyl recalls the converted plane had 'an ensuite bedroom, a bar, a lounge with a 42-inch plasma TV screen, a dining room, a kids' room with games and another

TV, then at the back staff quarters for eight staff. There were usually more staff on board than passengers.' When the music system was on, the bass thudded so loud in the cockpit Steyl worried his instruments would break. They stayed at 5-star hotels. He got a business-class flight home for two weeks' holiday every few weeks, plus a generous salary.

Mann called his friend in Bangalore, late in February, asking if he wanted a freelance job. Few would blame him for refusing. But Mann said the task would take just 'three or four days'. It would be like before, the thrill of Executive Outcomes again. Steyl, by chance, was due home in South Africa in March anyway. There are rumours that Mann offered him $1 million to fly the plane. So he accepted, bringing his holidays forward. 'I thought I'd take a few days off and do this thing and it turned into a big fuck-up.' He laughs contentedly. 'I knew it was something military, but not the details. I'd just be moving cargo from A to B. A pilot doesn't care what his passengers do when they get there. I wasn't going to do anything there. I expected to stay two or three days. But such details were never discussed.'

An idea was floated that he might set up an airline to shuttle between Johannesburg and Equatorial Guinea. 'Yes, that was possible. But I had a good job. I was just doing this in my holiday,' he says. 'I don't want the money. I said I would do it for the good of the cause and for the kicks.' He trusted Mann, and continues to trust him. 'I would do something with Simon again. But not for money, for the kicks. It's not "Hell, I'm never going to do this again". Life is for living. Sometimes there's a fuck-up.' Two other crew members, co-pilot Hendrik Hamman and flight engineer Ken Pain, were recruited, too.

So the month at least ended more hopefully for Mann. Despite failures there were now promising signs. The 727 was due from the United States. His old friend Niel Steyl would fly it. The delay had been put to some use: the footsoldiers, instructed by Horn and Carlse, practised urban fighting at a training ground near Pretoria. Brandishing wooden replica rifles they rehearsed house penetration for several days. Some extra officers were recruited: Witherspoon, who had already been up to Kolwezi, Louis du Prez and a third man called Leon Lotz. Du Prez later said he had heard the South African authorities had 'okayed the whole mission'. His lawyer said, 'They were told that Thabo Mbeki was looking forward to meeting the new president.'

To the plotters' delight, Equatorial Guinea's president was also coming under pressure. At the end of February, Obiang visited Riggs Bank, in Washington DC, to check on his millions of dollars. Obiang was the bank's single biggest client, with a long relationship, but he was told to close his accounts. An investigation into money-laundering called for some $360 million of Equatorial Guinean funds to be frozen until the source of the money could be identified. It was humiliating news. Perhaps it suggested the United States was hostile to the dictator.

And, finally, investors' money was flowing again into Mann's accounts. Logo Logistics, his firm registered in Guernsey, saw four big deposits. The first, just under $240,000, came from Wachovia Bank in the United States on 23 February. Then, on 2 March Crause Steyl's airline company passed on $100,000, thought to be the balance of funds from Mark Thatcher's helicopter payment. Then another transaction, through Hansard Trust Company (which oversaw Mann's various corporate entities), provided nearly $400,000, the amount needed for the plane. Finally, on 3 March, there was a transfer of nearly $135,000. This last payment would cause trouble later. It came from a J. H. Archer.

A Literary Coup?

There is much speculation about the mysterious donor of 3 March. Was he, in fact, the convicted perjurer and best-selling British novelist Lord Jeffrey Archer? If so, the money came barely a year after the disgraced peer was released from prison after serving a sentence for lying to a British court and perverting the course of justice. There is some circumstantial evidence. Lord Archer's initials are indeed J. H. (for Jeffrey Howard). He is a longstanding friend of Ely Calil and he also knows Mark Thatcher. A lawyer acting for Equatorial Guinea later said telephone records showed four calls from Calil's home to that of Lord Archer some weeks before the J. H. Archer transferred money to Mann's account. These calls, he suggested, 'provide substantial links between the conspirators around the time of the coup attempt'.

And – an insubtantial but entertaining point – Archer has long been interested in west Africa. Coincidentally, he wrote a short story, published in 1980, entitled 'The Coup', which describes a violent attempt to overthrow an oil-rich government in the region. It is a thin tale, based on Archer's knowledge of a military coup in Nigeria in the 1970s. One of his characters does make a relevant point for coup plotters to keep in mind, however: 'Pull off a coup and you're a national hero,' he suggests, 'fail and you're an evil criminal; in business it's the same difference between bankruptcy and making a fortune.'

Approached for this book, Lord Archer refused to comment on what appears, at least, to be an extraordinary coincidence. His secretary conveyed the message that 'he knows nothing about it and doesn't want to say anything about it'. Earlier he did deny any involvement in, or knowledge of, the coup attempt. His lawyers produced a carefully phrased statement that Archer had never 'issued a cheque in the sums mentioned'. They avoided the suggestion that the money was deposited in Logo Logistics' account using a bank transfer, not a cheque. As for the phone calls, the lawyers again produced a statement of limited use that begged further questions. They admitted that calls occurred between Calil's home and Archer's home, but suggested that at least one call did not involve Lord Archer. That was hardly a robust response. Plotters interviewed about the Wonga Coup shed little light on the mysterious J. H. Archer. It is hard to believe the novelist's denials, but one involved in the plot thinks funds were passed to Mann without J. H. Archer knowing what they would be used for. Perhaps Archer paid the money blind, possibly believing he was making a charitable donation.

The respected journal, *Africa Confidential*, once published what it called the 'Wonga List', naming those who would be asked questions about the financing of the Wonga Coup. It did not mention Archer, though the list predated publication of Mann's bank account showing the J. H. Archer payment. *Africa Confidential* estimated the coup had a budget of about $3 million. It suggested that five men would be asked about supplying ready cash for the March operation. Investigators in South Africa were said in *Africa Confidential* to be keen to ask Ely Calil if he invested $750,000, and four others – Karim Fallaha; the British property trader Gary Hersham; David Tremain; and Mann himself – if they each put in $500,000. The men, at least those ready to speak on the matter, denied investing. In addition, the journal reported claims that Wales routed 'unspecified payments' through one of Mann's accounts. But, to date, efforts to prosecute individuals named as suspected financiers – with one notable exception – have failed.

16

The Wonga Coup
(Mark One)

*'Have you seen Simon? What's he doing? I'm worried he's up to
his old tricks.'*

Mark Thatcher, speaking to a friend of Simon Mann, March 2004

Early in 2004 a man called Diosdado Nguema Eyi died in
Equatorial Guinea. The ex-chief of presidential security was
probably murdered. His death was typical of what befalls
those who know the secrets of a repressive government then
lose its favour. 'Officially, his car fell into a ravine in a freak
accident', reported *Africa Confidential* in March, '… but we
hear he had a bullet wound when he died and that his body
was not returned to his family.' Perhaps an old score had
been settled. Or perhaps Diosdado was suspected of plotting
against his ex-boss.

By March the government had every reason to expect a
coup attempt, the most serious of Obiang's 25-year rule. A
South African envoy to Malabo recalls, 'Everybody knew
there was a coup in the offing, from January onwards there
was much talk about security.' Obiang made a formal trip to
South Africa in December 2003 and met President Mbeki. His
second son, Gabriel Mbegha Nguema – the more likeable one

– then visited Mbeki in late February. These were new signs of cordiality. Intelligence was exchanged. Early in March, probably on Wednesday 3 March, a South African intelligence team chartered a plane to Malabo and warned of pending trouble. The information was imprecise, along the lines of 'Be careful, there is something in the air, keep an eye on South Africans', said a lawyer for Equatorial Guinea later. A day or so later, the minister of security, Nguema Mba (an uncle of Obiang), rushed to Angola to hear a more detailed warning. He was told a flying force would join a team of plotters already in place. Angola had its intelligence from spies in South Africa, and maybe from mercenary rivals to Mann.

By Thursday 4 March, when du Toit flew to Equatorial Guinea, his fate was sealed. He went in a private plane with Sergio Cardoso, Georges Allerson and Jose Domingos. The German Gerhard Merz was at the airport and took them home to Malabo. Oddly, du Toit sent text messages to friends suggesting that the coup attempt had been cancelled. Perhaps he had cold feet, though he had no chance to back out now. The wife of one of his men later forgave him, concluding that, indeed, du Toit 'never had a choice'. Perhaps he hoped to spread false information by saying the coup was off. He should have known others monitored his calls. Confirming he was once part of a planned attack was not a smart thing to do; at worst, eavesdroppers might deduce it was imminent.

The Canary Islands team gathered again. Crause Steyl and David Tremain took a commercial Spanish flight from South Africa. Tremain insisted they return to the Steigenberger hotel. Karim Fallaha, Greg Wales and Alex Molteno, the stunt pilot, joined them. Some suggest Wales brought a bag with a large bundle of dollars for emergency use, perhaps $500,000. He denies it. Others say Wales put a similar sum into Mann's bank account, and later had Kershaw help him withdraw it. He denies financing any operation for the richer Mann.

Records obtained from the Steigenberger hotel (both for the February and the March visits) show the men dined together in the hotel piano bar, sat by the pool, watched pay TV movies in their rooms, sipped mineral water (without gas), ate chocolate and played tennis. Wales, Tremain, Molteno and Steyl are all identified by name on the hotel records for this time. The men dined together, discussed tactics for the operation and dreamt up ways to unsettle Equatorial Guinea's rulers. 'Karim mentioned making confusion ... confusing the ministries with oil bids,' says Steyl. The idea was to cause a nuisance in the finance ministry in Equatorial Guinea by pretending to be oil men making bids for the country's oil. Steyl had a simpler tactic: 'I said we needed to get the radio station. If we don't do that, otherwise, we could fly the Boeing 200 feet over Malabo with the speed brakes on, the flaps open, and circle the town. The noise alone would be intimidating. Circle the town twenty times. The silence afterwards would be peace itself.'

The 727 was due in South Africa. A bill of sale between Dodson Aviation and Logo Logistics was recorded on a Federal Aviation Authority document of 3 March. Two days later, still registered as N4610, the ex-US coastguard plane left Mena, near Kansas. Some are suspicious at how easily the plane cleared United States airspace despite red tape, and suggest an American with close ties to US intelligence was aboard the plane at this stage.

Most of the plotters remained in South Africa: the officers and footsoldiers in Pretoria; Mann and a few others in Johannesburg. Mann briefly visited Harare to check his consignment of weapons was still available. Niel Steyl, the 727 pilot, arrived in Johannesburg, early for his holiday. Simon Witherspoon later told investigators he was formally recruited at this point. He recalled arguing with Mann, saying the black footsoldiers should be paid more. He later told investigators he was hired for a 'contract in Equatorial Guinea where there were some political problems. In this country, we were expected to assist the military and police of the new government.' He said he heard the governments of Zimbabwe, South Africa, Britain and Spain knew of the contract, 'and we, therefore, had nothing to worry about'.

On 5 March, a Friday, du Toit phoned Mann from Malabo to ask if the plot was going ahead. It was, but a day late, on Sunday. Someone – probably Mann – also phoned Mutize, the Zimbabwe Defence Industries man, and told him the weapons would be collected at 7 p.m. that day. A later call postponed collection to Sunday. At roughly the same time Mark Thatcher phoned a mutual friend of his and Mann's in Johannesburg and asked, 'Have you seen Simon? What's he doing? I'm worried he's up to his old tricks.' The friend knew nothing.

Mann undertook a final, rushed trip. He still thought the 727 might be late, and wanted a back-up plane. Perhaps he also doubted his deal in Zimbabwe. He might get a plane, weapons and support in Kinshasa, the sultry capital of Congo. If that were a new base, he would be in easy striking distance of Equatorial Guinea. Early on Saturday morning he told Witherspoon the job was going ahead. Then he boarded a Hawker Siddeley 125 jet, registration N90FF, apparently owned by Dodson Aviation, and flew to Congo. Horn and Carlse went with him. Horn said Ivan Pienaar flew the jet. Another source says a Dodson man took the controls. In Kinshasa Mann (he later said) met a contact, Tim Roman, who is close to Congo's president, Joseph Kabila. They discussed aircraft and weapons. Mann implicitly wanted backing for his coup attempt, but specifically asked for Roman to provide a second plane. There was no immediate response because Roman had first to 'consult his partner [President Kabila] before agreeing finally. However, he thought he would be able to do it.' Mann, Horn and Carlse flew south to Harare and checked in at the Cresta Lodge again. Mann later recounted: That evening Tim rang and said that his partner [ie Kabila] had refused his doing this job. However they would do it in the future and would be prepared to also supply 'equipment', in other words weapons.

By now Nigel Morgan was frantic. He had last dined with Mann on Thursday 4 March and knew of the plan to go to Kinshasa. Now signs indicated the coup would be launched any day. Morgan had missed the first attempt in February and was anxious to avoid repeating the mistake. That night in his remote country house he did not sleep, but sat up writing a detailed intelligence report saying the coup was at hand. He emailed it, encrypted, to an intelligence contact at dawn on Saturday morning. There followed frantic calls between assorted intelligence gatherers. According to one version, intelligence men and foreign policy experts held an emergency meeting that afternoon. It was a hectic time. South Africa was preparing for a general election – only the third since the end of apartheid – with Mbeki campaigning to keep the presidency.

A decision was needed: Should South Africa stop the plotters? Few would mourn Obiang's removal and letting a despot get booted out would serve the ends of justice, at least if a better ruler took over. There was every chance, too, that South Africa would enjoy good relations – and oil benefits – in a new Equatorial Guinea. But a stronger group of officials and politicians recoiled at the idea. South Africa had opposed the British–American invasion of Iraq, saying outsiders had no right to remove any government, however wicked, or however tempting its oil. The parallel was obvious. In Africa, Mbeki's much-repeated concern was promoting order and stability before all else. Only a stable continent could prosper, he argued endlessly. His government opposed mercenaries and any who would push for violent change of government, especially any based in South Africa. He would never tolerate a coup led by white Britons hungry for African oil. As for oil benefits for South African firms in Equatorial Guinea, a grateful Obiang might oblige.

The latter view prevailed. The next question was how to act. An option was to arrest the plotters before they left South Africa. While foiling the coup, it would be hard to prosecute them for breaking anti-mercenary laws. Another choice was to warn Equatorial Guinea to fight the mercenaries on arrival in Malabo. That was risky. Mann's invaders might yet triumph. Even if the hired guns were quashed, there would be bloodshed and another case of instability in Africa. A third option was to tell Zimbabwe, whose police could catch the plotters red-handed as they collected the weapons. The hired guns might be treated roughly, but that would set a lesson for others. 'We allowed things to go through ... We wanted to send a message. We stand for peace on the continent,' a government spokesman said later. A call was made to Harare.

Intriguingly, Zimbabwe's rulers seemed to believe Mann was a threat to them. Zimbabwe's government had grown increasingly paranoid and its relations with Britain, the old colonial power, were at their lowest point ever. Some Zimbabweans even worried that Britain might launch or sponsor a military attack on Zimbabwe itself. A senior official in the ruling party, Zanu PF, and close ally of Robert Mugabe gave an interview for this book. Efriam Masiwa spoke in an unlit room late one afternoon in Harare, in March 2005. He denied Zimbabwe had laid any trap to catch mercenaries, but said officials had been worried about Mann. They had suspected the former SAS officer might have been working for the wicked British. 'These guys wanted to put us in a corner,' he explained. Once Zimbabwe knew of a plan to attack Equatorial Guinea, such fears were confirmed. 'If they had succeeded it would be known that the weapons used to remove the Equatoguinean president were acquired from Zimbabwe', and that would 'authenticate the British [and American] thinking about Zimbabwe ... as an outpost of tyranny'. It is a convoluted argument, but Masiwa believes the Zimbabwean government 'would be blamed for the coup' in Equatorial Guinea. Thus: 'It was not us that trapped the Simon Mann group. It was the Simon Mann group that was trying to trap us.'

Back in Malabo, rumours of a coup had been spreading for weeks. Expatriate oil men knew to stay in their compounds. A foreign aid worker later told a French documentary team that 'everyone knew by March there would be a coup. Everyone knew. Moto couldn't keep a secret. And all knew that Madrid's intelligence was involved in the affair.' One expert on Equatorial Guinea says several senior people, including President Obiang, had slipped quietly out of the country by early March. The last to leave, said this source, was Gabriel, the moderate second son.

Du Toit recalls briefing his employees that Saturday, 6 March. He told his men to take cars to the airport, with bottled water. According to one version, they were to leave the keys in the ignition for the arriving team. By now they, too, should have noticed the swirling rumours of a plot and sensed a threat. Mark Schmidt, the youngest and least experienced of du Toit's forward team, later spoke to a South African reporter of an ominous atmosphere under Malabo's grey skies. 'On Saturday the soldiers and police were very busy all around us. We asked the people what was going on and they said they were arresting strangers.' It was obvious there were problems.

Sunday Dawns

At dawn on Sunday 7 March, the plotters were ready. After a long flight from the United States, via Sao Tome, the white Boeing 727 landed at Lanseria airport, near Pretoria. Its American registration, N4610, remained on the starboard side. Its chrome-rimmed engines glinted in the morning sun. From Lanseria it hopped the short distance to Wonderboom airport. There Niel Steyl and his assistants took charge, relieving the American crew.

That Sunday an ex-soldier called Raymond Archer was sitting down for lunch with his girlfriend in Pretoria. He had returned the night before from a bodyguard job in Haiti, in the Caribbean. He took a call from Harry Carlse. 'I've a job for you,' said Carlse. 'Leon Lotz has pulled out, we need you. You have two hours to get to the plane'. He gave no details but told Archer to go to Wonderboom airport. There would be a full explanation mid-air. Archer agreed and kissed his girlfriend goodbye. Lotz, witting or not, made a smart choice. Archer, the last recruit for the Wonga Coup, had just made a terrible one. 'He was the unluckiest guy,' concludes a relative of the Steyl brothers.

Lourens Horn organised a bus to get the footsoldiers to Wonderboom airport. There James Kershaw counted everyone on, noted names and checked each person's bank details. The plane was loaded with blue and black bags, each marked with the brand 'Carry All'. One was stuffed with new lace-up boots still bearing labels. Another held sandals. There were sleeping bags, bull horns, bolt cutters, a sledgehammer with a green head, radios, a first aid kit and a satellite phone. They filed on board, sixty-four men scattered about the cabin seats. Kershaw stayed behind.

At 4 p.m. the plane took off, heading due north. It barely had time to climb before landing again, this time in Polokwane, the dry town halfway to the Zimbabwean border. Everyone cleared emigration. It was a warm and sleepy afternoon, late on a Sunday and late in the summer. Back on board, the men settled down to doze, play cards or chat.

In Zimbabwe, Mann finished lunch with Captain Mutize of ZDI. He confirmed his technical problems with planes were over. A Boeing would collect the weapons that evening. He returned to Cresta Lodge and checked the others were ready. At 6 p.m. he sent a message, the last of several, to a contact in South Africa. He confirmed that all was going to plan and he was in position.

At 6.20 p.m. the Boeing lifted from the runway in Polokwane. It reached cruising height some twenty minutes later and crossed the wide Limpopo river, entering Zimbabwean airspace and speeding above the darkening farmland. A few stared from the plane's port side windows as the sun slipped below the horizon.

Niel Steyl, the pilot, radioed the air traffic control tower in Harare. A few days earlier permission had been obtained to land at the airport and proceed to its military zone. He says he called ahead to the airport, reporting a need to stop for fuel and to load cargo. In pilot's parlance, he wanted a 'technical stop'. He claims, too, he admitted to having sixty-eight passengers aboard, but none destined for Harare. 'We landed, refuelled, parked in the military area. We were still in the international airport, but a different apron. We crossed no gates, we were still in no-man's land. We waited two hours. I went to sleep in the cockpit.' Zimbabwean officials recount another story, saying Niel Steyl did not report his passengers, who were concealed in the darkened cabin of the plane. Written instructions were circulated telling the men to keep still and silent after landing. Lights were to remain off. One air traffic controller, Faith Gutsire, says she was told there were only 'three crew on board'.

One of the men on board describes the arrival:

We landed in Harare it was dark. All we knew was we're going to DRC [Congo]. They told us we're in Zimbabwe to get fuel and cargo. Some of us were asleep. Some were in economy class and could not hear. I was at the back, right at the back, back. They told us, 'This is not our destination, we are here to refuel.' There were no written instructions for everybody, just one piece of paper. The lights were on when we landed. Some of us were playing cards, some were drinking, some sleeping. We were three hours on the plane at Harare. We landed at 7 p.m. and stayed until 11 p.m. I was sleeping. Carlse and Loutjkie [Horn] came in and even Simon Mann came in with customs officials. I didn't see him, but he walked in and came out. He said, 'Everything is OK.' Then Hendrik Hamman, the [co]pilot, says he's coming back, he's just having a coffee and he'd be back.

Lourens Horn left Cresta Lodge, in Harare, and went with Mann and Carlse to the military part of the airport that Sunday evening. The 727 had already landed. Carlse spoke to some of the crew on the plane. An official 'told Simon Mann he would inspect the plane as a standard procedure', recalls Captain Mutize. Mann 'tried to resist' and offered a bribe, but Mutize assured him inspection was normal practice. Mutize says Mann first claimed there were only a couple of crew and cargo handlers aboard. Now the story changed. In fact, he said, there were over sixty men 'whom he claimed were medics and logistics personnel'.

Then Carlse, Horn and Mann were asked to inspect the weapons in crates atop pallets in a nearby hangar. Mutize continues: 'While inspection went on, I took Simon Mann and his assistants to the parachute training hangar, where a truck loaded with the arms and ammunition was [parked].' Horn recalls he and Carlse walked up to the crates in the hangar and looked at the weapons. The goods did not correspond to Mann's order, they complained. An operative of the Central Intelligence Organisation – a man called Nhamo Mutasa – was filming from the shadows.

17

The Wonga Coup (Mark Two)

'I woke with a barrel of a gun in my face.'

Footsoldier

Several thousand kilometres north of Zimbabwe, in the Canary Islands, the escort team was ready. From this launching point, Mann's close friend Greg Wales would fly with Severo Moto, the man who would be president, to Equatorial Guinea. They would be flown by Crause Steyl and another pilot, Alex Molteno. David Tremain, the British financier, and Karim Fallaha, the Lebanese investor, were coming along for the ride. This team would fly south east, converging with Mann's team as it flew north and west from Zimbabwe. If all went to plan, Moto would be brought into a secure Malabo airport roughly an hour after Mann had overseen Obiang's removal.

Moto's entourage had been scattered between different hotels on Gran Canaria. Now they gathered at a small coastal airstrip, Club Aeroport. The Beechcraft King Air, registration ZS-NBJ, was primed and ready. Crause Steyl's aviation company had hired it three months earlier in South Africa on a 'dry lease', meaning he provided his own crew and maintenance. Finally it would be used. But, to Steyl's dismay, the airstrip was busy.

That Sunday afternoon, motorbike enthusiasts were using the runway as a racetrack. The event could not be stopped. Steyl and the others were to leave without drawing undue attention to themselves, so could only wait. To their mounting frustration, the bikers droned on for three more hours.

Just before dusk the bikers cleared the strip. One of the men aboard the King Air plane says Molteno took the pilot position on the left of the cockpit while Steyl took the other seat. The cabin was small. At the front sat Tremain, facing sideways. Wales sat on the right, looking forward. At the back were four seats in a square. Moto took the furthest corner on the right side. He had a speech and an economic plan ready. The plan promised to get small things done fast, to show people a better life under the new president. Equatorial Guinea would be the 'star of Africa' and 'a new model for the continent'. The new 'state, discreetly but effectively present' would promote economic growth, cut poverty and push 'monetary orthodoxy'. It was stirring stuff. Opposite sat Karim Fallaha. On Moto's left sat his closest assistant. 'Sargoso was the main planner in the Moto group. He let Moto be as clean as possible, to play the part of Good King Wenceslas,' says one aboard. A minister in Moto's 'government', probably a man called Biyogo, took the last chair.

According to one source on the plane, though no one else volunteered this, another aircraft shadowed the King Air that night: 'There was also another plane on the way to Bamako and I suspect Tremain and Sargoso knew more about that one. It had more Spaniards and Moto's people on board. Sargoso was liaising between the planes.' The source adds obliquely that there were 'Spanish guys, serious ones ... [and] some serious American guys' on the Canary Islands. This plotter implies that the second plane and the unamed 'guys' in fact represented American intelligence, and thus some sort of American approval for the plot.

The take-off was thrilling. Alex Molteno took the controls, leaving Steyl in the co-pilot's seat. He wore a golf hat and explained that he would take the plane low – 'as low as you can go, over the wave tips and below radar for the first 120 miles'. The small aircraft lifted up from beach level, but just to the height of a single-storey house. The idea, explains a plotter, was to lie low beneath the radar screens of local air traffic controllers, allowing officials to say – honestly – there was no record of the plane's departure. 'Which is what the Spanish briefed us to do,' he says. The small flying club is at sea level and they were soon skimming past boats and over a calm sea. The sun was low and the passengers looking from the windows had a view as if they were in a speed boat. They passed two or three cruise liners, glancing up at their funnels and windows. Everyone was briefed not to move. 'If you need to go to the toilet, tough luck. If you need a drink, don't get up, get someone to pass it to you.'

Eventually, to save on fuel and once a safe distance had been reached, the pilot rose up again. Fly too long at a low level and the pilot risks losing a sense of proportion. Steyl explains: 'The danger is you can't judge height over water, there is no reference. A wave can be one centimetre or ten metres.' But for ongoing security the plane's radios were kept silent. There were rumours of a couple of F16 fighter jets in the Canaries, though no one expected them to be scrambled for a departing plane. There was a security lapse, says Steyl: 'An asshole at the airport, a manager at the Club Aeroport, he phoned the bigger tower at the main airport. He told them a plane has just taken off with no flight plan and flying low.' But by sunset the plane was heading towards mainland Africa, to the Moroccan coast and then to the western edge of the great Sahara. By the time the Atlantic had finally given way to desert, the night had set in. They flew 2000 km (1250 miles) to Mali. At this stage the pilots were relaxed, chatting about possible loot in Equatorial Guinea. Steyl had his heart set on some aircraft – 'P51s, Mustangs' – that were sitting somewhere in crates in Malabo. He heard there were three old planes: 'We'd sell one and keep two. We were making plans for how to get them.'

After four hours of flying they neared Bamako, capital of Mali. Steyl decided to pretend they were from a local airport. The plane dropped to 2200 metres (8000 feet) and the pilot announced they were completing a local flight from an airstrip with no tower. Steyl forgets where they claimed to be from – 'I'm not sure where, maybe Timbuktu' – but they landed and bought fuel. They spent an hour on the ground, anxious to make up time, reckoning they were some four hours behind the agreed schedule: 'So now we confirm with Jo'burg that the coup is in progress. But also we don't want to wait on the ground too long. This is a hot place. We try to establish the situation. [I] phone a mystery number for James Kershaw to ask what's happening. I use a secret number that Simon gave me. I say, "James, we've landed. What's next? Shall we go on?" Unfortunately James is not a military man, he's an accountant. He appears calm but clueless. His reply is "Fuck, I don't know, we have problems"'. Next Steyl contacted his brother Niel, the pilot of the plane in Harare. Niel sounded worried and explained he had no idea what was happening. 'He asked if I knew where Simon was. He'd seen him earlier in the evening but he'd disappeared for hours.'

Another man recalls that Sargoso stood alone at Bamako airport and used a satellite phone. He did not trust the others. The men stretched their legs by the runway and waited. A couple of Malian guards lingered nearby. Wales tried telling them jokes in French. Eventually he persuaded the soldiers, with a $100 bill, to slip back into the gloom. Then Sargoso called out. There were problems in Harare. Steyl got the same message from his brother in Harare: 'Then, the very next minute, I got an SMS. He said: "We are all being arrested".'

In Harare the junior ZDI official, Mutize, was unaware of the sting. At first there had been no plan to arrest Mann and the rest. But word had come from South Africa, perhaps that same day. Zimbabwean officials later claimed they planned to detain Mann anyway as he lacked an end user certificate for the weapons. But that notion was cooked up after the event. Probably Mann could have collected his guns in February, no questions asked. But by March, a few weeks on, South Africa had shared the intelligence provided by Morgan and other sources. There lay the difference between possible success and utter failure.

When officials demanded to look inside the 727, Mann admitted over sixty passengers were aboard and reportedly offered a $10,000 'gift' if they looked away. They refused. Mutize took Mann, Carlse and Horn to the parachute hangar, where they opened the crates. 'It was during the inspection that suddenly we were surrounded by armed men in civilian clothes,' recalls Mutize. 'I was confronted by the men who demanded to see the Government of Zimbabwe Authorisation Papers. I showed them the quotation and referred further questions to my superior, Colonel Tshinga Dube.' At that moment plain clothes police and soldiers stormed into the hangar, ordering Mann and the others to stand still. The men were handcuffed and dragged away to vehicles parked outside the hangar. Mann, Horn and Carlse were promptly bundled into separate cars and driven away. Mutize, recognised as a worker for ZDI, was soon freed.

Armed officials barged on to the plane. Niel Steyl says
he, like most of the others on board, was asleep when they
stormed in up the back entrance. Troops with AK-47s ran
up the aisle, seized control and forced the passengers and
crew off at gunpoint. Steyl was slow to catch on. 'I thought
maybe we would be taken to a hotel, I never thought I'd be
arrested until we were outside and I was handcuffed to the
flight engineer [Ken Pain]. Then I thought, OK, it's a problem,
maybe a couple of days.' Kashama Mazanga was also asleep,
in the passenger section. 'When I looked up there was just a
big barrel of a gun touching me and someone saying, "Don't
move."' He was startled and pushed out of the plane into the
warm, dark air. 'You just feel somebody grabbing you and
throw you on the ground and cuff you with leg irons. From
there to the truck.' Ken Pain, the flight engineer, was in shock:
'You just go cold ... wonder what comes next ...'

Niel Steyl calls the arrest an 'abduction', though the plane
was evidently in Zimbabwean territory. Another man did
not believe what was happening: 'I was one of the last to be
arrested. I woke with a barrel of a gun in my face. I thought
at first it was a joke. Some of the men were in military jackets
on top of civilian clothes.' It was unclear whether the officials
were soldiers or police. He was told to stand while his hands
were cuffed behind his back. The arresting men shouted,
in English, 'No funny jokes or we are going to shoot you.'
As the hired gun stumbled down from the American-regis-
tered plane, a bright light was flashed into his face. He saw
almost nothing, but on the side of a police car he read the
word Zimbabwe. The men were made to lie, face down, on the
tarmac and then were bundled into two army trucks, thirty or
so men in each.

Jonathan Samukange, an urbane lawyer, arrived promptly.

He says he was contacted by a lawyer in South Africa within a couple of hours of the plane landing in Zimbabwe, though the timing is suspicious. He was asked to act for Mann and the others. Investigators scrabbled over the Boeing 727. No weapons were on board, but they found military-related material in the Carry All bags and copies of various contracts – for the YKA mining company in Congo, and for the PANAC aviation group in Equatorial Guinea – that Mann hoped to use as a cover. They also found bags containing cash. One had some $30,000 in it to pay for aircraft expenses such as fuel and landing fees. Another, apparently Mann's, contained nearly $100,000. They also found a map of Malabo, with the pizza restaurant marked, the one du Toit had given to Harry Carlse.

Last Chance in Malabo

Late that evening du Toit was preparing to drive to the airport in Malabo when Crause Steyl phoned. 'When I speak to him he says "I was just about to get my boys ready." But I tell him there is something wrong in Harare. I suggest he should go somewhere else. I say, "I'd seriously consider going elsewhere."' Du Toit had the option, with two planes at the airport and a couple of fishing trawlers at his disposal, but he refused. 'In his mind, he didn't do anything wrong. In his legalistic way,' suggests Steyl. Du Toit thought he knew the élite in Malabo well enough and explained, 'It is not necessary to leave.' In that, as with many other things, he was wrong.

Du Toit probably heard the obvious advice from others, too: get out while you can. He was near the airport. Two men on the mainland could have crossed to Cameroon. But he chose to lie low instead, as he had done after the February coup attempt. Perhaps he did not realise how seriously the mission was broken this time. Those in Mali – Moto, Steyl, Wales and others – did not yet know the plot was over. They hoped it might be tried again a few days later. Even some in Harare, like Niel Steyl, thought they faced jail for a night or two at worst. And du Toit did not want to abandon his jealously guarded business, nor be caught while fleeing. Finally he might have hoped that his highly placed friends, notably the president's brother Armengol, would offer protection. For whatever reasons, du Toit called his men and told them to go home to their beds.

The team in Mali, at least, made a wise choice. Moto took the news of his aborted trip well enough. 'Moto was pissed off, but OK. He had thought this was the moment he'd long been waiting for ...' But in the middle of the night it still seemed possible to resurrect the plot one more time. Standing on the edge of the runway, they held a short and heated debate on what to do next. They gathered around a map, prodding at possible destinations. Steyl wanted to fly on to South Africa, perhaps going by Namibia. Moto and his aides preferred Europe, perhaps Malta. The men were irritable and hungry for sleep. Karim Fallaha also wanted to return to Europe. They chose what they knew best, the Canary Islands, a part of Spain. 'At least we know it. We'll get shit, but less shit to manage in Spain than elsewhere,' recalls Steyl.

Some aboard the King Air may not have realised it, but they came close to death soon after leaving Bamako. Steyl says the small plane rose into the darkness and told the control tower it was going to Sao Tome to the south. But with the lights off it turned and headed in the opposite direction, towards the Canaries. 'And as we are taking off, voom, just above our heads, passes a 727.' Africa has by far the worst air safety record in the world, in part because of reckless pilots like these.

Steyl believes it was a commercial airliner also heading for the Canaries, and it passed within metres of the smaller craft. 'Mid-air collisions over Africa, yeah, it wasn't a good thing. But in extraordinary circumstances you have to do this.'

They landed just before dawn at the larger airport on Gran Canaria, because the smaller airstrip, at Club Aeroport, has no lights. They were detained, locked in a basement interrogation room and told to wait three hours. The 'tired and drunk' staff at the airport were suspicious. Steyl had no passport and they noticed the plane had left the night before without a flight plan. But then a Spaniard in a crisp suit appeared. He spoke to Moto for fifteen minutes, then told everybody they were free to go.

Back in Pretoria, Kershaw panicked. The project was in tatters, and he had no idea what to do. Distraught, he phoned his friend Morgan, who told him to get every document relevant to the coup, pack it into his car and race several hundred kilometres south to Morgan's house. If Kershaw confessed all to the South Africans, he might avoid arrest. He drove through the night, reaching Morgan's home at dawn.

Johann Steyl – brother of Crause and Niel – was also disturbed in the middle of the night. Johann, yet another ex-pilot for Executive Outcomes, had known vaguely of the plot. Woken from his bed, he took a rushed call from Niel in Harare. Niel, now realising his plight, begged for a lawyer, just having time to add: 'I am going to be in Harare for a long time.' Johann called others in the family and said his brothers had been caught while 'flying a mercenary force to somewhere in Africa to overthrow some incredibly bad dictator'.

18

Playa Negra Pedicure

'In this game of crooks, who do you trust?'

Jonathan Samukange

By the morning of Monday 8 March the plot was over. But the misery of the plotters had just begun. Reaction to the coup attempt was fierce and furious in Malabo. Just as soldiers took to the streets in 1973 after the abandoned 'dogs of war' coup attempt, the mood darkened in 2004. Many innocent people were promptly rounded up. Equatorial Guinea draws large numbers of foreign workers – especially traders from Cameroon, Gabon, Ghana and Nigeria – to keep the economy moving. After the failed coup, many were intimidated and attacked. On 13 March Obiang said the coup plotters planned to turn 'our city into a blood bath'. He told his people to suspect all outsiders and ordered 'operation clean-up' to expel illegal immigrants. Rich foreigners, notably South Africans who had the misfortune to be in Malabo at the time, were put under hotel arrest. Gangs of xenophobic youths threatened migrant workers in the street, demanding their papers. Many ordinary people were chased from the country. A senior official later told the ruling party's newspaper, *Ebano*, that citizens should beware of foreigners and 'commandos', who 'are more highly trained than an ordinary military officer ... [and] were going to come into Equatorial Guinea under the effects of drugs, and so they were not going to have pity on anyone. Therefore, as Attorney General, I call on the population to be vigilant with foreigners, regardless of colour, because the target is the wealth of Equatorial Guinea, the oil.'

For du Toit and the others, it was the start of ten miserable days. That Monday morning, at 8 a.m., a local business partner told du Toit to show himself at the central police station to 'see about his passport'. He dutifully appeared and was pushed into a cell. Mark Schmidt, the youngest of du Toit's team, shared a house with the Armenian pilots. Shortly after du Toit's arrest, uniformed men surrounded their house and dragged away the Armenians. 'I didn't think anything about it. I thought that's just the way they handle transport problems around here,' he told a journalist later. But it was soon his turn. 'Suddenly there was military everywhere. It was so scary. The soldiers were reeking of alcohol and they were threatening us with weapons. They threw me down and put a gun to my head. I thought I was going to die right there,' said Schmidt.

Heavily armed gangs of soldiers snatched six of du Toit's team in Malabo (du Toit himself, Allerson, Boonzaier, Cardoso, Domingos, Schmidt), six Armenians, plus the German (Merz). Their hands cuffed tightly behind their backs, they were herded into a single cell in the dreaded Black Beach prison. The room was large, some 20 metres by 4 metres (60 feet by 12 feet), but 200 other foreigners – African traders rounded up from the streets – were already there. Allerson was pulled aside and thrown into solitary confinement. Police ransacked their homes in Malabo, stealing phones, money, televisions, music players and other goods. They found no weapons. That evening police on the mainland part of the country pulled two others – Abel Augusto and Americo Ribeiro – from their beds.

Handcuffed, they were brought to Malabo, as officials stole their satellite phones, money and other property. Later several Equatorial Guineans were also grabbed.

Abel Augusto describes conditions in Black Beach: 'Some of the guys were crying, begging for them to loosen the cuffs. Every time you turned, even a little bit, the cuffs tightened more. They'd just say "Too tight?" Then they'd tighten it some more.' For ten days they were beaten. Interrogation was the worst. While interrogators demanded answers they held a flame to the sole of a prisoner's foot. Oddly, the foreign prisoners were given takeaway food in the first week in jail. 'The food never tasted like anything because you were being beaten while eating,' said Augusto. The men would crouch on the floor and eat without using their hands. 'They'd say, "Eat!" So you eat and then, boom! They beat you, kick your plate over. Then they'd say, "Eat!" And it happens again and again,' said Augusto. The men learned to do everything staring at the ground. Eye contact with guards was seen as defiance and punished immediately. 'With your hands cuffed behind your back constantly, you can't do most things. Not even use the toilet. I had to wipe Bones's [Boonzaier] bum for him,' one prisoner later told a South African journalist.

Du Toit got most attention. Like the others, he had no lawyer and was not told why he had been arrested (he first heard the formal charges four months later on the radio). He thought he would be killed, either in jail by a guard, or at an execution. He was kept in solitary confinement much of the time, beaten and tortured. Interrogators from South Africa, Angola, Zimbabwe and Britain (Henry Page, acting for the Equatorial Guinean government) eventually interviewed him, again without lawyers being present. Various confessions were extracted. No prisoner could contact an embassy for help.

A day after his arrest, du Toit was taken to the ministry of foreign affairs. There he confessed to the coup plot before an audience of diplomats and a set of television cameras. The footage was broadcast all over the world. Wearing a green shirt, he was clean-shaven, his hair dark and matted. He implicated Moto, telling the camera that the exile's plane was due to arrive 'half an hour after the people landed with the force from South Africa. They will fly in Severo Moto and a new government from Spain. They will land here and then he will be here on the ground, then he can take over the government.' He said he was freely confessing and had not been tortured. Later he told a lawyer that a gun was being pointed at him and he was being told what to say, on pain of death. Others suffered similar threats. Lawyers who later acted for the detained Armenians said they were told: 'You are going to die. You are terrorists.'

The Malabo Manicure
Du Toit also implicated Mann and the others. The British lawyer working for the Equatorial Guinea government, Henry Page, though aware of the prisoners' conditions and intimidation, soon compiled a pair of long and detailed confessions, dated 24 and 25 March, from du Toit, in which he admitted much of the coup plot. Equatorial Guinean interrogators collected their own confessions from the detained men, usually in Spanish. Du Toit later withdrew some of what he said, and changed his mind on many details. A visiting interrogator from Zimbabwe promised him that full co-operation would mean unconditional release, otherwise he and the rest would simply be killed. Amnesty International and other human rights groups later condemned the

conditions. Du Toit's wife Belinda told the *Sunday Telegraph* of the prisoners' mistreatment. 'For the first four weeks they were hit with sjamboks [whips made from leather hides], kicked and hit. One of the guards stamped on Nick's foot so hard the toenail came off, and they forced handcuffs around his ankles even though they were too small and bit through the flesh …' This abuse was eventually dubbed the 'Malabo manicure' by observers and came to symbolise conditions in Black Beach (though the 'Playa Negra pedicure' would have been more accurate).

Eventually, du Toit was also put before a few foreign journalists to confess his guilt afresh. One, Barbara Jones, quoted the following admission from mid 2004: 'My role was to secure the control tower and change the frequency on the tower radio to 120 MHz to establish communication directly with the incoming aircraft from Harare, Zimbabwe. Then I would drive with another man in the lead car, with the others driving behind us. Another man would be taking one of the groups to the military base near the Haladji hotel. Others would be at the two military bases on the Luba road waiting for us.' According to Jones, other men were supposed to take the mercenaries to the house of Antonio Javier, the president's special adviser, and kidnap him. He would show them where the president slept that night. 'I wasn't in it for the kicks. I wasn't looking for anything but useful employment,' du Toit said. Other versions of du Toit's plan for the evening were published thick and fast. The official indictment later said he planned to attack the central police station, while Cardoso would attack the president's palace.

Either the torture was so bad that du Toit confessed falsely and in detail to the journalists. Or he was willing to spill the beans anyway, so the torture was inflicted as punishment. The worst beatings continued for ten days. One defendant wrote a graphic account on a cigarette packet that was smuggled from of Black Beach. It was dated 10 and 11 March, two days after the arrests. An Amnesty report later quoted it:

10/3 22h00–23h00 I was taken to the police station for interrogation. I had no lawyer. I was asked many questions. I had no answers for them.

1. *Handcuffs tightened and cut into my flesh, into bone of right hand. In the office.*
2. *I was beaten with the fist. I had no answers ... Beaten on head and jaw.*
3. *They took me to a small dark room down the stairs into the police courtyard. Here I was put on the ground. A dim light was burning. I saw Sergio Cardoso hanging, face down, in the air with a pole through his arms and legs. The police guard started asking questions which I still could not answer. Every question a guard would stand on my shin bone, grinding the skin and flesh of the right leg with the military boots. This carried on for at least 30 minutes. I was shouting, begging them to stop.*
4. *Later I begged them rather shoot me for I could not take the pain and agony anymore ... After no answers it stopped. I was taken back at 2 o'clock ...*
6. *11/3 about 15h00 I was tied to a bed with cuffs on my right hand. I was beaten and slapped ... my right thumb broke.*
7. *At my bed ... I was beaten with a blow unconscious.*
8. *The same afternoon I was burnt with a lighter.*
9. *At 17h00 I was taken to the police station and told to write everything I knew. Anything that came to my mind. I will have the same and worse treatment of the previous evening. I was terrified and wrote down as if I was involved in everything (which*

I was not) because they were to torture me again.

10. *About six weeks later I had septicaemia … pus was running out of my wound … my ankle was heavily swollen of the infection …*

They Must be Killed, the Devils

If Obiang did slip out of Equatorial Guinea at the time of the coup attempt, he was soon back and rubbing his hands with delight. He launched into a speech, roughly a week after the arrests, making it clear what du Toit and the others could expect. 'The terrorists, who have been arrested, will go through a fair trial,' he claimed, but if 'the actions towards us are judged as dreadful, the laws of Equatorial Guinea will determine how to punish them; if they have to be killed, they will be killed. Because Equatorial Guinea has not abolished the death penalty, we won't forgive them. If we have to kill them, we will kill them. If we have to give them life in prison, they will stay in jail for the rest of their lives in Equatorial Guinea, so this serves as an example and a lesson to others who try to do the same.'

But his belief in the rule of law was not convincing. He also told his countrymen to look out for others who may try a plot:

> … we have to eliminate these terrorists, we have to kill them without the need of taking them to justice. Nobody will ask us if they are killed in the act because they have come with bad intentions … I have been informed that there are others who are preparing themselves. Now that we know, they will not be detained, they will be killed immediately … Starting right now, whoever presents themselves as a mercenary, there will be no need to come let the President know, they must be

liquidated, they must be killed because they are the devils.

A few days later it became clear what treatment mercenaries could expect. By 17 March, Saint Patrick's Day, the men had endured ten days of ill treatment and most were crammed together in one cell. That day Gerhard Merz, the German arms trader and aviation contractor, was dragged out for interrogation. There are various versions of what happened next. Prison officials said Merz suffered an unusually quick attack of cerebral malaria. Johann Smith said the arrested men were 'manhandled', 'as you would expect', and Merz, overweight with a bad heart, could not cope. Smith thought him 'a heart attack waiting to happen'. Fellow prisoners later said Merz died in front of them, in the cell, after torture. Abel Augusto said Merz enraged the interrogators. 'When they hit him, he never said a word.' This provoked more severe battering. 'After one beating he started speaking in German, which he never did before'. Dumped back in the cell, he was in wretched shape. Fellow prisoners called for medical help but were ignored. He collapsed, apparently from a massive heart attack. 'We watched him die. We were waiting for our time also,' Augusto said later.

Amnesty later reported that Merz 'collapsed in the cell. The other detainees called the guards, who reportedly dragged him into the bathroom and poured water on him, apparently to revive him. He was then taken to hospital but he was already dead on arrival.' No autopsy was done and the body was only released three months later, in June, to German authorities. A German official saw Merz's body the day after his death and noted marks around the wrist and ankles (from cuffs) and bruises on the torso, apparently made during the resuscitation efforts. The official could not examine the entire body. When an autopsy was finally done in Germany, it was found Merz had not died of malaria.

But nobody much cared that Merz was dead. Germany has no embassy in Equatorial Guinea, and few – human rights groups aside – bothered to protest at the murder of a man named by the United States as a suspected trader in chemical weapons. The death sent out a powerful warning, though, both in Equatorial Guinea and in Zimbabwe. Those in Black Beach decided to co-operate fully, desperate to avoid the same fate.

19

Send Me a Splodge

'It may be that getting us out comes down to a large splodge of wonga!'

Letter from Simon Mann

The men arrested in Zimbabwe fared a little better. Most were bundled off together that night and taken to a maximum security prison, Chikurubi, outside Harare. Niel Steyl was thrown alone into a bare police holding cell. No inmate is supposed to spend more than twenty-four hours in one of those. He was there for a week. 'I had to bribe a policeman with US$100 for drinking water and so I could get access to my phone. I called my family and my girlfriend,' he said later. One text message he sent to his mother read: 'I am well, I am strong, I will survive. I love you.' His initial hope for a hotel turned into prolonged fear of death. Zimbabwe's foreign minister, Stan Mudenge, said he hoped to hang the foreign 'terrorists'.

By Tuesday, two days after his arrest, Mann had drafted and signed a handwritten statement, confessing in detail and giving information on others. He had no lawyer present and the confession was never used in court in Zimbabwe. He later retracted it, saying he was 'brutally and severely tortured and assaulted for several days', adding that others 'dictated to me what I should write and at every instance that I objected I was subjected to further torture and assaults. The police then typed the handwritten statement which was brought to my cell and which I was forced to sign ... I wish to make it quite clear that the version of events described in the statement is substantially untrue.' But Mann's lawyers are reluctant to discuss details of his torture, and a copy of the long and detailed statement in Mann's handwriting does not show any obvious signs of the author's distress. However, the SAS man was certainly threatened. 'I was taken to the airport and shown an aeroplane; I was told that it was ready to take me to Equatorial Guinea unless I did exactly what I was told.'

Others were equally horrified. Several interrogated in Zimbabwe promptly gave detailed confessions. Harry Carlse quickly admitted he was going to Equatorial Guinea to 'displace the president' and that a 'former politician who was violently disposed will be flown in to displace him'. He also confessed to training 'about sixty black guys' for the operation. He gave detailed descriptions of pay scales and the roles of others. Simon Witherspoon said he had been recruited by Mann and Kershaw and admitted being involved in a contract 'to assist the military and police of the new government' in Equatorial Guinea where 'there were some political problems'.

By mid March the plot was completely blown to pieces. Some hundred men were jailed in two African countries. James Kershaw escaped arrest by co-operating promptly with South African investigators, aided by Morgan. Later Crause Steyl followed suit, giving investigators a long account of his role. Ivan Pienaar, Carlse and Lourens Horn and others did so, too. Severo Moto and his aides returned to Madrid. He refused to speak about what happened beyond saying he had no role in a coup that did not happen. When a French documentary film crew asked why du Toit and others named him as a conspirator, he replied blithely that they must have been forced to lie. He and Calil refused to give interviews. A well-informed friend called Karim Kobrossi was supposed, much later, to set the record straight for Calil for the purposes of this book, with an off-the-record discussion. But at the last minute he grew nervous and withdrew, refusing to reschedule.

In London some pitiful efforts were made for those in jail. Steyl approached Tony Buckingham, Wales (now back in London) and others for funds to pay lawyers. The cigar-chomping Buckingham offered £2000, which an insulted Steyl refused. Steyl said he and Wales told Amanda Mann soon after the arrest of her husband. 'Amanda was pretty cool in the beginning. Greg spoke to her and said it's been a fuck up. I told her that he [Simon] might be dead. The Zimbabweans were not admitting they had him.' Rebecca Gaskin, the well-connected American friend of the family, rushed to her side. Wales, who is fond of masquerades, issued feeble statements on behalf of Mann's company, Logo Logistics, using the name Charles Burrows. (Though Wales has denied he is Burrows, phone and internet records suggest otherwise.) He claimed the men in Harare were mere guards due to work in Congo, briefly adding to public confusion. But a mining journal soon made it clear that the cover story was feeble. Mine owners in eastern Congo lined up to say that they would never need sixty machine-gun-toting foreigners. 'That's a mini army,' said one. Mostly they hired local, unarmed guards.

Phone records at this time showed a flurry of conversations between several people who crop up in the story of the Wonga Coup. There were the four calls between the homes of Ely Calil and Jeffrey Archer, the novelist, earlier that year; Archer's lawyers admitted that there were calls between

Calil's home and Archer's home, but suggested that at least one call did not involve Lord Archer. Then Wales made five calls to Mark Thatcher in the days after it. Henry Page, the lawyer who works for Equatorial Guinea's government, later suggested: 'The calls … provide substantial links between the conspirators around the time of the coup attempt.'

There were several other noteworthy phone conversations around this time, too. Greg Wales, by one reckoning, was in repeated contact with Mann, Calil, Karim Fallaha, Mark Thatcher, Crause Steyl, Morgan, Kershaw and others before the coup. Wales and Morgan, in particular, spoke endlessly, including six times in the two days after the arrests in Zimbabwe and Equatorial Guinea and roughly a hundred times in early 2004. Wales and Morgan spoke by phone at dawn, a few hours after Mann's arrest. Wales called Calil a dozen times in mid February, at exactly the time of the first coup attempt. He then called Fallaha fifteen times in the days before the March attempt. Phone records also show Calil phoning Moto more than a hundred times over many months before and after the coup attempt, plus some fifty calls to Mann, including many in the month before the March attempt was launched. Other records show constant contact between the various plotters. What is striking is how the flurries of phone calls between many of the plotters increase markedly on and around the dates of the two coup attempts.

By 15 March the Spanish prime minister, Jose Maria Aznar, retired and his ruling party, the Partido Popular (PP), suffered a surprise defeat at the polls. No one suggests the coup plot affected the result. Four days earlier, Islamists set off several bombs in Madrid, dispelling any thoughts of Africa. Though Equatorial Guinea continued to claim that Spain backed the coup plot – which seemed evidently true – few took notice.

The new government in Madrid refused to discuss any clandestine initiatives of its predecessor.

Some foreign journalists could visit Equatorial Guinea. They strolled by Malabo's yellow and red buildings, walked under palm trees and gazed over the harbour where rusting cannons pointed to the grey sea. Walls were turning black from mould. Tropical vegetation choked everything, plants sprung up from cracks in the road and seemed to grow as one watched. A few reporters tried to leave the city to see what rural Equatorial Guineans thought of the whole affair, but police turned them back, threatening arrest. They badly beat one locally hired interpreter. It was a sinister, unwelcoming place. One reporter, widely travelled in Africa, found an untypical 'disdain for foreigners'. Most Africans are enthusiastic and generous towards outsiders, but here the people ignored him, refusing to talk. Another found Malabo residents 'surly and arrogant'.

On 17 March President Obiang strode into a hall at the People's Palace for a press conference, a rare event. The palace had a Spanish atmosphere. Patterned tiles covered the base of many walls. Obiang stood before a wooden screen. His Moroccan guards scowled a few steps away. He explained that the crisis was over and reassured everybody that 'government morale was high' (an anxious world sighed with relief). He thanked Angola, South Africa and Zimbabwe. It was at roughly this time that prison warders beat the German to death. Despite evidence to the contrary, Obiang emphatically denied that his brother, Armengol, had any business relationship with du Toit or any part in the coup, saying that he would have known if it were the case. Some in government promptly grumbled that Armengol had been let off the hook.

Smelly and Scratcher

Now Mann and the rest had to make the best of a desperate situation. They faced long jail terms, possibly execution. Their best chance was if interest in the story withered, so that their wealthy or powerful friends could work quietly on their release. But for journalists, criminal investigators, lawyers and the general public, March 2004 was not the end of the tale but the first chapter of a gripping story. Various versions and details of the coup would leak out in the coming months. Arrests, trials and plea bargains drew renewed media attention to an improbable escapade that was, appropriately, dubbed the new Dogs of War, after Forsyth's novel.

A proud South African intelligence service did nothing to hide its role in foiling the coup plot. But evidence was left 'strewn on the battlefield, nobody buried the bodies', complained Morgan. Documents, witness testimonies and conflicting versions of the coup plot soon appeared in public. Then Morgan was asked to compile further reports about the coup plot by the South Africans. He flew to London and interviewed Wales, Calil and others connected to Mann. They may have been under the impression that Morgan was seeking ways to spring Mann from Zimbabwe. In fact, Morgan was collecting the background detail for his intelligence report for the South Africans. He would later be accused of betraying his friends, though he denied it. One South African prosecutor later suggested there might be recriminations against those who helped foil the plot: 'I don't know if there will be violence. I don't know the band of brothers so well. You won't get away with double-crossing the likes of Carlse and others. If you are a snitch, you are a snitch. I don't think they will smile for Nigel Morgan. But I don't know if they know of Morgan's role. At first Johann Smith was accused of being the snitch. I know he has been threatened many times.'

Later much information was leaked to the press. Wales planted his own stories. Henry Page passed on all sorts of evidence and tips to reporters, who willingly published what they were given. But the document that caused most excitement when it was leaked (though only some months later) was a handwritten letter from Mann in prison. It is dated 21 March, a few days before his first court appearance in Zimbabwe and some two weeks after his arrest. In it, he confirms he knew his cover story of hiring guards for Congo was feeble. He also implicates several others. The letter is addressed to four people: Amanda, his wife; James Kershaw, his assistant; Rebecca Gaskin, a well-connected American, and Morgan. A website address is included on one version of the letter that has been circulated (this has been carefully deleted on others), referring to a website run by Wales in London.

It is a plea for help. Mann worried that his lawyers, Alwyn Griebenow, a South African, and Jonathan Samukange, a Zimbabwean, were getting little co-operation or money.

Sunday 21st March 2004

Please! It is essential that we get properly organised. Please trust and work with Alwyn and Jonathan and the others. They are getting frustrated that they cannot deal with Amanda or with James. Apparently they have been told that they must deal with Rebecca and Nigel. That is fine in principle: but then they are told that Nigel and Rebecca are meeting on TUESDAY etc. etc.

Our situation is not good and it is very URGENT. They get no reply from Smelly and Scratcher asked them to ring back after the Grand Prix race was over! This is not going well.

What we need is maximum effort – whatever it takes – NOW. We seriously do NOT need the guys on the ground (Alwyn, Jonathan etc.) having their lives made more difficult! I am sure that is not what you are trying to do but it is the way it seems to them – which to us – is very upsetting.

The main point is this: do not accept that things are OK or that the local legal system is going to get us through OK. It will not.

I must say once again: what will get us out is MAJOR CLOUT. We need heavy influence of the sort that Rebecca, Smelly, Scratcher, Nigel, David Hart [have] and it needs to be used heavily and now.

Once we get into a real trial scenario we are f—d. The opportunity lies in our deportment from Z to SA. The window dressing for this is that in SA we will face the Foreign Military Assistance Act. That would be fine. This can suit Z because they look good and SA do – BUT it will only go with major influence being applied at BOTH ends simultaneously.

Everyone has to work together, NOW, to achieve this.

I know you are also trying your best – but so are these guys:

Please – cannot Amanda and/or Rebecca and/or Nigel actually come here and then talk to me with Alwyn present. That way we can get working together. We need to do so ASAP or it will be too late.

Love to all,
Simon Mann

The letter proved useful to prosecuters and journalists, but not to Mann. It never reached those it was intended for. Instead, it got to the indefatigable British press. The references to 'Smelly' and 'Scratcher' proved explosive. Nobody doubted that Mann meant Ely Calil when he complained that Smelly ignored calls from his lawyers. Though Calil denied the pungent nickname was his, he may not have known what others called him. Nor did anyone think Scratcher could be anyone but Mark Thatcher. He tried at first to reject the nickname, but his biography notes he was called 'Mork Scratcher' at school. And the refusal to be distracted from a car race by a desperate friend in prison sounds all too much like Thatcher.

One of Thatcher's friends relates the Grand Prix incident. Thatcher is a car enthusiast and soon after the coup attempt he was interrupted by a call from a gruff Afrikaner. The caller sounded threatening and asked for money. Thatcher said he did not give cash to strangers and told him to get lost, saying 'I'm watching the Grand Prix.' He later explained to *Vanity Fair* magazine that 'I tend not to give money to people whom I've never met and when I don't know what it's for'. He subsequently reported the incident to the police. But there were more calls, including some where the caller spoke of knowing 'where your children go to school'. Thatcher felt the caller was trying to extract money with menaces. Morgan eventually got a call, too. He also sensed a threatening manner.

Soon afterwards, one of Griebenow's assistants, Dries Coetzee, was in London. He met Wales at the Savoy hotel and asked for money to feed the prisoners in Zimbabwe and pay defence lawyers. He called himself the gatekeeper who had access to Mann, and claimed he was the 'only one doing anything about the welfare of the prisoners in Zimbabwe', who 'had to be fed', so 'where is the money coming from?' He also said Mann had authorised him to ask for money from certain friends and demanded $100,000. Wales refused.

Coetzee reportedly said, 'We are going to come after you people', which Wales took as a threat. Coetzee returned to South Africa with nothing. Eventually the defence did raise some funds by selling a plane, an Aerostar 600 that Mann had bought a year earlier for $350,000. It was a curious transaction. Mann gave Griebenow power of attorney on 14 March to let him sell it, to pay the lawyers and more. It was rumoured to be sold for a mere $75,000.

The 'major clout' that Mann wanted, possibly through Coetzee, was money for Zimbabwean officials to smooth their deportation to South Africa. To his credit he wrote not only about his own predicament but showed a concern for the others detained. In South Africa they could expect a trial under a decent legal system and, almost certainly, more lenient sentences. But South Africa did not want Mann and his band of men. A case was brought in South Africa's constitutional court, arguing that the government had a duty to seek the extradition of its nationals from prison in Zimbabwe. The case failed and the government refused to ask either Equatorial Guinea or Zimbabwe to deport their prisoners.

Wonga

Then a third page of writing was leaked. This was hand-written, too, apparently by Mann (though in block capitals). Scratcher is named again, along with one Gianfranco Cicogma, who may have promised to invest, and a 'GW'. The amount Mann and 'JK' believed each person owed, presumably in units of 1,000 US dollars, is marked in brackets. The page is not signed. It reads:

> ... this is a situation that calls for everyone to act in concert. It
> may be that getting us out comes down to a large splodge of

wonga! Of course investors did not think this would happen. Did I? Do they think they can be a part of something like this with only upside potential – no hardship or risk of things going wrong? Anyone and everyone in this is in it – good times or bad. Now its [sic] bad times and everyone has to f—ing well pull their full weight.

Anyway JK was expecting project funds inwards to Logo from 'Scratcher' (he of the 'Scratcher' suite) (200); from Gianfranco Cicogma (200) and GW (500). GW's was for last resort use only – this is the last resort. As I say, if there is not enough then present investors must come up with more.

Thus the word 'wonga' became closely associated with Mann and the coup plot. For most newspaper readers around the world, wonga meant nothing at all. The English slang baffled most who heard it. The term was used in England, first by Romany (gypsy) people to mean coal, then to mean money. The phrase 'a splodge of wonga' – a large pile of cash – is typical of the schoolboy idiom that Mann likes.

And how did the letter (or letters) come to be published rather than delivered? That probably came down to wonga, too. Mann handed it to someone in prison, and after that it went astray, most likely sold to the highest bidder. His lawyer in London, Anthony Kerman, says diplomatically: 'The person who was entrusted with the letter, I hypothesise, clearly the person who was entrusted with the letter was not very careful.' His lawyer in Zimbabwe, Jonathan Samukange, asks rhetorically: 'In this game of crooks, who do you trust?'

Nobody, of course.

20

Smiling and Dying

'I was extremely distressed, disoriented and extremely vulnerable.'

Simon Mann

The accused were shackled hand and foot, in pairs, and dressed in regulation prison garb of khaki shirts and baggy shorts, plus sandals. They walked, many limping, beside a high fence. Guards with swagger sticks kept them in line. Zimbabwe's authorities had decided to convene a court inside Chikurubi prison, in a former hospital ward, and try the plotters promptly. The courtroom was makeshift: rows of single-plank benches for the defendants and the same arrangement for the press. Mann, wearing small, round glasses and a short beard, looked more a scruffy professor than a snarling dog of war. The beefy Afrikaners were Hulk-like in their green prison clothes. At least one had sewn an extra patch of cloth into his shirt. Small handcuffs cut into their thick wrists.

Mann got no 'major clout'. It probably would have done him little good anyway. By late March he and the others saw the 'trial situation' begin, with the first of many court appearances. Samukange, the politically connected lawyer who took up the defence case in Zimbabwe, said the men were held for immigration offences, while prosecutors dreamt up other charges. Interviewed in Harare, Samukange explained: 'Initially they prepared ten charges, including ridiculous counts, such as contravening a UN resolution on terrorism and mercenaries that has not even been adopted by our parliament. There were many other crazy things, charges about coups, you name it, they thought of all sorts of things.' But it became clear it was impossible to charge anyone with more than relatively trivial charges: 'conspiracy to possess firearms, immigration offences and aviation offences'.

Zimbabwe has not entirely lost the rule of law under Robert Mugabe. But the state can strongly bend legal process in its favour. Samukange said he received a clear message as the trial got underway. If the accused did not plead guilty, the state would drag out the case for years. There would be many excuses to do so, given seventy accused. Whenever somebody fell sick, the trial could be postponed, leaving the accused to rot in jail. So Samukange advised most of his clients to plead guilty to the immigration and aviation offences, as these normally carry low sentences, usually fines. In return, he expected the more serious firearms offence to be dropped for most of them. 'Legally they should have pleaded not guilty, but a trial of seventy prisoners would take two years. Then they would be convicted, as it is a political case. "At the end of the day the magistrate is an ex-combatant selected to convict you," I told them. "Then you would appeal to the High Court, and your appeal would go on to the Supreme Court where another judge is waiting. So the quickest and wisest thing for you to do is to plead guilty." Already two of our guys were sick. The prosecution could say, "We delay the trial until they are well."'

So the men appeared in court and did what they were told. The first appearance passed smoothly. It was a chance for Zimbabwe to display its captured mercenaries. But behind the scenes things were not so calm: at the end of the month a dozen guards allegedly stripped fifteen of the arrested men and beat them with batons. Mann, too, was in an uncomfortable position. There was speculation he would be murdered by his embittered co-accused. Though he was probably unaware of it, some families of the poorest footsoldiers said they would like to see him killed for dragging their men into trouble. Yet those jailed with him recall that the black inmates continued to address Mann as 'Sir'. Instead, the white ones, notably Louis du Prez, 'wanted to kill him, to fight with him', explained an ex-prisoner later. Du Prez and Mann were separated.

Mann in particular endured weeks of intense interrogations. The British lawyer Henry Page, who worked for Equatorial Guinea, appeared in Harare and asked Samukange for permission to see the accused. Page wanted evidence against the financiers, the men discussed in the media as being on the 'Wonga List'. Samukange refused, but Page went ahead anyway. He spoke to Mann and produced a statement that Mann later said was given involuntarily. Mann was to testify that:

By the time I saw Mr Page I was extremely distressed, disoriented and extremely vulnerable. My physical and mental condition would clearly have been apparent to Mr Page. I informed Mr Page that I did not want to see him unless my lawyer was present. Mr Page informed me and kept on informing me during our 'interview' that it was not necessary for my lawyer to be present as our conversation was completely off the record. He said that he felt very sorry for me and undertook 'to sort out everything with the President of Equatorial Guinea' and that all I had to do was to speak openly with him. Mr Page then dictated to me a series of events to which I did not respond, he wrote on a piece of paper as he spoke.

Mann's lawyer in Zimbabwe, Samukange, said his client was put under enormous pressure to confess and name financiers to be prosecuted in a civil case in Britain. Samukange said conditions were 'very bad, terrible. He is kept in a cell with all the others. The guys from Equatorial Guinea tried to break him down. He slept chained to the bed from his ankle and from his arm. Henry Page came here ... They wanted Mann to admit, to get a confession.' A Guernsey court also expressed its 'concern that Mr Page as an English solictor had made almost no attempt to answer' allegations about his behaviour.

But the court was, at first, unaware of Mann's conditions and the situation in which Page had collected evidence. Page's legal team launched a civil case in London saying two companies and four individuals financed the plot: Mann's two firms, Logo Logistics and Systems Design Limited, as well as Mann himself, Greg Wales, Calil and Moto. On the basis of Mann's confession, Page won a legal order forcing the Royal Bank of Scotland to supply details of one of Mann's bank accounts to the prosecutors. In May the bank did so. Later, when the British judges were better informed of Mann's conditions, the ruling was reversed and the bank was told not to pass on any more bank details. But the information already gathered from Mann's Logo Logistics dollar account proved spectacular. The most juicy details, including the interesting payment from the mysterious J. H. Archer, soon leaked to the press.

The civil case was lodged with the English High Court. The claimants – the Equatorial Guinean government, notably Obiang – wanted financial damages from the accused for the 'conspiracy to overthrow the government so as to profit financially'. These were to be arrived at by calculating the costs of extra presidential security in Equatorial Guinea, and of detaining and trying the conspirators. The case was farcical. Prosecutors wanted a British court to order that Obiang – a fabulously wealthy and corrupt dictator who had himself snatched power in a coup and had his own uncle executed – be compensated for 'mental anguish'. To proceed, Obiang would supposedly appear in court in person and submit to a cross-examination of his own past and human rights record. Page claimed that Obiang was willing to do this.

But Page was busy in other areas. Most seriously, he wanted action from Britain's anti-terrorist branch, saying that those who plan a violent coup are terrorists and should be treated as such, even if they happen to be white, Eton-educated aristocrats, not brown-skinned Islamists. He also sought legal redress in Lebanon against companies registered there, which he said were involved in the coup plot.

Harare
Back in Zimbabwe, the prisoners suffered more miserable months. Chikurubi is a hellish place. Built by Rhodesia's whites decades earlier, it has always been brutal. By 2004 it was rundown and packed far beyond capacity: 3000 inmates crammed in cells designed for 900. Samukange called it a terrible place with no water. Prisoners drank a little water from cans; toilets were not flushed. 'The shit is piling up in the toilets. It is only a matter of time before there is a cholera outbreak,' explained Samukange.

One of the footsoldiers later said, 'Chikurubi was like a German concentration camp. A place of death, where you go to die. It is not a place of rehabilitation. We thought we'd perish there.' He recalled prisoners died in his cell almost every day. Some forty people were crammed into space for half the number. Many died simply of hunger: prison rations were typically a small portion of rice once a day. And though this is Africa, Harare is at a high altitude and gets icy cold in winter. Errol Harris recalls 'eating rats, eating pigeons which I killed in prison'. He 'received blankets, but we also received the lice'.

All the inmates were shocked by the lack of food. Niel Steyl describes a daily meal as 'just three bean pips and a spoon of cabbage. It takes a guy with no help from outside six months. Then his skin starts cracking, he loses his balance. [The disease is] called pellagra. None of them complain. It affects the brain. They are smiling and dying. They eventually have difficulty walking. They take one step forward, then another backwards. In time the other prisoners carry them out in the morning and back to the cells in the evening. Nothing is done for them. Then they die.'

Others noted how men lay down like sardines at night, and by morning found corpses among them. They soon learned not to try and wake men who appeared to oversleep. 'The strange thing was, the doctor comes to certify him dead. But even when they take the body away they put him in leg irons and handcuffs. There was no mortuary. Bodies were put in a room for as much as a week. They were decomposing. They just pile up the bodies. The smell ...' One footsoldier died, apparently of meningitis. Two more were released on medical grounds.

Wealthier men suffered less. Gifts from visitors – cheese, dried meat, fruit – meant that many ate better than their guards. Niel Steyl coped by keeping fit: 'I was in a section where you couldn't run. So I climbed instead.' Each morning he climbed a concrete bench in his cell 900 times, calculating that was the equivalent of walking to the top of the World

Trade Center and down again. But all feared death. His fifty-fourth day in jail was the worst. Apparently an escape was suspected so in the middle of the night five white plotters were dragged out of their cells.

I thought that they were going to stage an escape and shoot us. We were put in a vehicle and driven out. All of us were shit scared. In the van were Hendrik Hamman, Ken Pain, Raymond Archer, Louis du Prez and me. We were sitting there in our khaki shorts, khaki shirts. We thought, if this vehicle stops in the veld, they will open the back door. There wouldn't be many options. You couldn't run far or fast in leg irons. You couldn't offer a bribe or beg for your life. We thought we would get bullets in the back of the head.

[Instead they went to another prison.]

I was taken downstairs, along a long passage, then they threw open a door and pushed me through into a lit room. All over the floor were bodies, ninety-five men sleeping, lying on the concrete floor like worms. I stood a while. Then I sat in the space where the door had opened. I did nothing for half an hour. Then I saw a Gideon bible by someone and I asked if I could have it. I looked for the book of Job to find someone suffering more than I was. I read for half an hour. Then the warder opened the cell and removed my handcuffs. He went out again and a prisoner called over and said, 'You see, it works. If you just read some more he will come back and take off your leg irons!'

Prisoners mostly smoked the bibles, calling the cigarettes 'gumbototo'. The thin pages burn well. Cigarettes became currency. A 2-kilo (4-lb) bag of sugar cost a packet of twenty. A jar of peanut butter cost ten, and a bucket of water two.

Even starving prisoners gave up food for them. Steyl did not smoke, so used them to buy clothes off other prisoners' backs. He also bartered for fruit, milk powder and fresh bread. He also hired a servant. 'I had a butler. I paid him cigarettes to make my bed, wash my stuff. He is called Learnfirst Chipika. He's going to come and work for me. It's agreed. He gets out on 12 December 2010.'

Finally – a taboo subject – many prisoners practised unprotected sex. Zimbabwe has a terrifying rate of HIV: roughly one in three adults is infected. Prisons help spread the virus. More than half the inmates in Chikurubi were thought to have AIDS. Hunger combined with the disease produces terrifying death rates. Steyl explained: 'Homosexualism is rife, even among men who would not do it outside. It is only because there are no females around. It happens in the open.' Older men protected younger ones in return for sex. 'The youngster does it to survive.' But the punishment for doing so was brutal. 'At 8 a.m., with the whole prison watching, the guys who were caught having sex are made to lie on the ground with their feet in the air, feet facing up. Then the guards beat the soles of their feet with rubber batons. I have counted up to 300 shots on each foot. Every bone in the foot is broken. One guy's feet swelled up like elephants' feet. He couldn't walk for a week. Other prisoners had to carry him.'

Mann's conditions were marginally better than average, said Samukange in 2005. 'In Simon Mann's hall there are ten of them. He sleeps alone in his own cell ... He has a small mattress, a pillow. He is allowed books as long as they are not about escaping from prison.' He read the Complete Works of Shakespeare and was said to be writing his own book and learning Shona (the main language of Zimbabwe). Niel Steyl describes Mann's prison life. 'Each day he runs around a courtyard, he does 200 laps daily. Around the courtyard – I've been there and measured it out – is sixty metres. So that is a twelve-kilometre run each day. Then, once a month, he does a half marathon. In his cell one of the four walls is bars, a metal grid. So you can see across a passage and talk to the other guys. Simon is locked in his cell for nineteen out of twenty-four hours. But at least he can see out and talk to other guys.'

21

Riggs and the Oil Firms

*'Oil companies operating in Equatorial Guinea may have
contributed to corrupt practices.'*

US Senate report, July 2004

By mid 2004 Obiang had good reason to feel content. The
Wonga Coup had failed. Legal cases against his enemies were
underway in several countries. Some hundred plotters were
in jail. And his government, long shunned for human rights
abuses while poor, had found new friends. Most notably,
relations had improved with South Africa, the dominant
power on the continent. Then Spain grew friendlier, too. The
ruling party (of course) won the local elections in April. Obiang
visited South Africa late in April for Thabo Mbeki's reinau-
guration as president. After that, he visited Zimbabwe and
saw his new friend Robert Mugabe, too. According to some
reports, he even visited Chikurubi prison one night to observe
those who had planned to depose him; Niel Steyl believed it
was possibly the same night that he and the others had feared
they would be executed.

Back home Obiang decreed a campaign to improve Equatorial Guinea's international image. No longer would he be
seen as a bent dictator. He was a victim of foreign aggression,
the head of a 'fledgling democracy'. His was a plucky little

country that had defied foreign pillagers. Little matter that coups were made more likely by his own misrule. But just as Obiang began to enjoy his new, warmer image, trouble struck. In the middle of 2004 American investigators and the US Senate threw open Obiang's overstuffed Washington DC bank accounts to the public gaze, laying bare the unethical practices of despots, banks and oil companies alike.

In July 2004, the United States Senate released a report on a terribly dull issue: banking regulation. Due to the rise of terrorism and global organised crime, American banks were required to crack down on money laundering and other bad practices. No longer were they allowed to take deposits from someone – a tin pot dictator, for example – who might be expected to be corrupt, unless given proof the money was from a legitimate source. As a test case, an investigative committee in the Senate chose to look hard at a Washington DC bank, Riggs Bank, which did much business with embassies and foreign politicians. Riggs also had a reputation for taking some of its regulatory obligations lightly, and an investigation by the *Los Angeles Times* in 2003 suggested Obiang kept hundreds of millions of dollars in the bank.

Investigators were interested in at least six Riggs accounts held by former dictator Augusto Pinochet, who had long led the military regime that had overseen murder and torture in Chile. In 2004 investigators found his personal accounts at Riggs were crammed with dollars (the balance ranged from $4 million to $8 million over the years). They concluded that Riggs had not asked proper questions about the source of Pinochet's money and the bank had helped Pinochet set up 'shell' corporations to disguise his identity. The same investigation threw up 'troubling facts' relating to 150 accounts connected to Saudi Arabia, many of them controlled by a Saudi prince.

The investigators also looked at Riggs' largest client (by 2003), President Obiang. Equatorial Guinea had opened its first Riggs account in 1995, just as oil had been discovered. Over the next decade a triangle of partners had established bad habits: in one corner Riggs; in the next, Obiang and family; finally, some American oil companies. A Riggs manager, Simon Kareri, looked after some sixty accounts linked to Obiang and other members of the ruling family, sharing a cosy relationship with them and visiting Equatorial Guinea to give financial advice. He even had signing rights on one account himself. He brought to the bank suitcases crammed with dollars, which had been provided by officials and diplomats from Equatorial Guinea. There were scenes you would expect in a gangster movie. Twice such cash deposits by suitcase involved $3 million dollars, which meant the case weighed about 30 kilos (more than 60 pounds). The notes were usually in unopened, plastic-wrapped bundles. But the source was impossible to trace. The bank rarely asked anyway, and Obiang – or other account holders, like his wife – did not say.

Aggregate deposits in these Riggs accounts ranged from $400 million to $700 million. It was blindingly obvious that a dictator of a poor African country was stealing oil revenues and stashing them in his private accounts at a rate that would make Pinochet green with envy. And Riggs was helping him do it. While Obiang's family bought mansions and luxury cars, Equatorial Guinea spent the least of any government anywhere on health, education and other public services. An internal bank report noted Obiang's government was awful: 'management of the oil sector may even become more opaque, and standards of governance are like[ly] to remain poor ... Human rights have been an endemic problem ...' Yet Riggs happily set up new accounts, then tried to hide his wealth (as with Pinochet) in offshore shell corporations. Apologists said the benign despot planned to use this money to benefit his people later. He feared others would steal it, so he hid it in his own accounts. In fact, Obiang proved no different from his mad uncle Macias, who stuffed the national treasury in a wooden hut in the jungle.

Senate investigators concluded that Riggs behaved abominably. Its staff had 'turned a blind eye to evidence suggesting the bank was handling the proceeds of foreign corruption'. There were 'multiple personal accounts for the President of Equatorial Guinea, his wife and other relatives'. Riggs opened an account to receive legitimate payments from oil companies, but then allowed wire transfers of $35 million to other accounts, almost certainly to a company 'controlled in whole or in part by the EG President'. Senators queued up to condemn Riggs. A Democrat on the investigating committee, Carl Levin, concluded: 'It is a sordid story of a bank with a distinguished name which blatantly ignored its obligations under anti-money-laundering laws.'

Riggs paid a price. Kareri was sacked in January 2004. The next month, just as the first attempt at the Wonga Coup was launched, some of Obiang's accounts were frozen until evidence could be provided on the source of his income. He refused, so the accounts were eventually closed. The bank was fined $25 million early in 2004. In January 2005, Riggs pleaded guilty to criminal charges of failing to monitor suspicious financial deals and paid another fine of $16m. But the real damage was to its reputation. A venerable old establishment – which had provided gold for the US government to buy Alaska – was now the bank of choice for the dirty despot.

As the scandal grew, the bank's stock value slumped. Corporate predators prowled. In February 2005, PNC Financial

Services gobbled up Riggs. Eight months later PNC agreed to pay another $5 million to settle a shareholder lawsuit from the Riggs case. Late in May 2005, Kareri was charged with bank fraud and money laundering. Prosecutors said he had stolen over $1 million from his clients through kickback schemes, forged cheques and wire transfers. He was accused of funnelling money to yet another shell company that he and his wife, Nene Fall Kareri, had set up in the Bahamas. Other charges followed. If convicted – he has not appeared in court yet and no date has been set – he could face thirty years in jail, plus a fine of $1 million.

What of the other two parts of the triangle? For Obiang, the details of his thieving habits came at an inconvenient time. Just as he was posing as a fledgling democrat and victim of outsiders' aggression he was cast again as a crooked despot. More suspicious, if the Wonga Coup had succeeded, the new government in Equatorial Guinea would – by mid 2004 – have been busy discrediting the previous rulers. To Equatorial Guinea's government this suggested the American government had helped orchestrate the coup plot. The details from Riggs' accounts would have been valuable material for the new rulers.

Obiang tried to respond to the Senate investigation. In September 2004 his government produced an 82-point, 8,000 word rebuttal accusing the Senate investigators of 'conceptual confusions', 'repeated imprecisions' and 'unfounded extrapolations'. It also alleged a conspiracy between human rights campaigners, Severo Moto and others to besmirch the good name of Obiang. Though an effort was made to distinguish private and public accounts held in Riggs banks, the rebuttal gave no convincing evidence that the hundreds of millions of dollars kept in the Riggs accounts were stored for

public use rather than for the private benefit of Obiang and
his relatives.

The new scramble

How did the third part of the triangle fit? The Senate's
attention turned to the role of western oil companies in Equatorial Guinea. Its investigation provided a glimpse of how
attention-shy oil firms work in poor countries. It was an
extreme but revealing case. A wretched spot had had great
wealth thrust on it. Like a tramp who wins the lottery, it had
been ill-equipped to cope. Equatorial Guinea had seen its gross
domestic product (GDP) leap by an average of over 40 per cent
a year between 1997 and 2001. It all comes down to oil. Equatorial Guinea produces roughly a barrel of the black stuff for
each of its citizens, every day. Its oil is sweet, pure, nectar-like.
To hear experts talk, you could drink it like champagne. This
is in great demand from refineries, as it is not the thick sludge
used to tar a roof or to line a bear pit that some produce. With
rising demand from Asia – now 30 per cent of the total global
market – the scramble for supply has grown fierce. Energy
importers increasingly fret that the supply of oil and gas is
unstable. 'We're entering an era of energy insecurity' is an oft
repeated mantra of the American government. One response
is to see friendly oil companies – those of your own country
– secure as much supply as possible, especially in tempting
spots like Equatorial Guinea.

In 2005, the International Monetary Fund (IMF) said the
country again had the fastest growing economy anywhere,
with GDP up by 34 per cent. It has kept the top spot for most
of a decade. The tiny country is one of the largest recipients of
foreign direct investment in Africa: some $6 billion between
1998 and 2005. Roughly 3000 Americans, mostly oil workers,

are said to live there. A decade ago the country produced almost nothing. Now oil and gas account for 98 per cent of its exports and Equatorial Guinea is sub-Saharan Africa's third largest oil exporter.

But it is proving a manic-depressive economy, swinging from lows to highs, exploited by outsiders, its people getting little. In the oil rush only the elite has prospered. Some responsibility for that lies with the oil firms: Equatorial Guinea earns less from its oil than most countries; and those revenues are used badly. The oil companies have squeezed the toughest deals possible from the country's ignorant rulers. Even after a major renegotiation of production-sharing contracts in 1998, the country had a lousy deal. One expert, Jedrzej George Frynas, says Equatorial Guinea typically gets just 39 per cent of total revenues from its oil, while Gabon gets 78 per cent, Congo gets 76 per cent and neighbouring Nigeria 70 per cent. Equatorial Guinea did not milk oil companies for 'signature bonuses', when a firm pays tens of millions of dollars in advance of exploiting the oil. Thus contracts obviously favour the firms. Worse, audits show companies routinely fail to pay what they promised to the government. In 2003 the IMF noted oil firms underpaid by $88 million over five years. Only late in 2005 did Obiang's government finally talk of negotiating a better deal.

Second, little of the oil revenues is spent on ordinary Equatorial Guineans. Thieving leaders and hopeless government structures surprise nobody, least of all oil firms. In 2004 the US State Department noted that most wealth in Equatorial Guinea 'appears to be concentrated in the hands of top government officials while the majority of the population remained poor'. And conditions are worsening. The United Nations says the quality of life – judged by its index of life expectancy, wealth and education – shows the country in a worse position each year despite the rise in oil income. In 2005 the anti-corruption group Transparency International noted the three most corrupt countries in Africa were all oil producers: Chad was the most venal; Nigeria and Equatorial Guinea tied for the second worst spot.

The oil firms must take some of the blame, however. Bribe-payers do much to spread corruption and help the politicians divert funds from legitimate uses. And firms operating in Equatorial Guinea certainly do nothing to stop oil money being stolen. Worse, graft is actively encouraged. The investigation into Riggs Bank showed oil firms happily channelling funds towards private accounts of leaders like Obiang. Several oil firms have operated in Equatorial Guinea in the past decade, but three dominate: ExxonMobil, Amerada Hess and Marathon. The Senate committee's view of these firms is bold: 'Oil companies operating in Equatorial Guinea may have contributed to corrupt practices in that country by making substantial payments to, or entering into business ventures with, individual EG officials, their family members, or entities they control, with minimal public disclosure of their actions.'

The oil firms frequently give money to the leaders of Equatorial Guinea, and their families. Examples abound. ExxonMobil, one of the largest operators in the region, paid $385,000 directly into the personal account of Obiang's wife, Constancia Mangue Nsue. The same firm, plus Chevron-Texaco, another called CMS, Marathon, Triton and Vanco, gave as much as $275,000 each for 'student funds'. In total, more than $4m was paid by oil companies to support over a hundred students abroad, 'most of whom were the children or relatives of wealthy or powerful officials'. One firm, Triton, put more than $250,000 into a Riggs account to pay tuition fees for the children of Armengol Nguema, Obiang's brother and Equatorial Guinea's security boss. That looks remarkably like bribery.

The oil firms have close business ties with the ruling family. ExxonMobil leases buildings and land from Abayak, a firm owned by Obiang, and rents property from ministers. The Senate report notes that Amerada Hess paid some $300,000 to the same company controlled by Obiang, in exchange for vague 'security services'. In 1998 ExxonMobil formed an oil distribution business in the country, granting a 15 per cent share to Abayak. Asked to estimate how many deals it had made with such well-connected individuals, ExxonMobil said it needed to research some 500 payments. Marathon paid $2 million for a plot of land which almost certainly benefited the president directly. The oil firms use services of local companies – in construction, security and other areas – owned by members of the ruling family.

One striking story involves the 14-year-old godson of a minister in Equatorial Guinea's cabinet. Amerada Hess leased property from the teenager, passing nearly $500,000 to him, until a local court ordered the payments to stop in 2003. Then Hess was questioned by the minister concerned who wanted to know why the payments were no longer coming. The minister immediately phoned up the judge, who promptly reversed the order, and the payments from Hess started up once more. The oil firm could have been in no doubt that it was behaving unethically – it even had a court order making that fact clear – yet the firm happily restarted payments.

There is no doubt that oil firms pay generous bribes to crooked rulers, and in return enjoy extremely profitable terms of business in Equatorial Guinea. The only losers are the ordinary people. Rather than deny it, the firms claim they have no choice but to behave in this way. Equatorial Guinea is a tiny country. To do business there at all means signing deals with companies owned by members of the government. The only land to buy and the only properties to lease are owned by the extended ruling family. A representative of ExxonMobil told the Senate that 'it may be virtually impossible to do business in such countries without doing business with a government official or a close relative of a government official.' And is it the concern of oil firms if the government fails to spend money to benefit ordinary people? Foreign firms obey the law, pay taxes and (sometimes) meet the conditions of their contracts. That is where their responsibility stops.

In fact, the firms were caught red-handed. Under no circumstances could they justify paying a teenage relative of the president large sums of cash. It was plain wrong to put money, supposedly for oil revenues, into the accounts of Obiang's wife or other relatives. (One oil industry consultant close to Equatorial Guinea told the *Financial Times* in September 2004 that the multinationals had been 'stupid'. With greater care they could have hidden the beneficiaries of their payments. 'You [pay to] a company if you are asked to do that,' he says. 'You don't write it out to a name.')

As such they were conspiring with the crooked leaders of the country to defraud the people of Equatorial Guinea of revenues. And the firms seemed to admit as much. After the Senate report, and under threats of prosecution in the United States, the oil companies promised to change their behaviour in Equatorial Guinea. Some also adopted fig-leaf 'social programmes' – for instance, helping to eradicate malaria on the island part of the country – to polish up smeared reputations.

Here is a microcosm of corruption in Africa as a whole, and

perhaps other parts of the developing world. In a country where democracy does not function, elections are not free, journalists are unable to investigate crooked leaders and the rule of law is not respected, there are no means to hold corrupt politicians or crooked businessmen – foreign or local – responsible. There is no chance that the powerful are going to regulate themselves. The local politicians seek out short-term gains from the resources they control: backhanders to stuff into bank accounts, flashy cars, assets held abroad. They have no serious interest in developing their countries, in part also because they may expect to flee into exile eventually or be put up in front of a firing squad. In turn the investors do not expect to remain in the country for long. Equatorial Guinea produces generous quantities of oil today, but this is no Saudi Arabia. A couple of decades from now the oil will be exhausted. Yet the oil firms have no incentive to develop the local economy, as they profit by extracting resources and exporting them, not by developing stable and growing local markets. Thus, for those with power, as in the many parts of Africa where extracting minerals and oil quickly is the main economic activity, the rationale is to make a quick buck and move on.

By 2006, with oil prices reaching $70 a barrel, two things have become clear. Oil firms are struggling to find long-term supplies of oil and gas to replace that being sold and used. But, with high prices, they are making astounding profits measured in many tens of billions of dollars a year. Remote and repressive little countries, like Equatorial Guinea, prove profitable indeed.

22

The Price of Failure

'We've been chained like wild animals.'

Nick du Toit

Crause Steyl rests his feet on the coffee table, puts his hands behind his head and chuckles. From the office of his aviation business in Bethlehem, South Africa, he ruminates on the good life of being a mercenary. He thinks it is a smart career choice. 'I don't have perfect morals. I don't care too much what other people think. In essence, I think all men are mercenaries and all women are prostitutes. Men will kill for money and women will screw for money … For unattached people I'd recommend it. Given the opportunity, almost anyone would do a mercenary coup. If you have time on your hands, then why not? You need all sorts, not everyone carries a gun and shoots people.'

He has no regrets about the Wonga Coup. 'If it had been successful we would have done it again! If I'd gone through life without trying these things I'd have been a civil servant serving somebody stupid.' From the start he had reckoned the risk of the plot was not too grave and the potential reward huge. The price of failure, at worst, was death or a couple of years in an African prison. He felt that was an acceptable gamble.

That is easy enough to say. But Steyl himself faced neither death nor prison. He got a rap on the knuckles in South Africa, admitted after many months that he had broken an anti-mercenary law and paid a fine. In contrast Mann, in July 2004, was found guilty of two charges by the court sitting in Chikurubi prison. He had tried to buy firearms with no end user certificate. (The court did not ask why ZDI had been ready to sell without seeing the same certificate.) Mann had also broken a repressive law, the Public Order and Security Act. His two assistants, Carlse and Horn, were found not guilty and were freed. They returned to South Africa where – like Steyl later – they went through a plea bargain process, admitted breaking the anti-mercenary law, paid small fines and carried on as before.

Most of the accused in Chikurubi prison, the black foot-soldiers and the white 'team leaders', had pleaded guilty to immigration and aviation offences, as their lawyer Samukange advised. By September they had been behind bars for six months and awaited only sentencing. The men were chained together as usual, shackled hand and foot, doing what Piet Steyl and other visiting relatives now called the 'Chikurubi soft shoe shuffle'. They were herded into the old hospital ward that served as a court while an armoured car trained a machine gun at their backs. Yet the atmosphere was hopeful. Most expected to get a fine and immediate deportation home. After all, the smaller fry said they knew of no coup plot, and had merely sat on a plane before they were arrested. They broke immigration rules only because the pilot taxied to the military side of Harare airport. They disembarked at gunpoint. Samukange said he was confident of their release.

But, to their shock, the magistrate handed down jail terms for all. The sentences clearly related to an act – plotting a coup – for which none had been charged, tried or convicted. Samukange said later that the politicians had ordered an example to be made: 'The magistrate told us, "I am under pressure to sentence your guys", he called me to his office and said that. Political pressure, but he did not say from whom. He apologised to me and said he hoped I could find a way to reduce their sentences. But I was shocked when I heard the twelve-month sentence.' Most of the prisoners were told they would spend almost another year in Chikurubi prison as their six months on remand counted for nothing. To add insult to injury, they were fined, too: 2000 dollars each, or thirty US cents.

The 727 pilot, Niel Steyl, and his co-pilot, Hendrik Hamman, landed sixteen-month terms. Piet said his brother paled visibly as sentencing was pronounced. His knees shook in his khaki shorts and he was ready to collapse. Mann sat unshaven, with long, tousled hair. '[H]e looked rather dishevelled – quite aloof from his present surrounding,' noted Piet. When a television camera focused on the former SAS officer, he mouthed silent but indecipherable words and appeared to write with his finger on his chest. Mann stood to hear his sentence: seven years for the two offences (later cut to four on appeal); he also forfeited the Boeing 727 and $180,000 in cash that were grabbed on the night of his arrest. The same month his seventh child was born in Britain.

Amanda Mann kept her usual silence. But the wives of the black footsoldiers were outspoken. Many had scraped together money, or used a one-off payment from a lawyer (acting for Mann), to visit their husbands during the trial. By September most were back in Pomfret, the asbestos town in the desert. They live in a decrepit area dubbed Esperensa, with overgrown gardens, cracked walls, gates hanging off hinges. Roads are named 'Buffalo', 'Carpenter' and 'Carnation'.

Viviana Tchimuishi, wife of Eduardo, was desperate. 'We depend on people who have pity, and on the churches. We get food parcels,' she explains. Her daughter, Cecilia, says: 'We heard the sentence of my father on the radio. We were surprised. They told us they would come out now.' Tears appear in her eyes. She blames Mann and the financiers: 'Those people put us into trouble. We are suffering because they put our father into problems.' She wants Mann punished. 'I'm happy. Not to give him seven years, no, to give him death penalty. He deserves it.'

'We had no idea about Equatorial Guinea until after the men were arrested,' declares Viviana. Then, using the past tense, she adds that her husband was a good person. 'He didn't bug me. We always had food. He was a great person. When he was here the children were always studying. Now there is no money for school. It seems to me as if he already died. I don't know I'll see him again … It's just me. I'm mother and father to the children.' Neighbours are unsympathetic, blaming the men for what happened. 'They were rushing for money,' says one.

Felicia Shapoda, wife of Bonifatius Matheus, had been in court in Harare for the sentencing and hoped to return with her husband. Instead he would spend a year more in jail. 'I felt very bad because they are not guilty. Simon Mann, he was crying. I was feeling pity for him, I didn't understand what he had done.' She spent just five minutes with her husband, time only to give him some biscuits, cigarettes and milk.

Wild animals
The men in Zimbabwe had one consolation: they were not in Equatorial Guinea. The Malabo trial began late in August 2004. A conference centre on the edge of the capital became the

court, where du Toit and the others were kept handcuffed and in leg irons. Du Toit once called out: 'We've been chained like wild animals ... we've been tortured by police ... we haven't done anything wrong ... [if we had] we would have tried to run away.' Another group of Equatorial Guineans, including Severo Moto, were tried *in absentia*.

A feeble effort was made to follow legal process. An envoy from South Africa said Equatorial Guinea was under intense scrutiny, and asked for a decent trial and no torture. Lucie Bourthoumieux, a French lawyer working for the Equatorial Guinean government, argued the process was fair as the accused faced a civilian court. They were seen as terrorists, she says, and could have been caged, thrown before a military court or not tried at all, as Americans treat their suspected terrorists in Guantanamo Bay. But mistreatment elsewhere is no excuse for what happened in Malabo.

There were obvious problems. Amnesty International reported on a 'trial with too many flaws'. Lawyers saw their clients only three days before proceedings began. Du Toit later told a television journalist: 'I've seen a defence lawyer only once, he was only allowed a 40-minute interview with all of us. He came to the jail, he spoke to us very briefly and then the next time we saw him was in court and he was not allowed to speak to anybody. He was not allowed to visit us. He was not allowed to come and speak to us, give us advice or whatever.' The trial was in Spanish, with partial and often misleading interpretation. Only one of the presiding judges had practised law; two out of the three were Obiang's relatives. Complaints of torture were ignored. One defendant identified a man in court, saying he had inflicted torture, but was told it was the wrong place to raise such concerns.

The accused wore shorts, sandals and their irons. Du Toit,

in a blue shirt with rolled-up sleeves, was kept apart from the others. At first he repeated his early confession of March, saying that none of the others were involved. Then as the trial began in earnest, at the end of August, two things happened. First, a text message circulated from a hitherto unknown group calling itself the 'Military Committee for Liberation' and addressed to 'Comrades in the Armed Forces'. It accused Obiang's brother, Armengol, of being part of the Wonga Coup and called the trial a 'grisly farce'. Nobody knew who sent the message, but the government was startled by it. Mobile phones are known as useful tools against dictators. Popular uprisings in eastern Europe have been organised with cheap ones. This outburst startled officials who feared, as usual, another coup attempt, so the phone network was partly closed.

Then something else happened. In South Africa Mark Thatcher was arrested in connection with the plot, causing huge media excitement. The trial in Malabo was immediately suspended. Prosecutors said they would interview Thatcher and, perhaps, seek his extradition. Some thought this an excuse to stop the trial and find the mysterious military group 'inside the palace' who were campaigning against Armengol. Somebody had faxed details of his involvement with du Toit's business to journalists in London. There were cracks in the government.

The trial in Malabo did not restart until November, by when much had changed. It became obvious that a media battle mattered as much as the legal ones in South Africa, Zimbabwe, Equatorial Guinea, Lebanon and Britain. Many incriminating details were leaked to the press, with journalists quick to publish any details they could. For the sake of the propaganda scrap, officials let du Toit speak to a BBC news crew in Black Beach in late September. He had grown thin and changed his story, again. He accepted a coup was planned, but claimed he was not deeply involved in it. He had earlier confessed, he said, because he believed the prosecutors were after Moto and the financiers of the plot but would let him go (and the others on the ground).

Du Toit repeatedly changed his story. Early in October he signed another statement, three pages long. In this he elaborated on his first confessions given in English to Page, but denied others attributed to him. He talked of Kershaw and Tremain, and claimed that Thatcher had once 'wanted to buy arms for somewhere in the Middle East, machine guns, rifles and quite a lot of ammunition'. He admitted a limited role in the plot. Page hoped to use this statement to prosecute alleged financiers of the coup in Britain. Du Toit admitted he had 'reluctantly agreed to help Simon Mann and Greg [Wales]' in a coup plot, but only because he was 'short of work'. He claimed, implausibly, that he had no plans to be part of any military operation against Obiang. He also spelt out the goal of the Wonga Coup: 'The whole thing is about money. Oil was the motivation behind the attempted coup. That is what I understood from Greg and Simon. As for the backers ... the only other information I have of a factual nature is that one important backer was Ely, who I understood to be Lebanese.'

On 12 October the defence lawyer in Malabo collapsed and died, apparently from malaria. It was a reminder of the miserable conditions in Malabo. The trial finally restarted on 16 November, when du Toit's story changed yet again. He retracted all confessions, saying the death of the overweight German, Merz, had scared them into giving false testimony. 'I had to tell these people what they wanted. It was the only way to stay alive,' he claimed. But it was too late and du Toit's contradictory claims lent him little credence. Nor was there ever a chance the court would acquit the plot leaders: little evidence was considered at the trial, where most time was spent reviewing the military background of the defendants.

Sentencing came ten days later. To show justice at work, six men, including three locals, were acquitted. The freed foreigners were those with the least military experience: Mark Schmidt, Abel Augusto and Americo Ribeiro (the latter two had been arrested on the mainland bit of the country). They were released after eight months, two weeks and five days in Black Beach. The rest, including nine who were absent (Moto and company), were convicted and given terms as long as sixty-five years. The six hapless Armenians received sentences ranging from fourteen to twenty-four years. Two Equatorial Guineans were convicted of 'reckless behaviour', though they had not been charged with it, and received 16-month terms. Bones Boonzaier, Georges Allerson, Jose Domingos and Sergio Cardoso were told they would each spend seventeen years in jail. And would du Toit be executed? Despite Obiang's early threats, the court dispensed with a firing squad. He got a 34-year term – effectively a life sentence. His wife Belinda, in court to hear the verdict, cried, 'There's not a place in my body that's not aching ... How can they keep him here for thirty-four years? ... He won't survive that, he'll die. After another year ... he'll die.'

Black Beach

Playa Negra is a terrible place. Casual violence, the impunity of guards and the long history of brutal execution and torture give it an ominous atmosphere. Many Equatorial Guineans have spent time behind its walls and carry the scars of torture. Placido Mico, the most serious opposition leader still alive in Malabo, spent a year inside. He says his cell was a cupboard,

1 metre by 1.5 metres (3 feet by 4.5 feet). Some inmates were packed three to such a box. He was let out for 'one or two minutes a day. The rest of the time we had to live with our urine and excrement and the cockroaches, flies, ants and spiders.' Mico describes seeing and hearing other prisoners beaten with electric cables, as much as a hundred strokes at a time. He saw the sun twice in eleven months.

It was normal for inmates to have wrists, arms and legs broken, without receiving medical care. Amnesty International estimates that 90 per cent of inmates held for a trial in 2002 suffered 'inhumane practices'. Women were raped by officials. Health conditions were terrible: no mosquito nets, poor hygiene and a tropical climate conspired to spread the nastiest diseases. Amnesty calls jail terms there 'slow, lingering death sentences' and says prisoners all but starve. In December 2004 the prison cut rations from a daily cup of rice to a bread roll, sometimes two, per inmate per day. By February 2005, even that was irregular, with sometimes six days passing without food. The government responded by attacking Amnesty as a 'faceless organisation' only interested in the fate of mercenaries.

Again, those with money enjoy better treatment. Some rich inmates pay for visits by prostitutes. Some can walk around the prison at night. And deals can be struck with guards. Warders once took a group of Nigerian prisoners out for a night to steal cement from a construction site. One of the acquitted men, Mark Schmidt, told reporters there was even a prison shebeen, not the usual bar you find in jail. One evening he was 'drinking a beer when one of the soldiers apologised [for the torture] … He said he was just following orders.' 'The men who beat us are our friends now,' added Abel Augusto. Schmidt had been designated cook for the foreign inmates.

He visited Malabo every few days to shop for food. Another released man, Americo Ribeiro, described leaving the others behind. 'When I left them I was crying. We were all crying,' he stammered. 'We told them to be strong, keep on praying and we'll see you soon.'

23

Thatcher Falls

'I just feel in this particular case like a corpse that's going down the Colorado River, and there's nothing I can do about it.'
Mark Thatcher to *Vanity Fair* magazine

From late August 2004 onwards most media interest focused on just one man. For months after the arrests in March rumours circulated about Mark Thatcher. With hindsight, looking at his friends and business interests, it is baffling that nobody had confronted the former prime minister's son earlier. He had been close to Mann since 1997 and to Morgan (whom he calls Nosher, but no longer considers a friend) for longer. He had funded Cogito, the early project of Morgan and Johann Smith in Equatorial Guinea. He had dined with Mann as late as February 2004, then called friends asking anxiously after his whereabouts. Both Crause Steyl and du Toit met Thatcher to discuss obtaining helicopters. Half the plotters had been with him that Christmas in Cape Town. Thatcher had visited Ely Calil's home in London in 2003, in Mann's company. He was known to have active business interests in odd corners of Africa and in oil. A keen entrepreneur, he was always looking for new ways to make money.

Soon after the plot fell apart, in mid March, Crause Steyl was in London. He sent a cryptic message (in Afrikaans) to his brother Piet asking: 'Has there been any mention in the South African press of the Thatch Roof?' He followed up by saying: 'Mark Thatcher owes me $250,000 and I have proof. His mummy's people will give all we need, but now we cannot throw the baby out with the bathwater.' Crause Steyl would give the most direct evidence of Thatcher's involvement. Yet it took five months, until Steyl fully co-operated with the South African authorities, for the big celebrity news element of the Wonga Coup to break.

A more cautious man than Thatcher might have used that time to slip quietly out of sight. Neither Tremain nor Wales, for example, have dared set foot in South Africa since the plot collapsed. Morgan recalled asking Thatcher, soon after the March arrests, how much he really knew about the plot. He said he knew nothing. Yet he was in South Africa most of the time when Mann and the others were plotting their coup. He agreed to help fund a helicopter. He admitted later that he suspected it would be used for mercenary activity. In January 2004 he had sent $275,000 to Steyl. Mann referred to 'Scratcher' in his famous letter of 21 March. For some reason Mann also apparently wrote that 'Scratcher' still owed $200,000 as an investor in the project.

If Thatcher had admitted some of this – as he eventually conceded in a plea bargain – Morgan says he would have dragged him to an airport and sent him out of the country to avoid arrest. A quicker thinker might have left of his own accord. There were chances to take a hint. There was the menacing phone call while he watched the Grand Prix in March 2004. Many knew he was connected to Mann. There were rumours that Crause Steyl, along with Kershaw and Morgan, were telling all to the South African authorities. Yet still Thatcher did not leave. He and his wife Diane decided to send their children back to the United States for school later in the year. There were rumours that his house was up for sale, along with his cars. But for now he lingered, ostrich-like, in Cape Town.

Thatcher did go abroad in the middle of 2004, however, returning in mid August. On his arrival back in Cape Town an airport official said the police wanted to see him. Thatcher met his lawyer and friend, a genial man called Ron Wheeldon who wears round spectacles, flies jet planes and looks like a garden mole. When Wheeldon also asked if he had been involved in Mann's escapade, he again said no. In that case, said Wheeldon, co-operate with the authorities. Thatcher called Morgan and asked him to arrange a meeting with the intelligence service: Thatcher would say what he knew in exchange for immunity from prosecution, as Kershaw had done. On 19 August, Thatcher and Morgan went to Pretoria, the capital, and saw an intelligence official. It is not clear what Thatcher admitted, but afterwards he believed everything was OK. Thatcher understood he had been accepted as a South African intelligence source. He called his friend Wheeldon to say that all was sorted out.

But early the next Wednesday morning, a chilly 25 August, a special team of investigators – the Scorpions – pounded at Thatcher's door, with journalists and television crews in tow. Thatcher was startled. He had volunteered to give information – and, reportedly, to show his house – to a government intelligence unit. But the Scorpions are isolated from other arms of officialdom. It became clear that Thatcher had no immunity at all. The Scorpions were part of the national prosecuting authority. High profile and mainly used to fight corruption, they are modelled on the FBI. Journalists often accompany them on dawn raids, travelling in a black and red car, with a mean-looking scorpion painted on the side. A team of young men and women wear black, sporty clothes. Some brandish guns, others have clipboards and clear plastic bags. They usually descend on a bemused suspect's home while he is still in pyjamas, his breakfast half-eaten, then search his house. The Scorpions say they find evidence in the oddest places. At one Nigerian's home in Johannesburg, for example, fake passports were buried in a garden compost heap. So a routine raid means pulling out every drawer, checking every cupboard, trawling through every computer and examining all phone records.

Such was the raid on Thatcher's large home in Cape Town. The Scorpions arrived at about 7 a.m. with the Cape Town press corps. They demanded entry from armed guards at the front gate. Thatcher, roused from his bed, agreed to let them in after he had shaved and dressed. Three cars pulled into the large driveway with roughly ten investigators. They searched the house and sealed computers, including those of Thatcher's children. Many newspapers reported that the Scorpions stung just as the family was about to flee, with bags packed and waiting in the hall. Wheeldon denies it. 'There are stairs up from the garage, where the Scorpions entered. Mark always kept travel trunks sitting there. The police saw these empty trunks and thought Mark was ready to go.' Some newspapers also said Thatcher had a 'secure room', a sort of vault where he could retreat. That, at least, seems to be fantasy. There was an office, a set of garages and a bedroom known as the 'Africa room', where guests stayed. Beside that Thatcher had an office where a couple of assistants usually worked. His private office was connected to his master bedroom and, by a spiral staircase, to a dressing room (with a large collection of suits) and bathroom below.

After some two hours, and while the Scorpions scuttled over all the house, Thatcher was taken away. Footage of his arrest was promptly broadcast all over the world. In arrogant Thatcher style he barked at the driver, 'Come on, let's move', as if bossing his own chauffeur. The driver took care to linger so news crews could do their job. Thatcher was taken to a nearby police station in Wynburg, Cape Town. There are some reports that the former prime minister's son was locked in a cell where hardened criminals stole his shoes. Though a delightful detail, it is probably false. Wheeldon calls it nonsense. 'He was only in a passageway beside the cells, and that's where I consulted with him.' Thatcher otherwise sat in an office. 'Everyone was nice and humorous, there was no tense atmosphere.' He was kept for five hours, until about 2 p.m. Wheeldon's legal team negotiated Thatcher's release on bail. The police wanted security of 5 million rand (roughly $800,000) but agreed on 2 million. The money came soon after 'from England', almost certainly from his mother, Baroness Thatcher. Thatcher junior was warned to report each day to his local police.

Excitement among journalists was extreme. A day later the London *Evening Standard* published information from the bank account of Logo Logistics. It fingered J. H. Archer as a financier. Everyone assumed – despite denials by his solicitor – that this was the novelist Jeffrey Archer. The information 'appeared to have emanated from either Penningtons or their clients', stated a Guernsey court in April 2005; Penningtons denied that the firm, or its client, Obiang's government, had leaked the information. The next day, 27 August, Equatorial Guinea said it wanted Thatcher arrested and brought to trial with du Toit. Whether or not that was a serious prospect, the idea of Thatcher dragged before a kangaroo court in west Africa to be tried as a coup plotter sent editors and reporters into a frenzy. (A South African cartoonist, Zapiro, made the sharpest comment, depicting George Bush Senior on the phone to a furious Baroness Thatcher advising, 'Maggie, that son of yours can't go around toppling governments just to get the oil contracts ... unless he's in office! Now my boy ...')

All this kept Mark Thatcher at the centre of media attention. Every few days after his arrest a new detail, or allegation, was thrown out by the team working for Equatorial Guinea, keeping the story of the coup in the news. In November 2004, as the trial of du Toit and others restarted, authorities in Malabo confirmed they wanted Thatcher. The attorney-general, Jose Olo Obono, said they would seek his extradition for trial as a financier of the coup. The same month Equatorial Guinea accused Britain of backing the coup.

As the months passed, Thatcher's predicament worsened. He recalls being threatened with extradition to Malabo. 'I was told that if I didn't co-operate I'd be extradited to EG. This was political mugging of the first order.' By late November Crause Steyl's plea bargain made it clear that Thatcher had a role. Thatcher's own trial was due to start on 25 November. He was also supposed to answer a set of questions, in court, posed by Equatorial Guinean investigators. His twin sister Carol later said she was 'dismayed at the hurt and worry Mum was suffering because of Mark's involvement in the Equatorial Guinea plot ... I was annoyed with my brother for getting embroiled in it ...'

Both the court sessions were postponed. That was telling. Whatever the evidence against Thatcher it seems the prosecutors' case was not watertight. It is notoriously hard to convict anyone of breaking anti-mercenary laws anywhere, not least because it is difficult to define a mercenary. It seems that, unsure they could pin anything on the Briton, the prosecutors hoped to pile on the pressure by postponing his court appearances. As long as Thatcher awaited trial he could not travel. Several friends, including Morgan, were named as state witnesses, and were forbidden from meeting or communicating with him. As his wife and children left for the United States, Mark Thatcher became increasingly isolated.

Then a verbal deal was offered in November: according to Thatcher, if he agreed to postpone the trial, the state would return his passport so he could make essential trips. Thatcher agreed and the trial was delayed. But the prosecutors, says Thatcher, broke their word. He would not, after all, get his passport back. Worse, it was suggested that the trial would not proceed for another two years. Wheeldon explains: 'It became clear that the trial would not have happened until 2007. Not being able to travel until then would have killed his business, and his relationship.' Mann's lawyer in London, Anthony Kerman, believes Thatcher – and others who struck plea bargains – were pushed into giving untrustworthy testimony: 'There are people making confessions in terms of plea bargains. They don't impress me at all, they are all self-serving. As for Thatcher, he was put in a very difficult position. He was told his trial date was 2007, but told he could get out if he admitted guilt and paid some money. He was completely blackmailed into it. If you had a quarter of a million, or your mum did, what would you do? I know what I'd do.'

Thatcher later considered this a triple witching hour. He was well known and rich. Prosecutors thought they could 'ping' him, he recalls. 'I admitted guilt, by negligent conduct under intense pressure. I believe there was a witchhunt against me, led by very senior members of South African president Thabo Mbeki's government.' He suggests Mbeki had always disliked his mother, Baroness Thatcher (who supported the apartheid leaders in South Africa).

Mark Thatcher explains: 'There is no doubt that the pursuit of me was political. There are three reasons. The first was explained to me by a member of the investigating team who described how and why Mbeki bore such animus towards my mother. In 1977 he was at a conference and he spoke about the armed struggle in South Africa and the ANC's policies, which were highly socialist. Subsequently my mother spoke about her own political, market-based views. [She] eclipsed the ANC policy stance; for that, the Thatcher family supposedly earned Mbeki's eternal fury.'

Second, prosecutors needed a high-profile scalp so the anti-mercenary law would be taken seriously. 'And, third, they went after me with complete malice aforethought.' Thatcher says that the prosecution, under pressure from politicians, also sought to deny him bail. Such a complicated conspiracy might explain things. More likely Thatcher admitted funding a helicopter which he suspected would be used for mercenary activity, for a simpler reason: it was true.

Next he negotiated what fine to pay and what suspended sentence he would receive. He noted that Crause Steyl, who was deeply involved, had been fined 200,000 rand (about $30,000). Prosecutors said they wanted Thatcher to pay 1 million rand (about $150,000) and take a nominal 2-year sentence (if the fine was not paid). He agreed. But around December 2004 he believes the ministry of justice became involved. At a further meeting prosecutors said, 'We're not prepared to accept anything under 25 million rand: 5 million plus 20 million into the asset forfeiture account [a way of imposing a large financial penalty on organised criminals].'

Thatcher was furious, pointing out that he had no proceeds

– he had lost money in the venture. He reportedly told officials to 'fuck off'. Haggling ensued which Thatcher found 'hairy', but eventually the officials agreed on 3 million rand. He says: 'Originally the amount was one million. Subsequently at a drafting session to agree the documentation that amount was arbitrarily increased to five for the stated reason that I lived in a large house.' He was unamused: 'These are the standards of a mad house. Only after considerable further discussion did the amount then get agreed at 3 million.' He was told that the ministry of justice wanted a suspended sentence as this would 'look better in the press'. 'That's why exploiters/invaders never come down for the long haul. Africa is not creating an environment where investors want to bring money long term.' He later recalled: 'I took the plea bargain before it could change again, as it did almost daily.'

Around this time Thatcher lamented to a journalist from the magazine *Vanity Fair*: 'I will never be able to do business again. Who will deal with me?' He suggested the charges had 'destroyed' him. 'I just feel in this particular case like a corpse that's going down the Colorado river, and there's nothing I can do about it.' He noted that the world took an extraordinary interest. On the day of his arrest he said there were '18,500 Google hits about it. Who will want to deal with me after that?' Few sympathised. Most newspaper and magazine articles, including the *Vanity Fair* piece, gleefully described 'Scratcher's' troubled career and self-inflicted woes.

In January 2005 Thatcher finally struck his plea bargain. He would admit to helping to charter a helicopter he suspected 'might be used for mercenary activity'. Journalists waiting outside the Cape Town court noticed one resident had hung a cheeky banner from a nearby window. On it was daubed: 'Save me mummy.' Inside, the accused pleaded guilty under

Roman law of 'intention by gross negligence' – *dolus eventualis* – negligence so bad it is considered as strong as being deliberate. Though the main plea bargain made no mention of Equatorial Guinea, an 'Annexure C' to the plea bargain spelt out that 'during the period November 2003 to January 2004 and at Cape Town [he did] undertake to financially assist Simon Mann and Crause Steyl to charter a helicopter, which helicopter Mann, Steyl and other persons acting for them, planned to use in mercenary activity, as defined in section 1 of the Regulation of Foreign Military Assistance Act, 1988 (Act No.15 of 1998) (hereinafter referred to as 'mercenary activity') in Equatorial Guinea'.

Thatcher accepted a 3 million rand fine ($450,000), or five years in jail if the fine was not paid. He paid. He also received a four-year suspended jail term. His friends tried, rather plaintively, to insist that he really 'had no idea what was going on'. Morgan said he was at worst a 'voyeur' trying – and failing – to get close to the plot. Wheeldon said Thatcher believed he was 'investing in an air ambulance to operate in west Africa, including Equatorial Guinea ... Mark doesn't mind sailing close to the wind, but he severely minds breaking the law'.

Eventually, in February 2005, Thatcher sat in court for his final test. A stern magistrate posed over forty questions about the coup that were sent from investigators in Equatorial Guinea. To the sound of cell doors clanging nearby, Thatcher spent an hour answering the questions he would have faced in Malabo. In a thin voice he admitted meeting Mann several times and discussing Equatorial Guinea. However, he denied ever paying money into Mann's bank accounts or funding du Toit's company, Triple Options. He recalled meeting du Toit, on Mann's request, to inspect helicopters, though he denied ever dealing in arms. 'I'm not in the business of buying or selling any military hardware. I'm a director of a company which distributes fuel oil products,' he told the court.

Thatcher's business was not too badly hit, since many treated the coup attempt as an exotic joke. But there were some other costs. His marriage collapsed in September 2005, probably hastened by the strain of the Wonga Coup. By entering a plea bargain, paying a fine and accepting a suspended prison sentence, Thatcher became a convicted felon. He feared he might be blocked from the US, but 'soundings had already been taken with the US consul in Cape Town that this would not be a problem', he explains. He was told that the crime in South Africa was not recognised as one in the United States, so he could visit his family. But he was misinformed. Now he is barred from the United States. 'It's fair to say that the US ruling creates a fairly serious impediment' to a full family life, he concludes. It was not quite the misery of Chikurubi or Black Beach prison, but Thatcher's fall was spectacular.

Back in Britain, some members of parliament demanded that the disgraced Mark Thatcher be stripped of his honorary rank and no longer referred to as 'Sir'. Thatcher was increasingly unpopular. The principality of Monaco, where he tried to set up home, ordered him out. There was also renewed talk of a civil court case in Britain, with the government of Equatorial Guinea prosecuting.

Later Thatcher expressed his rage at how the prosecutors treated him. 'The application of the rule of law in Africa is selective for political purposes. Exhibit one: me, my case. Why was my fine seventy-five times greater than someone [Crause Steyl] who admitted having Severo Moto in his plane? Why haven't any of the 6,800 [South African mercenaries] in Iraq been arrested? The Prosecutors' Office itself gave me this figure, of 6,800. So they know about it. Why? Because it doesn't suit the President's political agenda.' But the prosecutors applied the letter of the law. They had convicted the most prominent man connected to the Wonga Coup, who had brought the greatest publicity to South Africa's anti-mercenary campaign. Despite his later denials, he had pleaded guilty to breaking the mercenary law because he was guilty of doing so.

The prosecutors wanted other financiers. Charge sheets were issued against Mann, Wales and Tremain. Wales and Tremain (charge sheet stamped and dated '2005-04-08', case number 14/954/05) were accused of conspiring and 'rendering foreign military assistance'. They were, according to charges lodged at a court in Pretoria – and not made public until now – part of recruiting, training, financing and engaging in mercenary activity. They were part of 'devising and attempting to implement an operational plan to engage and defeat the security forces and seize key points of the said Government in order to oust the president of EG'. The charge sheets suggested they conspired to 'make the necessary logistical arrangements for the instalment of a new *de facto* government on the 19 February 2004 and the 6/7 March 2004 by accompanying CRAUSE STEYL and others from the strategically placed Canary Island, from which they were meant to fly in the replacing President, SEVERO MOTO, after the coup had been successfully completed.' They confirm that, despite Wales's denials and Tremain's silence, the two men were deeply involved in Mann's plot. They also show how thoroughly Steyl (and other informers) spilled the beans to the South Africans.

One prosecutor explained in 2005 he wanted to 'go after the financiers, the organisers who sit in ivory towers, using guys from Pomfret to do their dirty work. Even the financiers will pay their dues ... Mark Thatcher, that was the beginning. The first step in the right direction ... It's not just poor black soldiers in Pomfret who are left to rot in jail, but guys with an oil platform who are looking to exploit others.' Calil, Wales, Tremain and Karim Fallaha have not set foot in South Africa since the coup plot collapsed.

24

Back from the Dead

'We suffered. What are they thinking of us, as dogs? It is like using a condom, use and throw. Or because we are blacks? Somehow they will pay.'

Footsoldier

In mid May 2005, the first prisoners were released in Zimbabwe. Described by some as the 'scum of the earth led by the fool of the family', sixty-one of Mann's footsoldiers were finally let out of Chikurubi prison. They had spent over fourteen months behind bars. Two had already been let out early, for medical reasons. Another died in prison. One man, Moses Moyo, was apparently removed from Chikurubi by the feared Central Intelligence Organisation for further interrogation. He was let go some weeks later.

The relief of the freed men was obvious. After several delays they were driven to the frontier with South Africa to a town called Beit Bridge. Many relatives gathered to meet them at the dusty border, where a long bridge crosses the Limpopo river. Ken Pain, the ageing flight engineer of the 727, was met by his wife Marge. She explained: 'I ran across, the cops just had to pull me away, and I cried and I was jumping around. I threw my arms around him, and *ja*, I just acted like an absolute idiot.' Pain himself was moved. 'Ah, it's incredible, hey, just watching Marge come ... just watching my grandson come running. You just can't describe what it feels like; it is just too much,' he told South African television at the time.

Mazanga Kashama was happiest to have clothes again. 'The moment you get in, you are stripped naked. They give you shorts and a shirt ... I spent 434 days without underwear. Now I have three days wearing underwear!' Like many others he expressed his pleasure at being free by describing the misery of jail, the blood-sucking wildlife behind bars and the starvation: 'These people, their skin peels off like a snake.' But the former footsoldiers were generally furious with Mann and the other plot leaders and financiers. One raged: 'If everything went all right they were going to benefit. Now our fingers are burnt. Employers don't want to hire us. They don't want to associate with mercenaries. We suffered. What are they [the financiers] thinking of us, as dogs? It is like using a condom, use and throw. Or because we are blacks? Somehow they will pay. They will have to pay us.'

Mann provided some food for the footsoldiers in prison, but it did little to buy off their bitterness. 'If I met Simon Mann, one thing's for sure, I'd kill him. He lied to us a lot ... We're just a sacrificial lamb. We protected his ass in Chikurubi. That was our mistake.' Those returning to Pomfret, the dilapidated asbestos town, were knocked again. South Africa's ministry of defence announced that it was to be bulldozed. There is nothing to endear one to the old army base, and the fear of asbestos dust should have seen it flattened years earlier. But the government clearly had another reason for acting: they wanted to crack down on the Buffalo Soldiers, the men of 32 Battalion who were such willing hired guns. One minister talked of South Africa as a 'cesspool for mercenaries'. A government insider said the veterans 'made the mistake of

fighting on the wrong side yet again'. Residents were promised
housing elsewhere, though scattered around the country. But
even with Pomfret razed, the problem of men being recruited
as private soldiers will persist. Ex-army types with no other
job prospects are sure to be lured into similar work in future.
'Soldiers-of-fortune are as old a profession as prostitutes,'
suggests a defence analyst in Pretoria.

For those released after fourteen months jailed in Zimbabwe,
there was soon something else to worry about. South African
prosecutors had seen Thatcher, Pienaar, Crause Steyl, Horn
and Carlse all strike plea bargains by admitting guilt. A
handful of others involved in conflicts elsewhere had also
struck plea bargains. In April 2005 charge sheets were drawn
up and lodged with a court in Pretoria against Mann, Wales
and Tremain should they ever set foot in South Africa. But the
country's anti-mercenary laws had still never been tested in
court.

The authorities chose to launch a test case against eight of
the men who had been released. These men were regarded
as officers, against whom a prosecution stood the best chance
of success. Raymond Archer, Errol Harris, Louis du Prez and
Simon Witherspoon formed one group. Their lawyer said the
men would not deny the plot, but could show that the South
African government gave the 'green light' for it to proceed. Four
black defendants, Victor Dracula, Mazanga Kashama, Neves
Matias and Maitre Ruakuluka (known as Celeste), formed a
second group. Prosecutors said privately that their political
masters wanted a trial to prove the law's worth. 'You should
never be blasé and think it wouldn't happen again, or to think
the law is going to stop these guys,' explained a prosecutor.
'A court case is the only way we get versions out. It would be
interesting if the defence calls witnesses sympathetic to them,

suggesting that there was a perception of a green light from government.' The trial was finally held in 2007, but the judge threw out the case after two weeks, noting that some defendants had believed that the South African government backed the plot.

Prosecutors wanted to crack down on them, in part to prevent them attacking each other, they said. There were fears that bitter men might settle scores between themselves. Smith had taken to sleeping with a Glock handgun under his pillow. Morgan added extra security to his remote, rural home. Smith regularly confronted drunk and aggressive 'moustaches' who said they were going to kill him. These were often friends and relatives of those behind bars in Zimbabwe and Equatorial Guinea. There were rumours of a hit list of those who had helped foil the coup. Morgan was advised his name was on it and told to take precautions. The police warned troublemakers they would be arrested immediately if there were any attack.

Another effort was made to stamp on mercenaries. As South Africa's 1998 law against them – one of few in the world – had proven so difficult to apply, the country's rulers promised a new act by 2006. It was even tougher, requiring anyone who sells any service in a conflict zone to be licensed. Intended to stop South African ex-soldiers fighting in Iraq, it could also hinder aid workers and journalists in war zones. Confusing matters, the law made an exception for 'freedom fighters' who joined an 'anti-colonial' war abroad. It promised to be no more useful than the old one: now both mercenaries and freedom fighters would have to be defined. South Africa also wanted to prosecute anyone visiting the country, even foreign tourists, who might have broken this law abroad. The chances of enforcing it looked slim.

At the end of July 2005, the pilots Niel Steyl and Hendrik Hamman were let out of Chikurubi. Apart from Mann, they were the last to be released from Zimbabwe. They were also driven to South Africa, to Beit Bridge. Grey-haired Niel agreed to an interview for this book four days later. His release was emotional. His brother Crause had flown to the border with Zimbabwe to collect him. 'We stopped at a liquor store and the television was on. I could watch the last three minutes of the rugby match against Australia. Our boys won!' He drank beer and flew home to a private runway near Pretoria, where a welcome party was thrown.

He gave a harrowing description of life behind bars, confirmed he had lost his job and missed some $170,000 of earnings. But did he regret signing up to the Wonga Coup? Not at all. 'I would do something with Simon again. But not for money, for the kicks. It's not "Hell, I'm never going to do this again." Life is for living. Sometimes there's a fuck-up.'

In Equatorial Guinea the first men were freed in mid 2005. Obiang marked his birthday with a decree pardoning the six bemused Armenian pilots. He called it a sign of goodwill. The less important inmates in Black Beach, such as Bones Boonazier, also hoped for early release. Officials were charmed by his wife, whom they found humble and unthreatening. Bones was reportedly allowed frequent visits and could even spend occasional nights with her at a Malabo hotel. It was rumoured that Bones and du Toit refused to speak to each other, Cardoso was depressed behind bars while Allerson handled the situation reasonably well. Bones was indeed released in 2006.

Where did that leave du Toit? A lawyer acting for Obiang suggested the president felt the men on the ground 'have been punished enough'. Du Toit was likely to be released last: he needed to be punished to set an example. But few expected him to serve more than a couple of years. And a gracious pardon could make Obiang look good, while ensuring he did not die of malaria or ill treatment in Black Beach. Unfortunately, officials in Equatorial Guinea took a fierce dislike to his wife, Belinda, reportedly calling her 'The Snake' because she dared speak in public about the awful conditions in Black Beach. They refused her the privileges enjoyed by Bones and his wife.

Mann's lawyers, and those jailed with him, said he coped well with prison life, charming the guards and other prisoners, and keeping fit. It was suggested that his lawyer, Samukange, brought him roast chicken to eat. The old Etonian continued to deny being part of a plot, to quote his London lawyer Kerman: 'Simon Mann has specifically said he was not involved in any plot to procure the violent military overthrow of the government of Equatorial Guinea.' Yet he was also said to be writing a book about the whole affair.

There was a flurry of excitement in mid 2005 when Zimbabwe's attorney general said he would extradite Mann to Equatorial Guinea to face trial for 'high treason'. Kerman said later he was deeply concerned by the prospect: 'I worry about it all the time. But President Mugabe has said, has given his word, that Simon Mann will not move as long as he is in Zimbabwe serving time for crimes in Zimbabwe. [But] in Africa, and in Russia, anything can happen. It's the sort of place that one morning Mugabe might wake up and say "Get rid of him".' Few expect extradition will happen, certainly not before Mann's term is complete in Zimbabwe. Mann himself is confident he will never set foot in Equatorial Guinea. He once boasted to a visitor he would be free by May 2006. It is widely thought by friends of Mann that regular payments made to senior prison officials in Zimbabwe keep the celebrity inmate treated well.

There have been rumours of efforts both in Zimbabwe and in Equatorial Guinea to break the men free. In Zimbabwe one idea was to arrange for Mann's extradition to South Africa in December 2004, for a payment under the table of some $5 million. It is unclear why, if the deal were really on offer, the money was not forthcoming from London. In Equatorial Guinea, Smith continued to peddle warnings of coup attempts against Obiang. He and others suggested there was a 'plan B' attack scheduled for mid 2004, with another intelligence report confidently predicting 'what will happen is that a bullet will be put in Obiang in the middle of this cacophony', provoking American intervention.

That did not happen, but in May 2005 there was a curious arrest at Malabo airport. A South African of Angolan origin, a man called Apollo Naria, arrived at immigration and declared he wanted to see his 'old friends' in Black Beach prison. Officials stared at him unbelievingly. Was the visitor a veteran of 32 Battalion, a Buffalo Soldier? He was indeed. A second lieutenant in 32 Battalion, he explained. The police promptly arrested and interrogated him. Fearing that he had come to do reconnaissance for a jail break they threw him into Black Beach prison, too. His fate, at the time of writing, is still not clear.

Epilogue

'You are a good friend and we welcome you.'
Condoleezza Rice, American Secretary of State, to Obiang,
Washington DC, April 2006

It is hardly appropriate to draw sweeping lessons about the whole of modern Africa as a whole from a story of a failed coup in a single small country. Too often writers try to comment on Africa without distinguishing between the great variety of people, politics, histories and cultures to be found there. Equatorial Guinea has little in common with well-run Botswana, for example, just as the aristocratic and minor celebrity plotters in the Wonga Coup have little in common with most outsiders who live and work in Africa. Yet this story touches on themes that are relevant not only to many resource-rich African nations, but to poor countries all over the world. The core message is simple enough: where the extraction of valuable resources like oil or diamonds is managed carelessly, as happens in too much of Africa, the consequences are usually grave.

The story of the Wonga Coup began, ultimately, in Angola's civil war. It was in Angola that the soldiers of 32 Battalion cut their teeth, and it was in Angola that Mann's Executive Outcomes was born. Angola's war, at least in the 1990s, was a battle for control of oil and diamonds, not one of ideology. Similarly, the scrap for Equatorial Guinea was all about controlling oil revenues: the dictatorial old guard of Obiang defended itself against a threatening new force that posed as democratic. But the rival sides shared a common goal of syphoning off short-term profits from the massive – and relatively new and poorly controlled – output of oil. Nobody intended to use the oil for a more decent purpose, such as developing an economy to lessen poverty and improve the lives of ordinary Africans. But at least the coup attempt threw into sharp relief how different participants in Equatorial Guinea's oil bonanza – usually the same actors present in other parts of Africa – behave. Not all African leaders are corrupt, but just as Obiang steals in Equatorial Guinea, crooked leaders rob their countries in Kenya, Nigeria, Cameroon, Angola and many other places.

Not all western banks are willing to stash the stolen funds of crooked leaders, but the exposé of Riggs Bank in America shows how easily it was done behind the respectable doors of a Washington DC institution. Few other banks have been subjected to the sort of scrutiny that eventually destroyed Riggs. If they were, others would surely be shown to be culpable, too. And, perhaps, not all oil companies are equally willing to pay bribes to crooked politicians. ExxonMobil, Amerada Hess and Marathon were exposed by the US Senate and shown to be channelling money in crude ways to the families of politicians in Malabo. Few would doubt they – but also other oil firms, mining firms, telecoms firms and so on – also pay bribes and fuel corruption in other parts of Africa. But we know about these payments because of the unusual scrutiny that fell upon one corner of Africa, in part because a group of mercenaries tried to snatch control there.

By 2005 the story of the Wonga Coup was near its end. The

men in Zimbabwe and Equatorial Guinea were behind bars. In South Africa Mark Thatcher struck his deal, admitted breaking the anti-mercenary law, paid a fine and left. He sold his Cape Town mansion making a good profit ('It washed its face,' he says grudgingly). Those involved had much time to ponder why the plot had failed so spectacularly. There were many reasons. From the outset it was too big and complicated: three teams co-ordinated over thousands of kilometres; roughly a hundred people to be marshalled to the target; weapons and ammunition bought on the way. The logistics were messy: a specialised plane from the United States; footsoldiers recruited in South Africa; guns from Zimbabwe; finance raised in Britain; an exiled politician in Spain; a launching pad in the Canary Islands; the target in Equatorial Guinea; abandoned plans to go via Uganda, Congo and Namibia. Crause Steyl concluded that trying to put together a 'semi-government' had proved over-ambitious and unwieldy.

As important, the plotters little understood what political backing they had. They repeatedly told investigators they believed that South Africa, Spain and the United States backed the plan. Mann had told them so. Mann believed that Spain's prime minister, Aznar, had met Moto three times and promised 3,000 civil guards to protect the new leader, and that he would give recognition and other diplomatic support. The Americans might have turned a blind eye if their oil interests had not been threatened. The British reaction was hardly relevant. But the African response was badly misjudged. Mann believed he had – at the last minute – got some support from Congo's Joseph Kabila to supply him with weapons for a later mission, if not for this one. It is quite likely that Mann planned to refuel in Kinshasa on his way to Equatorial Guinea. In South Africa, low-level intelligence officials might have encouraged Mann, but higher echelons, including President Mbeki, would not have approved. However, Mann believed that, a week before his arrest, the South African government contacted Moto and offered him support, even inviting him to meet Mbeki. In Zimbabwe, Mann and du Toit even deluded themselves they had an ally in Colonel Tshinga Dube of Zimbabwe Defence Industries and wrongly believed they had made friends in high places. The plotters also knew Nigeria's response mattered, but ignored rumours that hundreds of Nigerian marines were poised to invade if there was a coup. If that had happened, Mann and the rest might have been killed. Perhaps Moto also expected some political backing – or an uprising – in Equatorial Guinea itself, though it is not at all clear if he is popular there.

The plot was not kept secret. Details spread like gossip. The plotters were indiscreet and arrogant during the planning, then most spilled the beans immediately after their arrest. Smith's intelligence reports circulated widely enough that du Toit wanted the plot called off. Moto bragged to anyone who would listen that he would soon be president. Greg Wales trotted around oil firms spreading rumours of regime change. Morgan passed on information, documents and detailed warnings to South African officials, something Mann might have suspected. Mann passed some paperwork to Morgan and went on dining and drinking with his fellow Briton every few days in the months before the attempt. Information also leaked through James Kershaw, his office assistant. Du Toit also sent uncoded messages about the plot up to the last days.

Mann had developed a system of code words (using English place names to refer to parts of Africa and numbers to refer to items, people and places), but this was hardly used. In bars and restaurants men boasted of what they planned. The lower ranks were said to get drunk and loose-tongued in Pretoria's pubs. The plot was even debated at a semi-public meeting at Chatham House in London several weeks before it took place. One hired gun later said he refused to join the plot because it had become an open secret. 'There were also just too many people involved and it did not have the element of surprise you needed to pull off something of this proportion. This ... was the main reason for the coup to fail – I think.'

Yet Mann had pushed on. Various people were brought in, including Mark Thatcher and the mysterious J. H. Archer, even though that risked drawing yet more attention to the plot. He did so because he needed money. Like so many amateur coup plotters before him, even Mann the millionaire lacked resources. Under pressure, he took risks. He tried a daring freelance attack without the resources that Executive Outcomes would have used merely to support a government. Lack of time mattered, too. A deadline forced action by early March, when Prime Minister Aznar retired in Spain. Mann told Zimbabwean investigators he was under pressure to complete the plot by February. Under stress he made quick and bad decisions.

There was rotten luck of course (the damaged Antonov that was to be used to transport mercenaries and guns in the February attempt), but ultimately the problem was poor leadership. The burden of failure rests mostly on Mann – plus the financiers who pushed him on. One complained that Mann 'lost the plot' in the final weeks of the botched operation. Widely liked and respected as a soldier, he designed and fumbled a complicated operation. When it started to go awry, a braver or more cautious man might have dared to cancel. But he was propelled on by investors, by the need to recoup losses, by his belief he had political backing, by his own vanity and by his love of adventure. Lafras Luitingh, one of the early leaders of Executive Outcomes, later blamed the failure of the Wonga Coup squarely on those who led it. In a snide comment to a friend he noted that Buckingham and other leaders of the old corporate army (including himself) had not been involved: 'It's what you get when you play with the second team,' he said. Ultimately, there were too many bad decisions. 'If it was a coup, it was horrendously badly planned,' concludes a mutual friend of Thatcher and Mann.

But if the coup went badly, the prosecutions of those involved were hardly more professional. Henry Page's various efforts to prosecute the alleged financiers of the coup plot, namely Mann and his two companies, plus Wales and Calil, came to nothing. The case in Lebanon was thrown out. The courts in Britain dismissed his civil case. The ruling by the Guernsey court, in April 2005, proved uncomfortable for Page. It ordered that no more information from Mann's accounts should be passed to the lawyer representing Equatorial Guinea. The long judgment did not assess the details of the coup plot, but found the idea that Obiang suffered 'severe emotional stress' laughable, given his own background. It ruled that the request for damages 'cannot be regarded for the present purposes as a serious claim', not least because Obiang is a 'despot'.

Page's behaviour was criticised; the court spoke of exhibits that cast 'serious doubt on the factual allegations in Mr Page's affidavits.' His use of Mann's confession to obtain the bank details was frowned on: '[accepting] Mr Page's evidence at face value ... can now be seen to have been incorrect', it concluded. The court had a 'strong suspicion' that evidence sought for the civil case might instead be used for a criminal case. And it issued an implicit rebuke of Page's firm Penningtons and their client, the Equatorial Guinea government, for apparently using evidence obtained in a legal process to 'conduct litigious warfare in the media'. The court seemed unhappy that sensitive information Page obtained from Mann's bank accounts rapidly appeared in newspapers.

Other lawyers were unimpressed with Page. Anthony Kerman, fond of pinstriped suits and pacing the room, opposed him and offered none of the usual grudging respect for a fellow professional: 'I find it odd that an intelligent and educated man, as one must assume Page to be, would choose to act for somebody whose regime has become a byword for brutality and corruption, who has been so widely criticised by the US Senate … If this was a criminal trial and Obiang was the defendant, you could say he is, like Milosevic, like Saddam, entitled to the best defence he can get. But this isn't a criminal trial with Obiang as a defendant, but a civil matter with Obiang as the claimant and in a sense Page is choosing to prosecute his aims.' Many criticised Page, who also published a private statement from Johann Smith, who admitted that he had warned officials in the Pentagon and British security of the coup plot before it took place. 'I never thought it would come out. I was naive, I trusted him,' laments Smith. Once in Equatorial Guinea, he was also placed under enormous pressure to write a statement that implicated Morgan.

Interviewed for this book, Page says he recognises there were problems with the treatment of the men held in Equatorial Guinea. He had suggested that du Toit and the others should get defence lawyers from the start, but was assured the Spanish 'inquisitorial system' let defendants be held without them. Though he thought du Toit looked fit and healthy when they met, du Toit explicitly told him of being 'knocked about by guards'. And though Page is confident that du Toit confessed of his own free will and told the truth, there is no way a man in fear of torture and facing every chance of a violent death would be considered someone giving free testimony.

But others were hardly blameless. Morgan is left in a moral quandary: though he helped to foil the coup plot, and thus helped South Africa's government score an impressive intelligence victory, he effectively betrayed friends who believed they could trust him. Thatcher certainly grew embittered towards Morgan, but he is hardly on high moral ground either. Thatcher struck a deal with the South Africans that included his giving close co-operation to the prosecution and evidence on others involved, presumably on Mann in particular. Most plotters, including Steyl, Witherspoon and others, seemed willing to strike a deal that landed others deeper in legal trouble. To his credit, Mann seems the exception to this rule.

If you can't beat him

Equatorial Guinea's rulers did profit from the saga of the Wonga Coup. Obiang found warmer relations with other powers. As late as November 2004, senior State Department officials described American ties in Equatorial Guinea as driven by 'oil men' and confirmed that 'our ties are not good' with the country. By 2005 that had changed. US officials gushed about the need for a stable relationship. In June 2005, Paul Wolfowitz, an ally of George Bush and the newly appointed head of the World Bank, said of Obiang: 'I was very impressed at his leadership and his government's leadership.' He said he hoped Obiang would manage oil revenues 'according to the standard of transparency and accountability that will ensure that wealth goes to the benefit of the people'. Serving members of the US administration also met the despot as part of a carefully designed effort to recraft Equatorial Guinea's image. Several American lobbyists and public relations companies were given contracts to that end. One firm, Cassidy and Associates, is said to have earned $1.4 million a year polishing the country's reputation – a rate which some industry observers thought 'eye-popping'. Another firm, Barbour Griffith and Rogers, was paid $37,500 a month to do a similar job. In April 2006 Obiang visited Washington DC and was granted an audience with Secretary of State Condoleezza Rice, who stated 'You are a good friend and we welcome you'. In contrast Severo Moto's lobbying efforts have fallen quiet.

But it also became clear that Obiang's illness – cancer – was becoming more acute by 2006. He was rumoured to weigh just 50 kilos (110 pounds) as his body wasted away. He reportedly contacted Angola's government asking for peacekeeping troops to keep order in Equatorial Guinea for the moment when he expected to hand power over to his elder son, Teodorin, or at least to make him a vice president.

Spain was suddenly friendly. In March 2005, a year after the failed coup, Spain's new foreign minister, Miguel Angel Moratinos, visited Equatorial Guinea and vowed to help prevent any more troublesome plots. Relations cooled towards Moto. The exiled opposition leader said Spain had sold out so its oil company, Repsol, could get concessions in Equatorial Guinea. Spain's rulers retorted that the exile would lose his refugee status if he caused any more mischief. Then, in April 2005, Moto disappeared. Some said he had been assassinated, perhaps by an agent working for Obiang. His wife feared he was dead. Others thought he was plotting a new scheme, or sulking in an effort to get more attention. One rumour held he had gone on a religious retreat in Italy. Johann Smith produced a speculative report saying Moto met Wales and Ely Calil in London, moved on to Croatia where he saw a team of military men, then scuttled to west Africa to collect a $2-million shipment of weapons. These he planned to use to invade Equatorial Guinea, perhaps in league with a mysterious group called the Southern Cameroonian Liberation Front.

Several weeks later, Moto resurfaced in Croatia with a tale that was equally bizarre. He told a Croatian newspaper that the Spanish secret service had planned to kill him in order to placate Obiang: 'As opposition leader ... I have become an obstacle to the deals with Obiang and that is why they want to eliminate me.' He held a press conference back in Madrid and spun another yarn. He was seeking asylum in Croatia when villains forced him aboard a luxury yacht in the Adriatic Sea. There he was to be drowned. But a supposed $10-million payment from Obiang did not appear and the kidnappers – who were good Catholics – decided not to murder him. When they learned Moto was a priest, they repented and let him go. He scoffed at suggestions he was in Croatia to recruit more mercenaries or to buy guns for a new coup attempt.

The exile grew more isolated. Other opposition men, notably those who dared stay in Equatorial Guinea, were recognised by many observers as more serious leaders. To Obiang's pleasure, Spanish relations with Moto soured further. When Moto supporters protested outside Equatorial Guinea's embassy in Madrid they were criticised by Spain. In 2006 Moto lost his refugee status in Spain and was on the verge of being expelled by the Spanish government.

Silver lining

The failed plotters of the Wonga Coup might possibly have done the people of Equatorial Guinea a small favour. As international relations warmed, Obiang's new friends – notably Spain and South Africa – argued that coup attempts and instability would be discouraged if the nature of government changed. Obiang made some efforts to show that oil money would benefit a wider circle of people, though the standard of living of ordinary Equatorial Guineans continued to slide as the oil income rose. He also spoke of Equatorial Guinea as a 'fledgling democracy'. But to hatch into one, Obiang and the ruling clan need to be persuaded that their privileged life depends on the well-being of ordinary Equatorial Guineans. That means spending a serious portion of their oil wealth on schools, hospitals and other basic necessities for their people. Equatorial Guinea must establish the basics of a decent state: create a set of laws to forbid torture; allow freedom of speech and other democratic norms. Interested outsiders should be allowed to visit the country and talk openly to Equatorial Guineans. If efforts are made there, the chance of any future plotters getting outside support will decline.

Sadly, there is little sign that the rulers in Equatorial Guinea are ready to change. A poisonous atmosphere of suspicion lingers. Factions in government jostle for power, waiting for Obiang's cancer to force him out of office. As if this were a kingdom, Obiang's two sons may well scrap over who succeeds. Few doubt that the obnoxious elder son, Teodorin, is in the stronger position. He has the backing of many in Obiang's family. But the younger one (by a different mother), Gabriel, appeals more to investors and reformers. If Teodorin assumes office, it will be tricky to promote a better image of the country. In September 2005, Amnesty International again condemned Equatorial Guinea for ill-treating prisoners. That month twenty-three Equatorial Guineans were handed long jail terms, up to thirty years each, for plotting yet another coup a year earlier. Almost no outsiders had noticed that one. All but two of the defendants told the court they had been tortured.

Mann and du Toit were left with nothing to do but wait in their respective prison cells on either side of Africa. Mann's outlook was probably the more hopeful, unless he were extradited to Equatorial Guinea. He expected to know his fate by May 2007. If, somehow, he landed in South Africa, he could face arrest and a costly plea bargain, perhaps a trial. But he would do his best to avoid that by returning to Britain instead. Du Toit and the others in Malabo might be allowed to finish their sentences in South African prisons. The alleged financiers in Britain – Calil, Wales, Mann and Mann's companies – can expect no prosecution after the failure of the civil case. It seemed unlikely that South Africa will try to extradite them, or that Britain will be notably co-operative. Early in 2006 Thatcher understood that the government of Equatorial Guinea might attempt to prosecute him in a British court. But nothing of substance emerged.

Thatcher as a convicted felon is barred from the United States. His wife Diane has divorced him. He continues some trade in Africa and has found a home back in Europe, though he was asked to leave Monaco early in 2006. He believes he may be pardoned by the South African government. Asked how he felt about Simon Mann he replied, 'Simon *is* my friend, not *was* my friend. Of course I'll give him a bloody good kicking when he gets out and ask him what he thought he was doing.'

The rag-and-bone intelligence men continue to ply their trade in Africa, despite death threats from thugs. In March 2005 the government of Equatorial Guinea rewarded Smith, naming him 'Johann Smith, Hero of the Nation'. At a ceremony in Malabo he was granted the 'freedom' of the island part of the country and handed a cross encrusted with rubies, tanzanite and diamonds.

What of the oil firms? There has been talk of prosecution in the United States. Some plans have been put forward for promoting better ways of doing business in poor parts of the world. One idea is the Extractive Industries Transparency Initiative: mining and oil firms would have to state what they pay African governments, and governments would have to say what they get. Others could see where money went, and countries could see when they got a bad deal from the firms. The trouble? Oil firms say they cannot open up their accounts for rivals to look at. It would be business suicide. Even if every American and European oil company became transparent, rival oil firms from China, India, Malaysia and Africa itself would steal their business.

Other efforts have been made. In Chad, the World Bank has some influence on how oil funds are spent. But corruption has not been reduced. In 2005 Chad was named the most corrupt country in Africa. In Sao Tome and Principe, experts tried to set up an oil fund to collect revenues and release them slowly, to be spent wisely. Such funds exist in Norway, Alaska and in other better-run oil producing economies. It may work in Sao Tome, too. Almost anything would be better than Equatorial Guinea, where nobody knows how to spend wisely revenues of some $60 million a month.

In Zimbabwe, President Robert Mugabe continues happily in office. In 2005 he told this author, with a large grin, that he would stay in power until he was a 'century old'. Zimbabwe's economy continues to collapse and its people pour over the borders to better run bits of Africa, like Botswana, Mozambique and South Africa. Chikurubi prison in Harare continues to be one of the most unpleasant spots on earth, where prisoners die daily from AIDS and malnourishment. Local media report that Mugabe was given $20 million by a grateful Obiang.

The Wonga Coup was a spectacular effort by outsiders to overthrow an African government. It failed. Of ten coups attempted around the world in 2004, none succeeded. The rate of coup attempts – let alone successful ones – has declined everywhere. An Oxford University study suggests most forms of violent conflict are becoming less common, and coups are especially rare. Between 1963 and 2004 the average number of coup attempts seen each year in the world has dropped by nearly two-thirds. Though a domestic coup did succeed in 2005, in Mauritania, it was quiet, localised and barely noticed by outsiders. Not a single British novelist, old Etonian or grizzled hired gun took part.

Optimists draw hopeful lessons from the Wonga Coup. They point to successful co-operation in Africa. Four African countries – South Africa, Angola, Zimbabwe and Equatorial Guinea – shared intelligence and co-ordinated responses. For a continent long split between warring countries this is a rare example of a few of them working together. South Africa shows a readiness to crack down on its mercenaries, even if its legislation is clumsy and ineffective.

Ultimately Simon Mann has joined Mike Hoare and Bob Denard as a buccaneer of world renown who ended up in jail. Like them, he made an early fortune by fighting in Africa, then hired a team of soldiers to overthrow the government of a small island country in Africa. Denard pushed it too often in the Comoros; Hoare flopped in the Seychelles; Mann bungled it over Equatorial Guinea. They had much in common with a fourth man, Frederick Forsyth, who dreamt up the first 'Dogs of War' coup attempt in Equatorial Guinea in 1973.

The Wonga Coup is a remarkable epilogue to a story that Forsyth began three decades before. It looks very much as if Forsyth was involved in plotting a coup in Equatorial Guinea, especially given documents just released by the National Archives in Britain and his own admissions in interviews for this book. After that coup attempt failed, Forsyth wrote up the experience as a novel, *The Dogs of War*. In turn that inspired other mercenaries. But what Forsyth began, Mann did not necessarily end. It seems likely that someone, one day, will try a rent-a-coup again. Most likely the target will be small and oil-rich, probably an island state with few foreign friends. It may yet be Equatorial Guinea once more. Bored buccaneers, perhaps men who tasted war in Iraq and who are looking for new places to fight in, will dream up another Wonga Coup. Some involved in this one – despite trials, prison, lost earnings and hunger – say they joined the adventure for the kicks and would be ready, given the right plan, to do it all over again.

Writing *The Wonga Coup*

The first I heard of the detention in Zimbabwe of an American plane packed full of mercenaries was on Monday 8 March 2004. We foreign correspondents in Johannesburg had no idea if the story was true, and at first excited rumours suggested the hired guns had tried a coup in Zimbabwe itself. Gradually the evidence of a plot in Equatorial Guinea emerged as du Toit and the others were arrested in Malabo. Still, it was unclear whether this story should be treated as a joke or as something more serious. The putsch in Sao Tome a year earlier had soon blown over, but this one had an extra element: the involvement of a British aristocrat and ex-SAS officer, Simon Mann.

In the months that followed, all sorts of confusing claims and counter-claims were published. There were early rumours of Mark Thatcher's role. Many thought western intelligence agencies were behind the plot. And there was the lure of Africa's oil to consider. I met Johann Smith a few days after the coup plot collapsed, and he pointed to unnamed oil companies that were eager to profit from Equatorial Guinea's oil production. He outlined the nature of the regime in Malabo, but argued that Moto would have been no better. From there, following a path well beaten by other reporters, I drove seven hours through the fringes of the Kalahari desert to the dusty ex-military base of Pomfret to meet relatives of some of the men detained in Zimbabwe. I heard their bitterness towards

Mann and the coup plot leaders. The former asbestos-mining town turned military base was a wretched place and I saw no reason why anyone should mourn its removal. But it was an intriguing spot, too. In the previous years I had travelled to Angola several times and here I found families speaking Portuguese, braiding their hair, eating food and listening to west African music as if this were a little bit of Angola picked up and dropped in South Africa.

Thanks to Barnaby Phillips I crossed paths with Nigel Morgan at the Butcher Shop and Grill in Johannesburg, the plotters' favourite restaurant. Though it is hard to understand how and why Morgan behaved the way he did towards his friends, he has been generous to a fault with me and proved hugely enjoyable company. Over the course of a year Morgan described – in varying detail, and occasionally with different interpretations – his version of what happened. He also introduced me to some characters involved in or connected to the plot. As important, he provided me with a thick file of documents, newspaper clippings and his own intelligence reports, which have proved invaluable.

Late in 2004 I set off for Equatorial Guinea with a colleague from the *Guardian*. We intended to cover the trial of Nick du Toit and report on the expanding oil industry in the region. We flew to Douala, the foetid commercial port in Cameroon, where we expected to take a small plane to Malabo. But fate – or more accurately, vicious Equatorial Guinean officials – intervened. We were hauled aside by an angry immigration man; scowling diplomats told us that British journalists were no longer welcome. It seemed that too many had written that Obiang likes eating human testicles. We were booted out and left to sweat for a week in Cameroon, within spitting distance of Malabo. Over the next year I repeatedly called ministers, ambassadors and close contacts of the Equatorial Guinea government in Malabo, London and Pretoria. I spent several hours in conversation with a hostile ambassador in London begging for a visa. But I was ultimately told by one diplomat, in most undiplomatic language, that 'British journalists have fucked us over too many times', so I would never be allowed into Malabo.

After Malabo the hardest place to conduct interviews was Harare, Zimbabwe's capital. In my day job as the *Economist*'s man in southern Africa I have frequently travelled clandestinely to Harare and other parts of Zimbabwe, though British journalists have been denounced as imperial monsters and I have been personally accused of being a spy. But to my delight, early in 2005, Zimbabwean officials let me visit to report on the parliamentary elections. I took the chance to apply to see Simon Mann (he refused) in Chikurubi prison, conducted long interviews with his Zimbabwean lawyers and several others involved, and visited some of the places where Mann had been. Most notable, a senior member of Zimbabwe's ruling party agreed to discuss the coup plot with me.

Other research in South Africa proved far easier. The Steyl family – Crause and Niel, who were involved in the plot, as well as their brother Piet – were especially frank. South African prosecutors and defence lawyers, members of the intelligence fraternity, journalists who covered various aspects of the cases and many others were generous with their time and material. Johann Smith also submitted to at least half a dozen long interviews and provided thick folders of his intelligence reports and other documents. Several of those who were jailed and released gave me interviews, short or long, about their experiences before, during and after the plot. Hours spent lingering in and beside court rooms in Cape Town and Pretoria, long evenings teasing apart the story with friends in Johannesburg, and the useful testimonies given to me by mercenaries in Durban and elsewhere are all appreciated.

In Paris Henry Page was kind enough to explain events from his perspective and to provide me with yet more documents and material relevant to the case. Another lawyer, Lucie Bourthoumieux, was similarly helpful. On Mann's side, his London lawyer, Anthony Kerman, was forthright and opinionated.

Others were notably helpful. Mark Thatcher agreed to be interviewed three times by me for the purposes of this book, once in Johannesburg and twice in London, and provided much illuminating material as well as the odd (jocular?) threat to rearrange my teeth or have me walking on stumps if I portrayed him in an unpleasant light. Greg Wales, a thirsty man, volunteered for two long meetings in two London wine bars where he was startlingly frank about his role. Wales sent me some documents he had written and admitted authorship of others. I also acquired a manuscript copy of a novel he had written about an 'exciting coup attempt' in an oil rich west African country. His fictional sex addict hero flits between luxurious hotels in Johannesburg, London, Washington and the sweaty capital of the target country, a place that sounds very much like Equatorial Guinea. Under the comical working title 'Coups and Robbers', an early version portrayed the Wonga Coup from his point of view. He described Moto and how 'Simon's job was to provide him with a good enough guard force to keep him alive on his return to his ravaged country'. It was later given a less jolly title – 'Power and Terrain' – and was packed with quotations from a Chinese philosopher suggesting it is always wise to 'take a state intact'. I am grateful for his help.

Wales was perhaps trying to imitate Frederick Forsyth. Forsyth also kindly granted me three interviews, by phone, when we discussed coup plots present and past. But several of those involved in – or thought to be connected to – the latter-day events turned down requests for meetings or interviews. Ely Calil, Severo Moto, Jeffrey Archer and David Tremain all failed to respond to requests for meetings or simply rebuffed them. In Madrid some representatives of the Spanish government were helpful, but many phone calls were not returned by those who might have cast a clearer light on that country's role.

Others – diplomats, oil experts, journalists, friends, Africa experts, academics, politicians and writers – have been generous with their time, advice and suggestions. Anthony Goldman in London was particularly kind with books, documents and discussion of events. The investigative journalist Paul Lashmar spent many long hours tracing phone calls between plotters, and kindly provided me with an invaluable summary.

In addition to interviews, much of the information in this book is drawn from documents produced by the plotters, from intelligence reports and from material provided by fellow journalists. A list of some primary sources is set out below, along with a selected bibliography. There are several television productions and documentaries relating to this coup attempt, some of which are also listed below. Many publications followed the coup attempt far more closely than did the *Economist*, and I have also benefited greatly from the many newspaper articles – and thus thousands of hours of research by others – relating to this story.

In addition to everyone who gave interviews I would like to thank several people for their time, hospitality and help. My thanks are due first and foremost to Anne, my wife, who read chapters, put up with endless discussions and gave me advice. Many friends, colleagues and relatives have been extremely generous. There is little space to list them all here, but you know who you are. Clive Priddle and all at PublicAffairs, and Daniel Crewe, Andrew Franklin and all at Profile Books have been a delight to work with. Will Lippincott, my agent in the United States, got the ball rolling in the first place and invested huge energy and enthusiasm in the project. Julian Alexander, my agent in Britain, was as helpful on this side of the Atlantic. Thanks, too, to Bill Emmott, John Micklethwait and several others at the *Economist* for their support. Phil Kenny did a great job with the maps. In addition, thanks to Jo Wright, Catherine Moulton and others at the BBC who recruited me, briefly, as a consultant. Both Simon Robinson and Heidi Holland in Johannesburg read large parts of the manuscript and gave helpful comments, while Heidi has been the most inspiring friend one could hope to have. Errors and misunderstandings, of course, are my responsibility alone.

Select interviews

In Britain: Lucie Bourthoumieux; Richard Dowden; Frederick Forsyth; Anthony Goldman; Koosum Kalyan; Anthony Kerman; Paul Lashmar; Augustin Nze Nfumu; Melanie Riley; Patrick Smith; Mungo Soggot; Greg Wales. In France: Amir Ben Yamid; Henry Page. In Spain: Antonio Sanchez-Benedito. In South Africa: Raymond Archer; Henri Boshoff; Duncan Clarke; Richard Cornwell; Avelino Dala; Mr dos Santos; Victor Dracula; Peter Duffy; Christina Fernando; Johann Ferreira; Jendayi Frazer; Ann Grant; Alwyn Griebnow; James Kershaw; Peter Leon; Angela MacIntyre; Greg Mills; Nigel Morgan; Bruce Morrison; Chris Munnion; Ivor Powell; Torie Pretorious;

Martin Rupiya; Felicia Shapoda; Johann Smith; Crause Steyl; Niel Steyl; Piet Steyl; Cecilia Tchimuishi; Viviana Tchimuishi; Mark Thatcher; Neves Tomas; Piet van der Merwe; Margie Victor; Martin Weltz; Ron Wheeldon; Simon Witherspoon; Deon X; George X; 'Mr Amstel'. In Zimbabwe: Efriam Masiwa; Cris Chinaka; Beloved Dhlakama; Jonathan Samukange; Paul Tembo; David Ashford; The owners of Wild Geese Lodge; 'Maxwell', manager of Cresta Lodge.

Primary documents
From the National Archives in London: diplomatic dispatches regarding Equatorial Guinea in 1972, 1973 and 1974; special report on activities of mercenaries 1973.

Documents directly relating to the Wonga Coup in the author's possession:
'Assisted Regime Change', July 2003;
Agreement One and Agreement Two (Mann–Moto contracts), July 2003;
Contract Nick du Toit–Congolese 'PDD' rebels, July 2003;
Two investor agreements for Logo Logistics, November 2003;
Triple Options–Panac–Equatorial Guinea government agreement/business proposal, November 2003;
Two agendas for coup planning, November and December 2003;
codeword documents for communication among plotters, December 2003;
Logo Logistics–Triple Options finance agreement, December 2003;
Omega–Triple Options agreement, December 2003;
'Bight of Benin Company', January 2004;
YKA subcontractor agreement, January 2004;
Logo–Panac subcontractor agreement, January 2004;

Logo Logistics dollar bank account late 2003–early 2004;
Joint Venture agreement Sonage–Triple Options Trading,
    January 2004;
Zimbabwe Defence Industries quotation for arms and
    ammunition, February 2004;
Dodson Aviation correspondence, February 2004;
Logo–MTS subcontractor agreement, February 2004;
handwritten Mann letter from prison, March 2004;
handwritten Mann confession, draft and final, March 2004;
power of attorney agreement, Mann–Griebnow, March 2004;
assorted intelligence reports by Nigel Morgan, 2004;
assorted intelligence reports by Johann Smith, 2000–2005;
assorted charge sheets against Greg Wales, David Tremain,
    Simon Mann and others in South Africa;
assorted plea bargains and summaries of agreed facts for
    Mark Thatcher, Crause Steyl and others;
assorted witness testimony, agreement statements of fact and
    others used in Zimbabwe trial;
assorted typed confessions of Mann, du Toit, Witherspoon,
    Carlse and others;
undated documents: payroll for footsoldiers; du Toit budget
    documents; passport details of fifty-six footsoldiers;
    copies of Mann's passport;
ruling of Guernsey court, April 2005;
copy of Foreign Military Assistance legislation, 1998;
'Power and Terrain', unpublished manuscript by Greg
    Wales; also 'Coups and Robbers' and the 'LBW Coup',
    both by Wales;
unpublished manuscript of the Equatorial Guinea coup
    attempt, Piet Steyl, 2005.

Selected Bibliography

Amnesty International, assorted reports on Equatorial
Guinea.
Archer, Jeffrey *A quiver full of arrows* (Pan Books, 1980).
Bayart, Jean-Francois and others, *The Criminalization of the
State in Africa; James Currey* (Oxford University Press and
Indiana University Press, 1999).
Breytenbach, Jan, *The Buffalo Soldiers, the story of South
Africa's 32 Battalion 1975–1993* (Galago, 2002)
Burton, Sir Richard Francis, *Wanderings in West Africa, from
Liverpool to Fernando Po*, 2 vols. (1862) (reissued by The
Narrative Press, 2001).
Cabell, Crai, *Frederick Forsyth, A Matter of Protocol* (Robson
Books, 2001).
Carney, Daniel, *The Wild Geese* (Corgi Books, 1977).
Cilliers, Jakkie and others, *Peace, Profit or Plunder, the
privatisation of security in war-torn African Societies* (Institute
of Security Studies, 1999), the chapter by Khareen Pech.
Collins, Robert O., *African History* (Random House, 1971).
Cook, Robin, *Chromosome 6* (Pan Books, 1997).
Coote, Stephen, *Drake, the Life and Legend of an Elizabethan
Hero* (Pocket Books, 2003).
Crick, Michael, *Jeffrey Archer, Stranger Than Fiction* (Fourth
Estate, 1999).

Fegley, Randall, *Equatorial Guinea: An African Tragedy* (P. Lang, 1989).

Ferguson, Niall, *Empire, How Britain Made the Modern World* (Penguin, 2003).

Forsyth, Frederick, *The Dogs of War* (Viking Press, 1974).

Forsyth, Frederick, *The Making of an African Legend: The Biafra Story* (Penguin, 1969).

Frynas, Jedrzej George, 'The Oil Boom in Equatorial Guinea', *African Affairs* 103/413, (2004), pp. 527–46.

Gary, Ian and Nikki Reisch, 'Chad's Oil: Miracle or Mirage? Following the Money in Africa's Newest Petro-state', Catholic Relief Services and Bank Information Centre (February 2005).

Germani, Hans, *White Soldiers in Black Africa* (Nasionale Boekhandel Beperk, 1967).

Greene, Graham, *Journey Without Maps* (Vintage Classics, 1936).

Halloran, Paul and Mark Hollingsworth, *Thatcher's Fortunes. The Life and Times of Mark Thatcher* (Mainstream Publishing, 2005).

Harrison Church, R. J., *West Africa, A Study of the Environment and Man's Use of It* (Longman's Green and Co. 1957).

Hoare, Mike, *Congo Mercenary* (Robert Hale, 1967).

Hoare, Mike, *The Seychelles Affair* (Bantam Press, 1986).

Hochschild, Adam, *King Leopold's Ghost* (Macmillan,1999).

Hooper, Jim, *Bloodsong: First-Hand Accounts of a Modern Private Army in Action, Angola 1993–1995* (Collins, 2002).

Human Rights Watch, 'Some Transparency, No Accountability: The Use of Oil Revenue in Angola and Its Impact on Human Rights', vol. 16, no. 1 (January 2004).

Human Rights Watch on West African mercenaries between 1998 and 2005: hrw.org/reports/2005/westAfrica0405.

International Bar Association, 'Equatorial Guinea at the Crossroads', www.ibanet.org (October 2003).

Ives, Ryan A., 'Diversifying the Oil Supply: Recommendations for Productive US Involvement in Equatorial Guinea', *International Affairs Review*, vol. 11, no. 2 (summer/autumn 2002), pp. 54–71.

Jeune Afrique Economie, 'Guinee Equatoriale 1995' (1995).

Kingsley, Mary, *Travels in West Africa* (1897) Phoenix Press, (reissued by 1976).

Klitgaard, Robert, *Tropical Gangsters: One Man's Experience with Development and Decadence in Deepest Africa* (Basic Books, 1990).

Liniger-Goumaz, Max, trans. John Wood, *Small is Not Always Beautiful: The story of Equatorial Guinea* (Rowman & Littlefield, 1989).

Liniger-Goumaz, Max, *Who's Who de la dictature de Guinée Equatoriale, Les Nguemistes 1979–1993* (in French) (Les Editions du Temps, 1994).

Liniger-Goumaz, Max, *United States, France and Equatorial Guinea, the Dubious 'Friendships'* (Les Editions du Temps, 1997).

McGowan, Patrick, *Journal of Modern African Studies*, vol. 41, no. 3 (September 2003).

McLynn, Frank, *Hearts of Darkness: the European Exploration of Africa* (Carroll and Graf, 1993).

Meredith, Martin, *The State of Africa: A History of the Fifty Years of Independence* (Jonathan Ball, 2005).

Mills, Greg and John Stremlau, *The Privatisation of Security in Africa* (South African Institute of International Affairs, 1999).

Mockler, Anthony, *The New Mercenaries* (Garden City Press, 1985).

Munnion, Chris, *Banana Sunday: Datelines from Africa*, (William Waterman, 1993).

Musah, Abdel-Fatau and J. Kayode Fayemi, eds. *Mercenaries, An African Security Dilemma* (Pluto Press, 2000).

Nortje, Piet, *32 Battalion; The Inside Story of South Africa's Elite Fighting Unit* (Zebra Books, 2003).

Nze Nfumu, Augustin, *Macias: Verdugo o Victima?* (in Spanish) (self-published, 2004).

Roberts, J. M., *The Penguin History of the World* (Penguin Books, 1992).

Shearer, David, 'Outsourcing War', *Foreign Policy* (Fall 1998).

Shelley, Toby, *Oil, Politics, Poverty and the Planet* (Zed Books, 2005).

Singer, P. W., *Corporate Warriors, The Rise of the Privatised Military Industry* (Cornell University Press, 2003).

Singer, P. W., 'Outsourcing War', *Foreign Affairs* (March/ April, 2005), pp. 119–32.

Spicer, Tim, *An Unorthodox Soldier: Peace and War and the Sandline Affair* (Mainstream Publishing, 1999).

St Jorre, John de, *The Nigerian Civil War* (Hodder & Stoughton, 1972).

Sundiata, Ibrahim K., *From Slaving to Neoslavery: The Bight of Biafra and Fernando Po in the Era of Abolition 1827–1930* (University of Wisconsin Press, 1996).

United States Senate Report on Riggs Bank (2004).

Van Rensburg, A. P. J., *Contemporary Leaders of Africa* (HAUM, 1975).

Venter, Al J., *Soldier of Fortune* (W. H. Allen, 1980).

Waugh, Evelyn, *Black Mischief* (1932) (Penguin Books, 1965).

Waugh, Evelyn, *Scoop* (1938) (Penguin Books, 2000).

Wood, Geoffrey, 'Business and Politics in a Criminal State:
The Case of Equatorial Guinea', *African Affairs* 103/413
(2004), pp. 547–67.
Yergin, Daniel, *The Prize: The Epic Quest for Oil, Money and
Power* (Free Press, 1991).

Television documentaries/productions
BBC, *Coup!* (2006): comedy drama written by John Fortune.
BBC, *Review of 2003*, Barnaby Phillips on Sao Tome
(Christmas, 2003).
BBC, *The Money Programme*, interview with Nick du Toit
(October 2004).
BFC Productions, *La Nouvelle Fortune des Mercenaires*,
directed by Patrice Dutertre (2005).
Carte Blanche, ETV, South Africa (29 May 2005).
Channel 4 documentary, *My Friend the Mercenary*, directed by
James Brabazon (March 2005).
Channel 4 News, interview with Crause Steyl (January 2005).
SABC Special Assignment, 'Anatomy of a Coup', 8 February
2005.
60 Minutes (Sunday, 1 June 1997).

Selected newspapers and other media
Many newspapers proved useful. In South Africa: *This Day,
The Star, Business Day, Sunday Times, Sunday Independent,
Noseweek, Financial Mail, Mail and Guardian.* In Zimbabwe:
Zimonline, Herald. In Britain: newspapers: *Observer, Sunday
Times, Independent on Sunday, Guardian, Independent, Daily Mail,
Financial Times, Sunday Telegraph, Telegraph, The Times, Evening
Standard;* magazines: *New African, Africa Confidential, Private
Eye, Spectator,* the *Economist.* In the United States: *Baltimore
Sun, Washington Post, The New York Times, Los Angeles Times,*

Time, Newsweek, Newsday, Vanity Fair, as well as National Public Radio, MotherJones.com. In France: *Jeune Afrique*. In Spain: *El Pais* and *El Mundo*.

There are many informative websites, but two particularly useful ones are: www.afrol.com (news from Equatorial Guinea) and www.guinea-ecuatorial.org (Moto's website).

Index

PublicAffairs is a publishing house founded in 1997. It is a tribute to the standards, values, and flair of three persons who have served as mentors to countless reporters, writers, editors, and book people of all kinds, including me.

I.F. STONE, proprietor of *I. F. Stone's Weekly*, combined a commitment to the First Amendment with entrepreneurial zeal and reporting skill and became one of the great independent journalists in American history. At the age of eighty, Izzy published *The Trial of Socrates*, which was a national bestseller. He wrote the book after he taught himself ancient Greek.

BENJAMIN C. BRADLEE was for nearly thirty years the charismatic editorial leader of *The Washington Post*. It was Ben who gave the *Post* the range and courage to pursue such historic issues as Watergate. He supported his reporters with a tenacity that made them fearless and it is no accident that so many became authors of influential, best-selling books.

ROBERT L. BERNSTEIN, the chief executive of Random House for more than a quarter century, guided one of the nation's premier publishing houses. Bob was personally responsible for many books of political dissent and argument that challenged tyranny around the globe. He is also the founder and longtime chair of Human Rights Watch, one of the most respected human rights organizations in the world.

·   ·   ·

For fifty years, the banner of PublicAffairs Press was carried by its owner Morris B. Schnapper, who published Gandhi, Nasser, Toynbee, Truman, and about 1,500 other authors. In 1983, Schnapper was described by *The Washington Post* as "a redoubtable gadfly." His legacy will endure in the books to come.

Peter Osnos, *Founder and Editor-at-Large*